PASS TRAK®

W9-BYG-140

SERIES 6

Questions & Answers

Investment Company/
Variable Contracts
Limited Representative

17th Edition

 Dearborn
Financial Publishing, Inc.

At press time, this 17th edition of PassTrak Series 6 contains the most complete and accurate information currently available for the NASD Series 6 license examination. Owing to the nature of securities license examinations, however, information may have been added recently to the actual test that does not appear in this edition.

This publication is designed to provide accurate and authoritative information in regard to the subject matter covered. It is sold with the understanding that the publisher is not engaged in rendering legal, accounting, or other professional service. If legal advice or other expert assistance is required, the services of a competent professional person should be sought.

Executive Editor: Kimberly K. Walker-Daniels
Managing Editor: Nicola Bell
Associate Development Editor: Barry Dempsey
Associate Product Editor: Brian K. Fauth

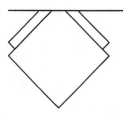

Contents

Acknowledgments

Special thanks to the following persons for their efforts in reviewing this book:

Marcia Burak

Howard Carstens

Joan McGillivray

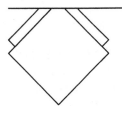

Introduction to PassTrak® Series 6

Welcome to PassTrak® Series 6. Because you probably have a lot of questions about the course and the exam, we have tried to anticipate some of them and provide you with answers to help you on your way.

The Course

How is the course structured?

PassTrak Series 6 is divided into two volumes: a textbook and an exam book. The textbook, titled *Principles & Practices*, consists of five chapters, each devoted to a particular area of investment company/variable contract products (IC/VC) trading and regulation that you will need to know in order to pass the IC/VC Limited Representative Qualification Exam (the Series 6). Each chapter is divided into study sections devoted to more specific areas with which you need to become familiar.

The exam book, titled *Questions & Answers*, contains review exams that test the topics covered in *Principles & Practices;* it concludes with three comprehensive and three final exams composed of questions similar to those you will encounter on the Series 6 exam.

What topics are covered in this course?

The information needed to pass the Series 6 exam is covered in PassTrak Series 6 through the following chapters:

Chapter 1: Securities and Markets, Investment Risks and Policies
Chapter 2: Investment Companies, Taxation and Customer Accounts
Chapter 3: Variable Contracts and Retirement Plans
Chapter 4: Securities Industry Regulations
Chapter 5: Tracking Traded Securities

How much time should I spend studying?

You should plan to spend approximately 30 to 40 hours reading the material and working through the questions. Your actual time, of course, may vary from this figure depending on your reading rate, comprehension, professional background and study environment.

Spread your study time over the two to three weeks prior to the date on which you are scheduled to take the Series 6 exam. Select a time and place for studying that will allow you to concentrate your full attention on the material at hand. You have a lot of information to learn and a lot of ground to cover. Be sure to give yourself enough time to learn the material.

What is the best way to approach the exams?

Approach each exam as if you were preparing to take the actual Series 6 test. Read each question carefully and write down your answer. Then check your answers against the key and read the accompanying rationale. Making yourself go through all of these steps (rather than simply reading each question and skipping directly to the rationale) will greatly increase your comprehension and retention of the information in the book.

Do I need to take the final exams?

The final exams test the same knowledge you will need in order to answer the questions on the Series 6 exam. By completing these exams and checking your answers against the rationale, you should be able to pinpoint any areas with which you are still having difficulty. Review any questions you miss, paying particular attention to the rationale for those questions. If any subjects still seem troublesome, go back and review those topics in *Principles & Practices*. At the end of each rationale, you will find a page reference that directs you to the page in *Principles & Practices* where the information is covered.

The Exam

Why do I need to pass the Series 6 exam?

Your employer is a member of the National Association of Securities Dealers (NASD) or another self-regulatory organization that requires its members and employees of its members to pass a qualification exam in order to become registered. To be registered as a representative qualified to sell investment company and variable contract products, you must pass the Series 6 exam.

What is the Series 6 exam like?

The Series 6 is a 2-hour-and-15-minute, 100-question exam administered by the NASD. It is offered as a computer-based test at various testing sites around the country. A paper-and-pencil exam is available to those candidates who apply to and obtain permission from the NASD to take a written exam.

What topics will I see covered on the exam?

This course covers the wide range of topics that the NASD has outlined as being essential to the IC/VC representative. The NASD exam is divided into four broad topic areas:

	% of Exam
Securities and Markets, Investment Risks and Policies	23%
Investment Companies, Taxation and Customer Accounts	36%
Variable Contracts and Retirement Plans	16%
Securities Industry Regulations	25%

What score must I achieve in order to pass?

You must answer correctly at least 70% of the questions on the Series 6 exam in order to pass and become eligible for NASD registration as an IC/VC representative.

How long does the exam take?

You will be allowed 2 hours and 15 minutes in which to finish the exam. If you are taking the computerized version of the exam, you will be given additional time before the test to become familiar with the PROCTOR® terminal.

Are there any prerequisites I have to meet before taking the exam?

There are no prerequisite exams you must pass before sitting for the Series 6.

How do I enroll for the exam?

To obtain an admission ticket to the Series 6 exam, your firm must file the proper application form with the NASD, along with the appropriate processing fees. The NASD will then send you a directory of Certification Testing Centers and a PROCTOR® enrollment valid for a stated number of days. To take the exam during this period, you must make an appointment with a Certification Testing Center as far in advance as possible of the date on which you would like to sit for the test.

What should I take to the exam?

Take one form of personal identification that bears your signature and your photograph as issued by a government agency. You are not allowed to take reference materials or anything else into the testing area. Calculators will be available upon request; you will not be allowed to use your personal calculator.

Scratch paper and pencils will be provided by the testing center, although you will not be permitted to take them with you when you leave.

What is the PROCTOR® System?

The Series 6 exam, like many professional licensing examinations, is administered on the PROCTOR® computerized testing system. PROCTOR® is a nationwide, interactive computer system designed for the administration and delivery of qualifications examinations. Included with your PROCTOR® enrollment, you will receive a brochure describing how the exam is formatted and how to use the computer terminal to answer the questions.

When you have completed the exam, the PROCTOR® System promptly scores your answers and within minutes displays a grade for the exam on the terminal screen.

How well can I expect to do on the exam?

The examinations administered by the NASD are not easy. You will be required to display considerable understanding and knowledge of the topics presented in this course in order to pass the Series 6 exam and qualify for registration. If you study and complete all of the sections of the course, and consistently score at least 80% on the review and final exams, you should be well prepared to pass the Series 6 exam.

1 Common Stock Exam

1. The holders of which of the following securities are considered owners of the corporation?

   I.   Mortgage bonds
   II. Convertible debentures
   III. Preferred stock
   IV. Common stock

   A. I, II and III only
   B. III and IV only
   C. IV only
   D. I, II, III and IV

2. A corporation needs shareholder approval for which of the following?

   A. Cash dividend
   B. 4-for-1 split ✗
   C. 10% stock dividend ⋏
   D. The repurchase of 100,000 of its own shares

3. When trading common stock, either at an exchange or over the counter, the typical size of the trading unit is how many shares?

   A. 10
   B. 50
   C. 100
   D. There is no standard unit.

4. Equity ownership of a corporation is split into two types. These types are commonly referred to as

   A. stocks and bonds
   B. common stocks and preferred stocks
   C. preferred stocks and bonds
   D. common stocks and convertible bonds

5. A company may pay dividends in which of the following ways?

   I.   Stock of another company
   II. Cash
   III. Stock
   IV. Product

   A. I only
   B. II and III only
   C. III only
   D. I, II, III and IV

6. TCB stock is $10.00 par value and is selling in the market for $60.00 per share. If the current quarterly dividend is $1.00, what is the current yield of TCB?

   A. 1.0%
   B. 1.6%
   C. 6.6%
   D. 10.0%

7. TCBS currently has earnings of $4 and pays a $.50 quarterly dividend. The market price of TCBS is $40. What is the current yield?

    A. 1.25%
    B. 5%
    C. 10%
    D. 15%

8. Common stockholders' rights include a

    I.   residual claim to assets at dissolution
    II.   vote for the amount of stock dividend to be paid
    III. vote in matters of recapitalization
    IV.   claim against dividends that are in default

    A. I
    B. I and III
    C. II and III
    D. III and IV

9. A company that has paid its common stockholders a dividend would be required to also have made distributions to which of the other securities issued by the company?

    I.   Bonds
    II.   Convertible bonds
    III. Preferred stock
    IV.   Convertible preferred stock

    A. I and II only
    B. I and III only
    C. II and III only
    D. I, II, III and IV

◆ Answers & Rationale

1. **B.**   Common and preferred stock are equity securities, while bondholders are considered creditors of the corporation.   (Page 3)

2. **B.**   Shareholders have a right to vote on such items as mergers, reorganizations, recapitalizations and stock splits.   (Page 3)

3. **C.**   Common stock trades in round lots of 100 shares each.   (Page 3)

4. **B.**   Equity ownership comes with two types of securities. These are common and preferred stocks.   (Page 3)

5. **D.**   A company may pay a dividend in any of the ways listed.   (Page 4)

6. **C.**   The quarterly dividend is $1.00; therefore, the annual dividend is $4.00. $4 divided by $60 (market price) equals 6.6% annual yield (current yield).   (Page 4)

7. **B.**   The quarterly dividend is $.50; therefore, the annual dividend is $2.00. $2 divided by $40 (market price) equals 5% annual yield (current yield).   (Page 4)

8. **B.**   As the corporation's owners, common stockholders would have the lowest claim against a company's assets at dissolution or bankruptcy. The owners of cumulative preferred stock have a claim against any dividends that are in default. Holders of common stock are entitled to vote on matters that affect their proportionate ownership. Recapitalization—the alteration of a corporation's capital structure—is an example of a situation that requires a vote of the stockholders.   (Page 5)

9. **D.**   Because common stock is paid last (most junior), other securities issued by the firm will receive distributions (interest payments on debt securities and dividends on senior equity securities).   (Page 5)

2 Preferred Stock Exam

1. Which of the following are considered to have an equity position in a corporation?

    I.   Common stockholders
    II. Preferred stockholders
    III. Convertible bondholders
    IV. Mortgage bondholders

    A. I and II only
    B. I, II and III only
    C. II and III only
    D. I, II, III and IV

2. In a portfolio containing common stock, preferred stock, convertible preferred stock and mutual funds, changes in interest rates would be most likely to affect the market price of the

    A. common
    B. preferred
    C. convertible preferred
    D. mutual funds

3. If interest rates are increasing and the market prices of bonds are decreasing, what happens to the value of preferred stock during this period?

    A. Its value increases.
    B. Its value decreases.
    C. Its value remains the same.
    D. Interest rates and the price of bonds have no impact on the value of stock.

4. An owner of preferred stock has which of the following rights?

    I.   Right to determine when dividends will be issued
    II. Right to vote at stockholders' meetings or by proxy
    III. Right to a predetermined fixed portion of the corporation's profit in cash when declared
    IV. Right to buy restricted securities before they are offered to the public

    A. I, III and IV
    B. II, III and IV
    C. II and IV
    D. III

◆ Answers & Rationale

1. **A.** Owners have equity positions. Common and preferred stockholders are owners.   (Page 7)

2. **B.** Preferred stock has the closest characteristics to bonds and would be most affected by a change in interest rates.   (Page 7)

3. **B.** Preferred stocks are interest rate sensitive as are other fixed-interest rate investment vehicles such as bonds. Because the dividend amount is fixed, if interest rates are increasing, the return provided by the dividend may be less than the return provided by other investments. The value of preferred stock will decrease.   (Page 7)

4. **D.** The preferred stockholder generally has no right to vote but carries a prior right to dividends if and when declared. A restricted security is one that has prescribed limits on resale generally requiring registration.   (Page 7)

3 Debt Securities Exam

1. Corporate bonds are considered safer than corporate stock issued by the same company because

    I. bonds represent equity in the company
    II. the company is more likely to back the original investors
    III. bonds are senior to common stock
    IV. the holder of a corporate bond is a debtor to the company

    A. I and II
    B. II, III and IV
    C. III
    D. III and IV

2. Which statement would be true for an investor who purchased $50,000 face value of 5.10 bonds at par due in 2002 and held them to maturity?

    A. The investor would receive $50,000, the final two interest payments and 5.10 market gain at maturity.
    B. The investor would receive $50,000 less 5.10 market discount at maturity.
    C. The investor would receive $50,000 plus 5.10 at maturity.
    D. The investor would receive $50,000 and the final interest payment at maturity.

3. Quantum Rapid Search, Inc. issued Mortgage Senior Lien bonds at 8 7/8, price 96.353. These bonds pay annual interest, per $1,000 bond, of

    A. $85.00
    B. $85.51
    C. $88.75
    D. $96.35

4. An investor has bonds maturing in two weeks. The investor plans to purchase new bonds with a 10% coupon rate. If interest rates decline in the period before the investor can purchase the new bonds, the investor can expect the income to be received from the new bonds to

    A. increase
    B. decline
    C. stay the same
    D. balloon

5. An investor's portfolio includes ten bonds and 200 shares of common stock. If both positions increase by 1/2 of a point, what is the gain?

    A. $50
    B. $105
    C. $110
    D. $150

6.   Your customer holds a 10M MCS 6s bond
     callable at 102 in 1995 and maturing in 2001.
     How much money will the customer receive
     in total at the debenture's maturity?

     A. $10,000
     B. $10,200
     C. $10,300
     D. $10,600

◆ Answers & Rationale

1. **C.** A bond represents a legal obligation to repay principal and interest by the company. The holder of a corporate bond is a *creditor* of the company.   (Page 9)

2. **D.** Because the 2002 bonds were purchased at par ($1,000 per bond) and will be redeemed at par ($1,000 per bond), the investor will receive $50,000 plus the final six-month interest payment of $1,275 at maturity.   (Page 9)

3. **C.** A coupon of 8 7/8 represents an annual interest payment of 8 7/8% of $1,000, or $88.75.
                                              (Page 9)

4. **C.** Fluctuations in interest rates may affect the price of a bond but will not affect the income payable from the bond. The percentage interest payable for use of money is stated on the face of a bond and is part of the bond indenture, a legal obligation on the part of the issuing company.
                                              (Page 9)

5. **D.** The gain would be $50 for the bonds (1/2 point for one bond is $5 times 10 bonds) and $100 for the common stock (1/2 point is $.50 times 200 shares).   (Page 9)

6. **C.** 10M bonds denote $10,000 in principal amount to be received by the bondholder at maturity. Each bond pays 6% annual interest of $60; thus, ten bonds pay a total of $600 per year in two semiannual payments of $300. At maturity, the bondholder will receive the $10,000 face amount plus the final semiannual payment ($10,000 + $300 = $10,300).   (Page 10)

 **4** **Characteristics of Corporate Bonds Exam**

1. Which of the following statements about mortgage bonds are true?

   I. They are secured by a mortgage or a lien.
   II. They are secured by the good faith of the issuing corporation.
   III. They are considered to be a safer investment than preferred stock.
   IV. They have a senior claim to the corporation's assets when compared to common stock.

   A. I and III only
   B. II, III and IV only
   C. II and IV only
   D. I, II, III and IV

2. Collateral trust bonds may be secured by

   I. real property of the issuing corporation
   II. equity and debt securities of a subsidiary corporation
   III. equity and debt securities of another corporation
   IV. installment payments based on the corporation's accounts receivable

   A. I
   B. II
   C. II or III
   D. II or IV

3. Which of the following corporate bonds is usually backed by other investment securities?

   A. Mortgage bond
   B. Equipment trust certificate
   C. Collateral trust bond
   D. Debenture

4. Which of the following statements about debentures are true?

   I. They are secured by a mortgage or a lien.
   II. They are secured by the good faith of the issuing corporation.
   III. They are considered to be a safer investment than preferred stock.
   IV. They have a senior claim to the corporation's assets when compared to common stock.

   A. I and III only
   B. II, III and IV only
   C. II and IV only
   D. I, II, III and IV

Use the following information from Moody's bond page to answer question 5.

TCBS ZR '12 54 1/4
FLB 5's '93 78 7/8

5. The annual interest received on the TCBS bond is

   A. nothing until the bond matures
   B. $ 12.00
   C. $ 24.00
   D. $ 54.25

6. Which of the following statements are true regarding corporate zero-coupon bonds?

   I. Interest is paid semiannually.
   II. Interest is not paid until maturity.
   III. The discount must be prorated and is taxed annually.
   IV. The discount must be prorated annually, with taxation deferred to maturity.

   A. I and III
   B. I and IV
   C. II and III
   D. II and IV

7. An investor who purchases a Treasury STRIP is assured of

   I. a locked-in rate of return
   II. a lump-sum payment of principal and interest at maturity
   III. lower taxes because the returns would be taxed at the lower capital gains rate
   IV. little or no reinvestment risk

   A. I
   B. I, II and III
   C. I, II and IV
   D. II and IV

8. Which of the following does NOT expose the investor to reinvestment risk?

   A. Treasury stock
   B. Treasury bonds
   C. Treasury STRIPS
   D. Treasury notes

◆ Answers & Rationale

1. **D.** Mortgage bonds are secured by the good faith and credit of the issuing corporation evidenced by a pledge of real estate or a similar asset. They are senior to stock ownership, have a senior claim to assets over other debt issues and are considered a safer investment. (Page 11)

2. **C.** A collateral trust bond is backed by securities of a subsidiary corporation or another company's securities. A mortgage bond is backed by real property. (Page 11)

3. **C.** Collateral trust bonds are backed by other securities, while mortgage bonds are backed by real estate. Equipment trust certificates are backed by equipment. Debentures are secured by the company's promise to pay. (Page 11)

4. **B.** Debentures are secured by the good faith and credit of the issuing corporation. They are senior to stock ownership, have a senior claim to assets and are considered a safer investment. (Page 12)

5. **A.** The TCBS bond is a zero-coupon bond (ZR), meaning that no interest payments are made. These bonds sell at a deep discount and the tax law requires annual accretion of the discount. (Page 12)

6. **C.** The investor in a corporate zero-coupon bond receives his return in the form of growth of the principal amount during the bond's life. The bond is purchased at a steep discount and the discount is accrued by the investor and taxed by the government annually. (Page 12)

7. **C.** Even though an investment in a Treasury STRIP does not yield a regular cash flow, paying all of its interest at maturity, the difference between the purchase price and the mature value is still taxed as ordinary income and must be accrued on a yearly basis. (Page 13)

8. **C.** STRIPS are special bonds issued by the Treasury department and split into individual principal and interest payments, which are then resold in the form of zero-coupon bonds. Because zeros pay no interest, the investor realizes gains in the form of increased basis as the bond matures and there are no income payments to reinvest. (Page 13)

5 Bond Pricing and Yields Exam

1. Which of the following securities is(are) issued with a fixed rate of return?

    I.   Bonds
    II. Preferred stock
    III. Common stock
    IV. Convertible preferred stock

    A. I, II and IV only
    B. III only
    C. IV only
    D. I, II, III and IV

2. The difference between par and a lower market price on a bond is called the

    A. reallowance
    B. spread
    C. discount
    D. premium

3. Klaus Bruin purchases $50,000 of 10% corporate bonds at par. At the end of the day, the bonds close down 1/2 a point. The investor has a loss of

    A. $25
    B. $250
    C. $2,500
    D. $5,000

4. How do you calculate the current yield on a bond?

    A. Yield to maturity ÷ Par value
    B. Yield to maturity ÷ Dollar market price
    C. Annual interest payments ÷ Par value
    D. Annual interest payments ÷ Dollar market price

5. The current yield on a bond with a coupon rate of 7 1/2% currently selling at 95 is approximately

    A. 7.0%
    B. 7.4%
    C. 7.9%
    D. 8.0%

6. A customer purchased a 5% corporate bond yielding 6%. A year before the bond matures, new corporate bonds are being issued at 4% and the customer sells the 5% bond. The customer

    I.   bought it at a discount
    II. bought it at a premium
    III. sold it at a premium
    IV. sold it at a discount

    A. I and III
    B. I and IV
    C. II and III
    D. II and IV

7. A bond at par has a coupon rate

    A. less than current yield
    B. less than yield to maturity
    C. the same as current yield
    D. higher than current yield

8. A municipal bond is quoted at 6 1/4%. Currently its yield to maturity is 6 3/4%. From this information it can be determined that the municipal bond is trading

    A. flat
    B. at par
    C. at a discount
    D. at a premium

9. Which of the following statements about a bond selling above par value is(are) true?

    I.   The nominal yield is lower than the current yield.
    II. The yield to maturity is lower than the nominal yield.
    III. The yield to maturity is lower than the current yield.
    IV. The nominal yield always stays the same.

    A. I and IV only
    B. II, III and IV only
    C. III only
    D. I, II, III and IV

10. If interest rates are changing, which of the following terms would best describe the relationship between prices and yields for corporate bonds?

    A. Reverse
    B. Inverse
    C. Coterminous
    D. Coaxial

11. You notice that the total assets of ALFA, a regulated open-end investment company, went down 28% last year. You also notice that the stock in which ALFA deposited its capital did very well. Lastly, you notice that ALFA holds a large number of bonds. Which two of the following most likely occurred?

    I.   ALFA was holding too much cash.
    II. Interest rates went up.
    III. ALFA paid huge commissions to agents for their extra sales effort.
    IV. A large number of ALFA shares was redeemed.

    A. I and II
    B. I and III
    C. II and III
    D. II and IV

12. Which of the following would be the best time for an investor to purchase long-term fixed-interest rate bonds?

    A. When short-term interest rates are high and are beginning to decline
    B. When short-term interest rates are low and are beginning to rise
    C. When long-term interest rates are low and are beginning to rise
    D. When long-term interest rates are high and are beginning to decline

13. Which of the following statements about a bond selling below par value is(are) true?

    I.   The nominal yield is higher than the current yield.
    II. The yield to maturity is higher than the nominal yield.
    III. The yield to maturity is higher than the current yield.
    IV. The nominal yield always stays the same.

    A. I and IV only
    B. II, III and IV only
    C. III only
    D. I, II, III and IV

14. A mutual fund previously invested in bonds with a medium-length maturity. As the bonds matured, the fund reinvested the proceeds and purchased long-term bonds with maturities of up to 20 years. What would have happened to the fund if the reinvestment had occurred during a period when interest rates were rising?

   I.   Decrease in yield
   II. Decrease in income
   III. Increase in yield
   IV. Increase in income

   A.   I and II
   B.   I and IV
   C.   II and III
   D.   III and IV

15. With fluctuating interest rates, the price of which of the following will fluctuate most?

   A.   Common stock
   B.   Money-market instruments
   C.   Short-term bonds
   D.   Long-term bonds

16. What happens to outstanding fixed-income securities when interest rates drop?

   A.   Yields go up.
   B.   Coupon rates go up.
   C.   Prices go up.
   D.   Short-term fixed-income securities are affected most.

◆ Answers & Rationale

1. A. Bonds and preferred stock are typically issued with a stated payment, either in interest or dividends. Common stockholders are entitled to receive a variable distribution of profits if and when a dividend is declared.   (Page 14)

2. C. The difference between the par (or face) value of a bond and a market price lower than par is known as the bond's discount from par.
                                                            (Page 14)

3. B. The investor holds 50 $1,000 bonds. If each bond decreases by 1/2 point, the loss is $5 per bond multiplied by 50 bonds equals $250.
                                                            (Page 14)

4. D. The current yield of a bond equals the annual interest payment divided by the current market price.   (Page 15)

5. C. Each $1,000 7 1/2% bond pays $75 of interest annually.

$$\text{Current yield} = \frac{\text{Annual interest}}{\text{Bond market price}}$$

$$= \frac{\$75}{\$950} = 7.89\%$$

7.89% is approximately 7.9%.
                                                            (Page 15)

6. A. If the current yield of a bond is higher than its coupon rate, the bond is selling at a discount from par. If interest rates of newly issued bonds are lower than the rate of a secondary market bond, it is likely that the older bond could be sold at a premium.   (Page 15)

7. C. When a bond is selling at par, its coupon rate, nominal rate and current yield are the same.
                                                            (Page 15)

8. C. The YTM is greater than the nominal yield, meaning the price must be less than par. The bond is selling at a discount.   (Page 15)

9. B. Nominal yield is fixed and stays the same on all bonds. A bond selling above par is selling at a premium, so the current yield and yield to maturity will be less than the nominal yield.
                                                            (Page 16)

10. B. As yields increase, the price of outstanding debt decreases and vice versa. Because the face and coupon on a debt instrument remain unchanged, the market value fluctuates to account for changes in yields.   (Page 16)

11. D. Because ALFA has a portfolio composed of bonds, if interest rates increase, the value of the bonds will decline. If shares are redeemed, the value of the portfolio will decline as the money is paid out. Commissions are paid from sales charges collected; they are not an expense of the fund.
                                                            (Page 16)

12. D. The best time to buy long-term bonds is when long-term interest rates have peaked. In addition to the high return, as interest rates fall the value of existing bonds will rise.   (Page 16)

13. B. Nominal yield is fixed and stays the same on all bonds. A bond selling below par is selling at a discount, so the current yield and yield to maturity will be more than the nominal yield.
                                                            (Page 16)

14. D. The longer the maturity of a bond, the greater the risk to the investor. As a result, long-term bonds pay higher interest rates than medium- or short-term bonds. If the fund replaces medium-term bonds with long-term bonds, you would expect the long-term bonds to pay higher interest rates and thus more income. Additionally, as interest rates increase, so do yields. For example, the fund has a medium-term bond paying 8%. The income from the bond is $80 annually. The bond matures and the fund receives $1,000 as a return of principal. The fund is purchasing a long-term bond paying 9%, or $90, annually (income to the fund will increase by $10). Additionally, if interest rates are rising, price is declining. Thus, the 9% long-term bond will not cost $1,000, but say $950. Therefore, the current yield of the 9% bond will be 9.47% ($90 ÷ $950)—yield is up.   (Page 17)

15. **D.** Long-term debt prices will fluctuate more than short-term debt prices as interest rates rise and fall. When one buys a note or a bond, one is really buying the interest payments and the final principal payment. Money has a time value: the farther out in time money is to be received, the less it is worth today. With a 10% five-year bond, an investor buying at market interest rates will pay $1,000 for one bond. If interest rates go to 15%, the bond price will fall to approximately $800. As payments move out to later years, they are worth less and less, due to the interest rate compounding effect. This same compounding effect causes longer term bonds to increase or decrease more in value (as interest rates change) than short-term bonds. (Page 17)

16. **C.** When the interest rates drop the coupons on new issue bonds will decline to offer lower yields. The price of outstanding bonds will rise to adjust to the lower yields on bonds of comparable quality. (Page 17)

6 Special Securities Exam

1. A corporation's capitalization includes $1,000,000 of 7% preferred stock and $1,000,000 of 7% convertible debentures. If all the convertible debentures were converted into common stock, what would happen to the company's earnings?

   A. They would increase.
   B. They would decrease.
   C. There would be no change.
   D. It cannot be determined.

2. All of the following will remain relatively stable in value in a period of stable interest rates EXCEPT

   A. convertible preferred stock
   B. senior preferred
   C. participating preferred
   D. cumulative preferred

3. Hedda A. Legge owns a convertible bond for IBS Corp. She is, therefore,

   A. an owner
   B. a creditor
   C. both owner and creditor
   D. neither owner nor creditor

4. The market price of a convertible bond will depend on

   A. the value of the underlying stock into which the bond can be converted
   B. current interest rates
   C. the rating of the bond
   D. all of the above

5. Which of the following is NOT true concerning convertible bonds?

   A. Coupon rates are usually higher than nonconvertible bond rates of the same issuer.
   B. Convertible bondholders are creditors of the corporation.
   C. Coupon rates are usually lower than nonconvertible bond rates of the same issuer.
   D. If the underlying common stock were to decline to the point where there is no advantage to convert the bonds into common stock, the bonds would sell at a price based on their inherent value as bonds, disregarding the convertible feature.

6. What is the conversion ratio of a convertible bond purchased at face value and convertible at $50?

   A. 2:1
   B. 3:1
   C. 20:1
   D. 30:1

7. Acme Zootech has issued both common stock and convertible preferred stock. The convertible preferred has a par value of $100 per share. It is convertible into the common at $25 per share. Acme convertible is trading at 110. What is the parity price of the common?

A. 25
B. 27 1/2
C. 35
D. 37 1/2

8. A 12% corporate bond issued by the TIP Company is due in ten years. The bond is convertible into TIP common stock at a conversion price of $20 per share. The TIP bond is quoted at 120. Parity of the common stock is

A. $20
B. $24
C. $50
D. $60

9. Which of the following affect the parity of a convertible bond with the underlying stock?

A. Interest rates
B. Company earnings performance
C. Stock market movement and trends
D. All of the above

10. A corporate offering of 200,000 additional shares to existing stockholders is a

A. tender offer
B. secondary offering
C. preemptive offer
D. rights offering

11. Stock rights (also called *subscription rights*) are

I. short-term instruments that become worthless after the expiration date
II. most commonly offered in connection with debentures to sweeten the offering
III. issued by a corporation
IV. traded in the securities market

A. I and II
B. I and III
C. I, III and IV
D. II, III and IV

12. If a corporation wanted to offer stock at a given price for the next five years, it would issue

A. rights
B. warrants
C. callable preferred stock
D. put options

13. Which of the following is(are) actively traded?

I. Warrants
II. Nondetachable rights
III. Common stock
IV. Options on stock

A. I, III and IV only
B. II only
C. II and IV only
D. I, II, III and IV

14. Which of the following statements is(are) true regarding rights and warrants?

I. Warrants are issued with an exercise price higher than the underlying stock.
II. Rights are issued with an exercise price lower than the underlying stock.
III. Warrants are long lived, may even be perpetual and may be issued to anyone.
IV. Rights are short lived and issued only to present shareholders.

A. I only
B. I and II only
C. II and III only
D. I, II, III and IV

15. All of the following pay dividends EXCEPT

    A. common stock
    B. preferred stock
    C. convertible preferred stock
    D. warrants

16. Which of the following best describe warrants?

    I. Short-term instruments that become worthless after the expiration date
    II. Most commonly offered in connection with debentures to sweeten the offering
    III. Issued by a corporation
    IV. Traded in the securities market

    A. I and II
    B. I and III
    C. I, III and IV
    D. II, III and IV

17. An investor will be in a position to acquire stock under which of the following circumstances?

    I. She is a buyer of a call.
    II. She is a buyer of a put.
    III. She is a seller of a call.
    IV. She is a seller of a put.

    A. I and III
    B. I and IV
    C. II and III
    D. II and IV

18. An investor will be in a position to sell stock under which of the following circumstances?

    I. He is a buyer of a call.
    II. He is a buyer of a put.
    III. He is a seller of a call.
    IV. He is a seller of a put.

    A. I and III
    B. I and IV
    C. II and III
    D. II and IV

19. Which of the following option investors are bearish?

    I. Buyer of a call
    II. Writer of a call
    III. Buyer of a put
    IV. Writer of a put

    A. I and II
    B. I and IV
    C. II and III
    D. III and IV

◆ Answers & Rationale

1.   **A.**   Bond interest is an expense of the firm, and when it is paid, it reduces the earnings of the firm. If the bonds were to convert, there would be no more interest payments; therefore, the company would have higher earnings. There will be more shares of common stock outstanding, and this will normally translate to lower earnings per share for the common. Interest costs would be reduced, earnings would increase and the number of shares would increase.   (Page 18)

2.   **A.**   Because interest rate movements drive the prices of preferred stocks, in a period of stable interest rates, preferred stocks will not fluctuate in value. However, convertible preferred stocks will fluctuate with movements in the price of common stock into which the preferred can be converted.   (Page 18)

3.   **B.**   A bondholder is a creditor (whether or not the bond is convertible). Only after the bond is converted to stock is she considered to be an owner.   (Page 18)

4.   **D.**   All of the factors listed affect the price of a convertible bond. The rating of a bond reflects the issuing company's health and therefore indirectly affects the value of the investment.   (Page 18)

5.   **A.**   Coupon rates are not higher; they are lower because of the value of the conversion feature. The bondholders are creditors, and if the stock price falls, the conversion feature will not influence the bond's price.   (Page 19)

6.   **C.**

$$\frac{\$1{,}000 \text{ par value}}{\$50 \text{ conversion}} = 20 \text{ shares per bond}$$

(Page 19)

7.   **B.**   Acme preferred may be converted into four shares of common ($100 \div \$25 = 4$). With the convertible preferred trading at 110, the common stock must be trading at 27 1/2 for four shares of common stock to be of equivalent value with one share of preferred. To calculate the parity price of the common stock, divide the current market price of the preferred stock by the number of shares of common stock that would be received for converting to the preferred ($110 \div 4 = 27$ 1/2).   (Page 19)

8.   **B.**   The bond is quoted as 120; therefore, it is selling for $1,200. Parity of the stock in which the holder of the bond can convert is equal to $24 as follows. The bondholder would be able to convert the bond into 50 shares of stock (face amount $1,000 \div \$20$ per share = 50 shares), because the bond has a current price of $1,200; dividing this amount by 50 equals parity price of the underlying stock.   (Page 19)

9.   **D.**   Parity is the equivalent value between a convertible bond and the underlying common stock into which the bond may be converted. Imbalances can occur when sudden moves in interest rates affect the value of the bond, when company earnings affect the stock's price and when bond or stock market movements affect the value of an individual security traded in the respective market.
                    (Page 19)

10.   **D.**   The question defines a rights offering.   (Page 20)

11.   **C.**   Rights are issued by the corporation that give the subscriber the right to purchase stock within a short period of time at a price lower than the stock's current market price. Rights do not have to be exercised but may be traded in the secondary market. Warrants are commonly used as a sweetener in debenture offerings.   (Page 21)

12.   **B.**   A warrant is a purchase option for stock for a long period of time. The warrant allows the holder to purchase common stock for a set price. Rights and options have a short life.   (Page 21)

13.   **A.**   Warrants, common stock and options all have an active secondary market.   (Page 21)

14. **D.** Warrants are usually issued as a sweetener to a deal. For example, if a company wants to issue bonds at an interest rate lower than general market rates, it could throw in some warrants to make the bonds more attractive. Warrants are usually issued with a very long life and give the holder the right to purchase stock above the current market price. When a corporation has common stock outstanding and wants to issue more common stock, it must offer the shares to the current shareholders first (preemptive rights). (Page 21)

15. **D.** Warrants do not pay dividends under any circumstances. The other instruments listed will pay dividends when declared by the board of directors. (Page 21)

16. **D.** Warrants are commonly used as a sweetener in debenture offerings and carry a long life. Rights are issued by the corporation to give the subscriber the right to purchase stock within a short period of time at a price lower than the stock's current market price. Warrants do not have to be exercised but may be traded in the secondary market. (Page 21)

17. **B.** The holder of a call has the right to buy stock at the strike price; the seller of a put is obligated to buy stock at the strike price if exercised. (Page 22)

18. **C.** The holder of a put has the right to sell stock at the strike price; the seller of a call is obligated to sell stock at the strike price if exercised. (Page 22)

19. **C.** Options investors who are in a position to sell the stock (put buyers and call writers) have a bearish outlook. Remember that diagonal positions (those positions that are total opposites, such as buys versus sells and puts versus calls) are on the same side of the market. (Page 22)

7 U.S. Government Securities Exam

1. Treasury bills can be described as

    A. issued at par
    B. callable
    C. issued in bearer form
    D. registered

2. Which of the following maturities is available to investors in newly issued Treasury bills?

    A. One week
    B. One month
    C. Six months
    D. Nine months

3. What is the maturity of a T bill?

    A. 20 years
    B. 10 years
    C. 5 years
    D. 1 year or less

4. If interest rates in general are rising, the price of new T bills should

    A. rise
    B. fall
    C. remain steady
    D. fluctuate

5. Which of the following statements is(are) true of Treasury bills?

    I. They are sold at a discount.
    II. They pay a fixed rate of interest semiannually.
    III. They mature in one year or less.
    IV. They mature in ten years or more.

    A. I, II and III
    B. I and III
    C. II and IV
    D. III

6. A customer who watches the T bill auctions noticed that the average return to investors in the latest T bill auction fell to 4.71%, down from 4.82% at the previous week's sale. When he asks you for your interpretation, you tell him that

    A. the decline in yields indicates that the supply of short-term funds has decreased relative to demand
    B. investors who purchased bills at this auction paid more for them than purchasers at the previous week's sale
    C. investors who purchased T bills twelve weeks ago paid less than purchasers since that time
    D. the federal funds rate and other short-term interest rate indicators are probably rising

7. The newspaper indicates that T bill yields have gone down. This means that T bill prices

    A. are up
    B. are down
    C. are mixed
    D. cannot be determined

8. Which of the following choices lists T bills, T bonds and T notes in ascending order of maturity?

    A. notes, bills, bonds
    B. bonds, notes, bills
    C. bills, bonds, notes
    D. bills, notes, bonds

9. One of your customers would like to invest in a fairly safe security, but is not interested in regular income. Which of the following securities are offered at a discount and would meet his needs?

    A. GNMA certificates
    B. FHLB securities
    C. FNMA certificates
    D. U.S. Treasury STRIPS

10. Which of the following Treasury securities allows an investor to lock in a yield for an extended period of time by minimizing reinvestment risk?

    A. Treasury bill
    B. Treasury STRIP
    C. Treasury bond
    D. Treasury note

11. Your clients would like to have $40,000 set aside when their child starts college, but do not want to invest in anything that could endanger their principal. In this situation, you should recommend

    A. zero-coupon bonds or Treasury STRIPS
    B. corporate bonds with a high rate of interest payment
    C. municipal bonds for their long-term tax benefits
    D. Treasury bills

12. All of the following are true of a Treasury receipt EXCEPT

    A. it may be issued by a securities broker-dealer
    B. it is backed by the full faith and credit of the federal government
    C. the interest coupons are sold separately
    D. it may be purchased at a discount

13. Bea Kuhl owns several Series EE bonds. She wishes to redeem them after three years. She would

    I.   pay federal income tax on the interest she has earned
    II. sell them through her broker
    III. receive the same rate of interest as she would have had she held the bonds to maturity

    A. I only
    B. I and II only
    C. II and III only
    D. I, II and III

14. An investor is looking into the purchase of Series EE bonds through payroll deduction at his place of employment. If the investor decides to purchase the Series EE bonds, he will receive the interest earned

    A. monthly
    B. semiannually
    C. annually
    D. at redemption

15. Which of the following is a nontransferable government instrument?

    A. T bond
    B. T bill
    C. T note
    D. EE savings bond

16. Which type of nonmarketable security pays semiannual interest?

    A. Series EE bonds
    B. Treasury bonds
    C. Series HH bonds
    D. Agency issues

◆ Answers & Rationale

1. **D.** A registered security is any security for which ownership is recorded in files maintained for this purpose. Even though T bills are book-entry securities (no certificates are issued), ownership records are maintained and, therefore, they are considered registered. (Page 25)

2. **C.** Investors can acquire Treasury bills at the weekly T bill auction in denominations of $10,000 and up with maturities of three months, six months and twelve months. The U.S. government can issue nine-month certificates, but currently does not. (Page 25)

3. **D.** A Treasury bill matures in one year or less. (Page 25)

4. **B.** Bill prices decrease as interest rates rise. (Page 25)

5. **B.** T bills are sold at a discount and have maturities of up to one year. Although they mature at face value, it is not considered interest. (Page 25)

6. **B.** As rates for T bills drop, T bill prices climb; T bill rates and prices have an inverse relationship. T bills are priced at their yield, so an investor who bids 4.71% is actually paying more for a T bill than one who bids 4.82%. (Page 25)

7. **A.** If the yields have gone down, that means that the discount has been reduced; therefore, the dollar cost of bills has gone up. (Page 25)

8. **D.** T bills mature in one year or less. T notes mature in one to ten years. T bonds mature in ten years or more. (Page 25)

9. **D.** U.S. Treasury STRIPS (Separate Trading of Registered Interest and Principal of Securities) are direct obligations of the U.S. Treasury issued in the form of zero-coupon bonds. Zero-coupon bonds pay no interest. They are issued at a discount and appreciate in value each period until maturity. (Page 26)

10. **B.** This is actually a three-part question pertaining to locking in yield, a long period of time and reinvesting with minimum risk. The long time aspect is easily handled in that bonds are longer term securities than notes or bills. STRIPS (Separate Trading of Registered Interest and Principal of Securities) are T bonds with the coupons removed. The choice between bonds and STRIPS is simplified when reinvestment risk is considered. STRIPS don't pay interest; instead, they are sold at a deep discount and mature at face par value. Consequently, there are no interest payments to be reinvested and no reinvestment risk. This is also how the investor locks in a yield. (Page 26)

11. **A.** Zero-coupon bonds represent the lowest risk coupled with the highest return of all the investments listed. They offer no current income. (Page 26)

12. **B.** Although the Treasury securities underlying Treasury receipts are backed by the full faith and credit of the federal government, the stripped securities are not. (Page 26)

13. **A.** A Series EE bond is a nonnegotiable instrument. The bond is redeemed by the government (usually through a bank). The interest received by the bondholder will be less if the bond is redeemed prior to maturity. The difference between purchase price and redemption value represents interest, which is taxable at the federal level. (Page 27)

14. **D.** Interest on Series EE bonds is received at redemption of the bonds. (Page 27)

15. **D.** An EE bond is nontransferable. It may only be redeemed by the owner of record. (Page 27)

16. **C.** Series EE bonds are sold at a discount and mature to face value; T bonds and agency issues are marketable debt. HH bonds are nonmarketable and pay interest semiannually. (Page 27)

8 Agency Issues Exam

1. A client could be assured of federal government backing for an investment in which of the following agencies?

    A. Federal National Mortgage Association
    B. Inter-American Development Bank
    C. Government National Mortgage Association
    D. Federal Intermediate Credit Bank

2. In describing GNMAs to a potential investor, you should tell him that

    A. the certificates have the full faith and credit guarantee of the U.S. government
    B. each bond is backed by a pool of insured mortgages
    C. interest payments received by the investor are exempt from both local and federal income taxes
    D. a GNMA can be purchased for as little as $10,000

3. An investor interested in monthly interest income should invest in

    A. GNMAs
    B. Treasury bonds
    C. stock of a utility company
    D. corporate bonds

4. Which of the following securities pays interest monthly?

    A. T bill
    B. Commercial paper
    C. Municipal general obligation bond
    D. Government National Mortgage Association pass-through certificate

◆ Answers & Rationale

1.   **C.**   Only the Government National Mortgage Association issues securities backed by the full faith and credit of the U.S. government. The remainder are considered government agencies and, although their securities are considered second only to U.S. government issues in safety, they do not have direct U.S. government backing.

(Page 29)

2.   **A.**   The certificates issued by GNMA represent interests in government-insured mortgages pooled by mortgage brokers (who guarantee the monthly cash flow), but it is the U.S. government that actually "backs" GNMA pass-through certificates. GNMA pass-throughs are issued in minimum denominations of $25,000, and all interest earned is subject to federal income tax. (Page 29)

3.   **A.**   The mortgages underlying GNMA modified pass-through certificates pay interest on a monthly basis. GNMA then passes this monthly income through to investors in GNMA pass-through certificates.   (Page 29)

4.   **D.**   Government National Mortgage Association (GNMA) pass-through certificates pay investors interest and a return of principal on a monthly basis. Treasury bills and most commercial paper are sold on a discounted basis and mature for a par amount. The dollar difference between the discounted amount and par is the earned interest. Municipal bonds pay interest on a semiannual basis.   (Page 29)

9 Municipal Bonds Exam

1. The doctrine of reciprocal immunity for municipal bonds originated in

   A. U.S. Supreme Court decisions
   B. state laws
   C. federal laws
   D. IRS interpretations

2. The interest from which of the following bonds is exempt from federal income tax?

   I. State of California bonds
   II. City of Anchorage bonds
   III. Treasury bonds
   IV. GNMA bonds

   A. I and II only
   B. I, II and IV only
   C. III and IV only
   D. I, II, III and IV

3. Sadie Longhorn lives in Detroit, Michigan. She is interested in purchasing bonds that are exempt from state income tax. The interest from which of the following bonds is exempt from Michigan state income tax?

   I. State of California bonds
   II. Michigan Toll Authority bonds
   III. Treasury bills
   IV. Treasury bonds

   A. I and II only
   B. I and IV only
   C. II, III and IV only
   D. I, II, III and IV

4. Investors buy municipal bonds for which of the following reasons?

   I. The interest is federally exempt for qualifying issues.
   II. The interest is locally and state exempt.
   III. Issues and maturities may be diversified.

   A. I
   B. I and II
   C. I and III
   D. II

5. The formula used to determine the tax-equivalent yield between a taxable and a nontaxable bond and to compare corporate return with municipal return is

   A. nominal yield divided by 100% minus the investor's tax bracket
   B. nominal yield plus 100% minus the investor's tax bracket
   C. nominal yield multiplied by 100% minus the investor's tax bracket
   D. nominal yield minus 100% minus the investor's tax bracket

6. A taxpayer in the 28% bracket would net the highest aftertax income from a

   A. 5% municipal bond
   B. 5 1/2% T bill
   C. 6% income bond
   D. 6 1/2% corporate bond

7. Municipal bonds are issued as either revenue bonds or general obligation bonds. The characteristics of general obligation bonds are

    I.   interest from general obligation bonds is exempt from federal income taxes
    II. interest is payable only from the revenue of the facility being financed
    III. these bonds do not have to carry a legal opinion of counsel
    IV. the principal of these bonds is backed by the full faith and credit of the issuing municipality

    A. I and II only
    B. I and IV only
    C. II and IV only
    D. I, II, III and IV

8. Which of the following sources of funds back revenue bonds?

    I.   Federal revenue sharing
    II. Special taxes on tobacco and alcohol
    III. Rental payments under leaseback arrangements
    IV. Tolls and fees

    A. I and III only
    B. II, III and IV only
    C. III and IV only
    D. I, II, III and IV

9. Cities and states issue both revenue bonds and general obligation bonds. Which of the following are characteristics of revenue bonds?

    I.   Interest from revenue bonds is exempt from federal income taxes.
    II. Interest is payable only from the revenue of the facility being financed.
    III. These bonds do not have to carry a legal opinion of counsel.
    IV. The principal of these bonds is payable only from the revenue of the facility being financed.

    A. I and II only
    B. I, II and IV only
    C. IV only
    D. I, II, III and IV

10. What secures an industrial development revenue bond?

    A. State tax
    B. Municipal tax
    C. Trustee
    D. Net lease payments from the corporation

◆ Answers & Rationale

1. **A.** The doctrine of reciprocal immunity, or mutual exclusion, was determined in the Supreme Court Case of *McCulloch v. Maryland.* (Page 31)

2. **A.** Municipal bonds are exempt from federal income tax. Treasury bonds are exempt from state tax. GNMAs are subject to federal and state income tax. (Page 31)

3. **C.** Municipal bonds are exempt from federal income tax and from state tax only within the state of issue. U.S. Treasury issues are subject to federal income tax, but would be exempt from state taxes. The California bond would be exempt from state tax in California but not in Michigan. (Page 31)

4. **C.** Because municipal bonds typically are serial bonds, it is easy to diversify maturities. The interest on municipal bonds is exempt from federal income tax, but subject to state and local tax. (Page 31)

5. **A.** Tax-equivalent yield on bonds issued between municipalities and corporations is determined by dividing the municipal bond's nominal yield by the difference in the investor's tax bracket. In reality, since municipal securities are quoted in yield to maturity, the truest measure of equivalency uses the bond's yield to maturity. (Page 31)

6. **A.** Municipal bonds are exempt from federal taxation and in most cases from taxation by the state in which they are issued. This particular investor would be taxed at the 28% level. The equiva-lent yield on a corporate bond would be 6.94% (5% ÷ 72%). (Page 32)

7. **B.** All municipal bonds must carry a legal opinion of counsel affirming that the issue is a municipal issue and interest is exempt from federal taxation. Interest and principal of a revenue bond will be paid only if the facility financed produces the revenue necessary to pay. A GO is a municipal issue backed by the full faith and credit of the municipality. (Page 32)

8. **B.** Typical sources of funds for revenue bonds include user charges, special taxes, payments under leaseback arrangements, lease revenues, and tolls and other fees from the operation of the facility. Federal revenue sharing is not a funding source for revenue bonds. (Page 33)

9. **B.** A revenue bond is a municipal issue sold to raise funds for the purpose of constructing a revenue-producing facility. All municipal bonds require an opinion of specialized bond counsel stating that the issue does indeed represent a municipal obligation and that interest payments are exempt from federal taxation. The interest and principal payments are backed to the extent the facility produces enough revenue to make payments. (Page 33)

10. **D.** IDRs are issued by municipalities to construct a facility that will be used by, or is being constructed for the benefit of a corporation. When this is done, the corporation is required to sign a long-term lease. Although classified as a municipal security, IDRs are backed by the revenues of the corporation participating in the project. (Page 33)

10   The Money Market Exam

1. Which of the following are characteristics of money-market instruments?

    A. They are backed by promises to repay a sum of money within a stated period of time.
    B. They are used to borrow money for short periods of time.
    C. They are issued by corporations and governmental bodies.
    D. All of the above

2. Which of the following is a money-market instrument?

    A. Short-term debt
    B. Long-term debt
    C. Short-term equity
    D. Long-term equity

3. One of the most important functions of a banker's acceptance is its use as a means of

    A. facilitating trades in foreign goods
    B. facilitating trades of foreign securities in the United States
    C. assigning previously declared distributions by foreign corporations
    D. guaranteeing payment of an international bank's promissory note

4. Which of the following are characteristics of commercial paper?

    I. Backed by money-market deposits
    II. Negotiated maturities and yields
    III. Issued by commercial banks
    IV. Not registered as securities

    A. I and II
    B. I, II and III
    C. II and IV
    D. III and IV

5. Corporations issue commercial paper with maturities ranging from as little as 1 day to as long as

    A. 7 days
    B. 90 days
    C. 270 days
    D. 365 days

6. Which of the following types of corporations typically do NOT issue commercial paper?

    A. Commercial banks and holding companies
    B. Investment and finance companies
    C. Industrial and service companies
    D. Brokerage and insurance firms

◆ Answers & Rationale

1. **D.** Money-market instruments are unsecured short-term debt instruments used by corporations and federal, state and city governments to borrow money. (Page 34)

2. **A.** A money-market instrument is short-term debt with one year or less to maturity. (Page 34)

3. **A.** A banker's acceptance is a time draft typically used to facilitate overseas trading ventures. It is guaranteed by a bank on behalf of a corporation in payment for goods or services. (Page 35)

4. **C.** Commercial paper represents the unsecured debt obligations of corporations in need of short-term financing. Both yield and maturity are open to negotiation. Because commercial paper is issued with maturities of less than 270 days, it is exempt from registration under the act of 1933. (Page 35)

5. **C.** Commercial paper is issued by corporations with a maximum maturity of 270 days, in part to avoid certain registration requirements under the act of 1933. (Page 35)

6. **A.** Commercial paper is unsecured short-term debt issued by corporations as a means of financing short-term needs. It is issued at a discount from face value and generally matures within 270 days. Commercial banks issue CDs and BAs. (Page 35)

11 Securities Markets and Broker-Dealers Exam

1. Which of the following statements about transactions in the different securities markets is(are) true?

   I. Transactions in listed securities occur primarily in the exchange markets.
   II. Transactions in unlisted securities occur primarily in the OTC market.
   III. Transactions in listed securities that occur in the OTC market are said to take place in the third market.
   IV. Transactions in listed securities that occur directly between customers or institutions without using broker-dealers as intermediaries are said to take place in the fourth market.

   A. I only
   B. I and II only
   C. II and III only
   D. I, II, III and IV

2. Which of the following trades occur(s) in the secondary market?

   I. Specialist on the NYSE buying stocks for his own inventory
   II. Municipal bond syndicate selling new issues to the public
   III. Registered representative buying unlisted securities for a client
   IV. Insurance company buying municipal bonds directly from another insurance company

   A. I, II and III
   B. I, III and IV
   C. II and III
   D. IV

3. The bulk of the securities trading over the counter are

   I. listed registered securities
   II. unlisted nonexempt securities
   III. registered unlisted securities
   IV. unregistered exempt securities

   A. I and II
   B. I and III
   C. II and III
   D. II, III and IV

4. What is the function of Nasdaq?

    I.   It is a computerized system available to market makers allowing the subscriber to access bid and ask quotations and quotation sizes for all market makers in the OTC market.
    II. It is a computerized system available to market makers allowing them to complete trades in the OTC market.
    III. It is a computerized system allowing OTC market makers to complete transactions on the floor of the NYSE.
    IV. It is a computerized system allowing clients to trade directly with OTC market makers.

    A. I only
    B. II only
    C. II and III only
    D. I, II, III and IV

5. An open-ended investment company bought preferred utility stock from a bank through INSTINET. This trade took place in the

    A. primary market
    B. secondary market
    C. third market
    D. fourth market

6. Securities trading on the NYSE can be best characterized as taking place in a(n)

    A. floor fracas
    B. Dutch auction
    C. double auction market
    D. blind and closed bid market

7. The over-the-counter market could be characterized as which of the following?

    A. Auction market
    B. Double-auction market
    C. Negotiated market
    D. None of the above

8. Your firm, Serendipity Securities, has received an order from one of your customers to buy 300 shares of DWQ at the market. Serendipity goes into the market, buys 300 shares of DWQ from another broker-dealer, and delivers them to the account of your customer. Serendipity's role in this transaction was that of a

    A. broker acting as an agent for a commission
    B. dealer acting as a principal for a profit
    C. broker acting as an agent for a profit
    D. dealer acting as a principal for a commission

9. When a broker-dealer is holding money and/or securities in its own account, it is

    A. underwriting
    B. hypothecating the securities
    C. taking a position
    D. engaging in none of the above

10. When a client gives a broker-dealer an order to buy securities, the broker-dealer may

    I.   act as the client's agent by finding a seller and arranging the sale
    II. buy the securities, mark up the price and resell them to the client on a dealer basis
    III. sell the shares from its own inventory to the client if it has the security in inventory

    A. I only
    B. I and II only
    C. II and III only
    D. I, II and III

◆ Answers & Rationale

1. **D.** Listed securities traded on exchanges compose the exchange market. Unlisted securities traded over the counter are the OTC market. Listed securities traded OTC compose the third market. Securities bought and sold without the aid of a broker-dealer compose the fourth market. INSTINET is a reporting service used by many institutions to locate other parties for fourth-market equity transactions. (Page 37)

2. **B.** Underwriters distribute new issues in the primary market. The secondary market is the trading market. In the trading market, a trade can take place on a stock exchange; in the unlisted or over-the-counter market; by trading listed securities in the over-the-counter market (the third market); or in a direct institution-to-institution trade without the services of a brokerage firm (the fourth market). (Page 37)

3. **D.** The SEC governs the securities that are to be traded in the over-the-counter market through registration requirements. Companies with 500 stockholders and $5 million in assets must register with the SEC. Registered securities that are not listed on an exchange constitute the bulk of the volume of trade of OTC equity securities. Municipal bonds and government securities are exempt from SEC registration requirements. The primary market for these unregistered, exempt securities is the OTC market. (Page 37)

4. **A.** Nasdaq is available on three levels of service, but it is primarily a method for obtaining information on prices (bid and ask) and inventories of OTC-traded securities. (Page 37)

5. **D.** The fourth market consists of direct trades between institutions, pension funds, broker-dealers and others. Many of these trades use INSTINET. (Page 38)

6. **C.** Listed markets (such as the NYSE) operate as double-auction markets. Floor brokers compete among themselves to execute trades at prices most favorable to the public. (Page 38)

7. **C.** The New York Stock Exchange is an auction market, and the OTC market is a negotiated market. (Page 39)

8. **A.** Your firm was acting as the customer's agent in acquiring the 300 shares of DWQ. The best way to remember the difference between brokers and dealers is through the letters BAC/DPP. They stand for "Brokers act as Agents for Commissions/ Dealers act as Principals for Profits." *Profit* is another way of saying *markup*. (Page 39)

9. **C.** When a dealer is holding securities for its own account, it is considered to be taking a position. (Page 39)

10. **D.** The broker-dealer can buy and sell securities either as an agent, charging a commission on a transaction and having no risk, or as a dealer, charging a markup or markdown and sharing the risk. (Page 40)

 **12** **The Underwriting Process Exam**

1. Which of the following actions is(are) the responsibility of an investment banker?

   I. Distributing large blocks of stock to the public and to institutions
   II. Buying previously unissued securities from an issuer and selling them to the public
   III. Raising long-term capital for corporations by underwriting new issues of securities
   IV. Lending money to corporate clients that require debt financing

   A. I, II and III only
   B. I, II and IV only
   C. III only
   D. I, II, III and IV

2. Which of the following is NOT a basic responsibility of an investment banker?

   A. Distributing large blocks of stock to the public and to institutions
   B. Providing a secondary market for securities that have been issued
   C. Giving advice to corporations on the best way to raise long-term capital
   D. Buying previously unissued securities from an issuer and selling them to the public

3. This Can't Be Sushi (TCB) will be offering $7,000,000 of its common stock in its home state and in three other states. For the offering to be cleared for sale by the SEC, TCB must file a(n)

   A. offering circular
   B. registration statement
   C. letter of notification
   D. preliminary prospectus

4. Consolidated Codfish would like to offer its new issue of 1,000,000 shares of common through Churnim, Burnum, Spernem to investors in the three states in which it has customers. What registration and sales restrictions will apply?

   I. The offering needs to be registered only in Consolidated Codfish's home state.
   II. COD shares can only be sold by registered reps licensed to sell securities in those states.
   III. CBS must arrange to have tombstones published in each of those states.
   IV. The offering must be blue-skyed in each of the three states in which the issue will be sold.

   A. I and III
   B. II, III and IV
   C. II and IV
   D. III and IV

5.   Which of the following is(are) the responsibility of an underwriter?

I.   Managing the distribution of large blocks of stock to the public and to institutions
II.   Selling a predetermined share of an offering to its customers
III.   Raising capital for corporations by assisting in the distribution of a corporation's new offering
IV.   Lending money to corporate clients that require debt financing

A.   I, II and III only
B.   I, II and IV only
C.   II only
D.   I, II, III and IV

6.   Which of the following would be underwriting an issue of securities?

A.   Chip Bullock sells his stock in ALF through his broker.
B.   Joe Kuhl, a director of Acme Zootech, purchases Acme stock.
C.   Fleecem Runn Skippe, a broker-dealer, sells a block of outstanding stock in Datawaq to Acme Sweatsocks.
D.   The Moneyflow and Cash Co., a broker-dealer, sells a new issue of KLP Bonds to the public.

7.   Which of the following activities are characteristic of a primary offering?

I.   Raising additional capital for the company
II.   Selling previously issued securities
III.   Increasing the number of shares or bonds outstanding

A.   I and II only
B.   I and III only
C.   II and III only
D.   I, II and III

8.   A secondary distribution is

A.   a distribution that is accomplished without an investment banker
B.   used to achieve a better price than the current market
C.   a method of redistributing a large block of stock without significantly affecting the market price
D.   a new issue of stock or bonds that is being offered by a "second tier" company

◆ Answers & Rationale

1. **A.** "Investment bankers" is another term for "broker-dealers." They do everything listed except lend money to corporate clients that require debt financing.   (Page 41)

2. **B.** The main functions of an investment banker are raising intermediate and long-term capital for corporations through the distribution of securities, buying securities from an issuer and reselling them to the public, distributing large blocks of stock and giving advice to corporations on the best way to raise long-term capital. It is not the responsibility of the investment banker to provide a continuing secondary market for securities once they have been issued.   (Page 41)

3. **B.** Because TCB's $7,000,000 issue is over $5,000,000, it must file a standard registration statement. If the issue were under the $5,000,000 Regulation A filing limit, it would have to file only a letter of notification.   (Page 41)

4. **C.** In order to sell an issue in any state, the broker-dealer, the registered reps and the security itself must each be registered in that state. Registering an issue in a state is known as *blue-skying* the issue.   (Page 41)

5. **A.** An underwriter manages the offering and helps the corporation to raise capital.
(Page 42)

6. **D.** Underwriting is the effort of a broker-dealer to market and raise capital for a company issuing new securities. The money raised goes to the issuer, as opposed to the seller of a previously outstanding security (secondary transaction) as is the case in answers A, B and C.   (Page 42)

7. **B.** A primary offering involves the sale of previously unissued securities. The issuing company receives the proceeds from the sale. Of course, once the securities are sold, there will be more securities outstanding and in the hands of the public.   (Page 42)

8. **C.** A secondary distribution is the sale of stock that has been previously issued and owned. A key purpose of a secondary distribution is to redistribute a large block of stock without significantly affecting the market price. Like a primary distribution, an underwriting manager makes distribution arrangements and a syndicate may be formed. In a secondary distribution, the securities are usually offered at a fixed price that is closely related to the current market price so as not to upset the market significantly.   (Page 43)

13 Market Terms Exam

1. If Joe Kuhl fails to make payment for the ATF Mutual Fund shares within the required amount of time, the broker-dealer could

   I.   cancel the order
   II. fine Joe based on the dollar amount of the sale
   III. sell the securities and charge Joe for any loss

   A. I and II only
   B. I and III only
   C. III only
   D. I, II and III

2. A customer confirmation must

   I.   contain all relevant information concerning the trade
   II. be sent within 24 hours of the trade
   III. be sent by settlement of the trade
   IV. accompany the delivery of the stock certificate

   A. I
   B. I and III
   C. II
   D. II and IV

3. Under the Uniform Practice Code, regular way transactions settle on the

   A. same day as trade date
   B. fourth business day following trade date
   C. third business day following trade date
   D. seventh business day following trade date

4. Lotta Leveridge wants to place an order to sell 20 TIP bonds. She currently has no TIP in her account. As her registered rep, before accepting the order you must try to determine which of the following?

   A. Name of the broker from which the security was purchased
   B. Where the securities are currently held and whether they can be delivered in three business days
   C. Willingness of Ms. Leveridge to deliver other securities from her account should she fail to deliver the TIP
   D. Whether she will pledge her other securities as collateral to secure a loan to effect timely delivery

5. When accepting a client's sell order, a broker-dealer must determine all of the following EXCEPT

   A. if the securities are in deliverable form
   B. the location of the securities
   C. if the client can make delivery promptly
   D. if the securities have been accepted by the transfer agent

6. The final determination on good delivery is made by the

   A. NASD or MSRB
   B. transfer agent
   C. member firm's cashiering department
   D. SEC

7. The regular way ex-dividend date for stock is the

   A. second business day preceding the record date
   B. fourth business day following the record date
   C. fourth business day preceding the settlement date
   D. fifth business day preceding the record date

8. Adam Grizzly owns 100 shares of CowTec. A dividend is declared on August 30th. The dividend will be paid to stockholders of record on Thursday, September 15th. When will the stock sell ex-dividend?

   A. September 11th
   B. September 12th
   C. September 13th
   D. September 15th

9. Hugh Heifer buys shares of the ACE Fund shortly before the ex-dividend date. Before he buys the shares, Hugh should understand that

   A. the price of the shares will decline on the ex-dividend date by the amount of the distribution
   B. if he reinvests the dividend, he will not be liable for taxes on the dividend received
   C. there is a great advantage to his purchasing the shares immediately so that he can receive the dividend
   D. all of the above may occur

◆ Answers & Rationale

1.   **C.**   If Joe fails to pay for the shares within five business days, the broker-dealer must sell the shares to pay for the transaction. Any gain or loss will be settled between the broker-dealer and Joe. The order has taken place and cannot be canceled.   (Page 44)

2.   **B.**   A customer confirmation must contain information on price, quantity, identity and commission or markup and must be sent by settlement. Broker-to-broker confirmations must be sent within 24 hours (the day of or the day after the trade).   (Page 44)

3.   **C.**   Under the Uniform Practice Code, regular way trades settle three business days after the trade date.   (Page 45)

4.   **B.**   The rep should ascertain the location of the securities as well as whether the customer can deliver within three business days, so the firm can make timely delivery. The broker from which the securities were purchased and the security holdings of the customer are immaterial.   (Page 45)

5.   **D.**   A broker-dealer must determine answers A through C. Acceptance by the transfer agent is not a factor when placing a sell order.   (Page 45)

6.   **B.**   The final determination on good delivery is made by the transfer agent because it ultimately accepts or rejects the certificate.   (Page 45)

7.   **A.**   The regular way ex-dividend date is two business days before the record date. This is the date on which the value of the stock is reduced by the dividend.   (Page 46)

8.   **C.**   The ex-dividend date is always two business days before the record date. In this case the record date is Thursday, September 15th, so the ex-date will be Tuesday, September 13th.   (Page 46)

9.   **A.**   Share prices decline on the ex-dividend date. Dividend distributions cause a tax liability, and so the purchase of shares right before an ex-dividend date is not a good idea because of this.   (Page 46)

14 Economics and Government Economic Policy Exam

1. Arrange the following economic phases in the normal order in which they occur.

   I. Contraction
   II. Expansion
   III. Peak
   IV. Trough

   A. I, II, III, IV
   B. II, III, I, IV
   C. III, II, I, IV
   D. IV, I, III, II

2. What term do economists use to describe a downturn in the economy that lasts more than two consecutive quarters?

   A. Inflation
   B. Stagflation
   C. Depression
   D. Recession

3. An economic downturn that lasts for six months is called

   A. a recession
   B. a depression
   C. progressive
   D. regressive

4. If inflation momentum is decreasing, the value of fixed-income securities would be

   A. stable
   B. increasing
   C. decreasing
   D. fluctuating

5. Which organization or governmental unit sets fiscal policy?

   A. Federal Reserve Board
   B. Government Economic Board
   C. Congress
   D. Secretary of the Treasury

6. What organization or governmental unit sets economic policy?

   A. Federal Reserve Board
   B. Government Economic Board
   C. Congress
   D. Secretary of the Treasury

7. Which of the following are responsibilities of the Federal Reserve Board?

   I. Acting as an agent for the U.S. Treasury
   II. Regulating credit
   III. Serving as the nation's central bank
   IV. Setting the prime rate

   A. I, II and III only
   B. I and III only
   C. II and IV only
   D. I, II, III and IV

8. Federal funds are used primarily by

   A. large commercial banks
   B. mutual insurance companies
   C. independent broker-dealers
   D. savings and loans

9. Which of the following statements best describes the federal funds rate?

    A. It is the average rate for short-term bank loans last week.
    B. It is the rate charged by major New York City banks.
    C. It is a rate that changes daily and that banks charge each other.
    D. It is the rate major New York City banks charge broker-dealers.

10. Federal Open Market Committee activities are closely watched by Wall Street because of the effect of its decisions on all of the following EXCEPT

    A. money supply
    B. interest rates
    C. exchange rates
    D. money velocity

11. In its attempt to increase the money supply, the Federal Open Market Committee is purchasing T bills. This action should cause the yield on T bills to

    A. increase
    B. decrease
    C. fluctuate
    D. stabilize

12. If the Federal Open Market Committee has decided that the rate of inflation is too high, it is MOST likely to

    I.   tighten the money supply
    II. loosen the money supply
    III. lower the discount rate
    IV. raise the discount rate

    A. I and III
    B. I and IV
    C. II and III
    D. II and IV

◆ Answers & Rationale

1. **B.** Economists consider expansion (recovery) as the beginning of the business cycle, followed by the peak (prosperity), contraction (recession or deflation) and the trough.
(Page 48)

2. **D.** An economic downturn that lasts for more than two consecutive quarters (six months) is known as a *recession*. (Page 48)

3. **A.** When the economy is bad for six months (or two consecutive quarters), we are in a recession; if it continues, we go into a depression. (Page 48)

4. **B.** When the rate of inflation is declining, the coupon rate of new issue bonds will be less and yields will decline. The price of outstanding bonds will rise to adjust their yield. (Page 49)

5. **C.** Congress sets fiscal policy, while the FRB sets monetary policy. (Page 50)

6. **C.** Congress sets fiscal policy, while the FRB sets monetary policy. (Page 50)

7. **A.** The Fed is the nation's independent monetary authority and central bank. It acts as the fiscal agent for the Treasury and attempts to maintain monetary stability and regulate credit. The prime rate is set by commercial banks, not by the Federal Reserve. (Page 50)

8. **A.** The federal funds rate is the rate of interest at which member banks of the Federal Reserve System can borrow excess funds from other members, usually on an overnight basis. (Page 50)

9. **C.** The federal funds rate is what banks charge each other for overnight loans. It can fluctuate hourly. (Page 51)

10. **C.** The FOMC is one of the most influential committees in the Federal Reserve System, and its decisions affect money supplies, interest rates and even the speed at which dollars turn over (money velocity). The foreign exchange rate is set in the interbank market. (Page 52)

11. **B.** The purpose of the FOMC purchase is to increase the attractiveness (market price) of T bills. Because the price will be driven up by an increased market demand and a decreased supply, yields should decrease. (Page 52)

12. **B.** If the FOMC decides that it is in the economy's interest to lower the inflation rate, it can encourage this to occur by raising the discount rate, which in turn will tighten the money supply.
(Page 52)

15 Analyzing Financial Risks and Rewards Exam

1. June Polar wishes to buy Datawaq bonds. You, as her representative, have advised her that the trade is unsuitable. If she decides to go ahead with the purchase, you must

   A. execute the trade specifically as she has directed you to do
   B. execute the trade if the NASD approves
   C. execute the trade only if Mrs. Anderson has previous trading experience in similar securities
   D. not execute the trade

2. Any recommendations made to customers by a broker-dealer must be suitable for the customer based on an investigation of the customer's

   I. investment objectives
   II. financial background
   III. tax status

   A. I only
   B. I and II only
   C. II and III only
   D. I, II and III

3. If a customer is concerned about reinvestment risk, which of the following securities would you NOT recommend?

   A. Treasury bills
   B. Project notes
   C. 10-year corporate bonds
   D. 18-year municipal bonds

4. Which of the following statements about corporate bonds are true?

   I. They represent ownership in the corporation.
   II. They generally involve less market risk than common stock.
   III. They pay a variable rate of income.
   IV. They usually mature ten or more years after issue.

   A. I and III only
   B. II and III only
   C. II and IV only
   D. I, II, III and IV

5. Bondholders face the risk that the value of their bonds may fall as interest rates rise. This is known as

   A. credit risk
   B. reinvestment risk
   C. marketability risk
   D. market risk

6. Credit risk involves

   A. safety of principal
   B. fluctuations in overall interest rates
   C. the danger of not being able to sell the investment at a fair market price
   D. inflationary risks

7. A newly issued bond has call protection for the first five years after it is issued. This feature would be most valuable if, during this five-year period, interest rates are generally

    A. fluctuating
    B. stable
    C. falling
    D. rising

◆ Answers & Rationale

1.   **A.**   If a customer wishes to purchase a security that the registered representative feels is unsuitable, the trade may be executed if the customer specifically directs it. The ticket should be marked "Unsolicited." (Most firms require that the customer sign a nonsolicitation letter for this type of trade, meaning that the customer was not solicited to do this trade by the firm.)   (Page 56)

2.   **D.**   The MSRB requires that financial status, tax bracket and objective be taken into consideration when recommending a security.   (Page 56)

3.   **D.**   Reinvestment risk is the danger that interest rates will change over the life of the debt instrument. This risk is greatest for long-term bonds.   (Page 57)

4.   **C.**   Bonds represent a creditor relationship; stock represents an ownership interest. Normally bonds are issued with a stated rate of interest and mature in ten or more years.   (Page 57)

5.   **D.**   Market risk is the risk of losing some or all of one's principal due to price volatility in the marketplace. Prices of existing bonds can fluctuate with changing interest rates.   (Page 58)

6.   **A.**   Credit risk is the risk of losing all or part of one's invested principal through failure of the issuer.   (Page 58)

7.   **C.**   In this case "call protection" means that the bonds cannot be called by the issuer for at least five years. If interest rates are falling, the issuer would have reason to want to call the bonds in and, perhaps, issue new bonds at a lower interest rate. Therefore, the call feature protects the investor for a specific period of time.   (Page 59)

16 Know Your Customer Exam

1. An oral recommendation by a registered representative must be

   A. followed by a statement of risks
   B. followed by an example of the strategy recommended
   C. followed by a prospectus
   D. approved by a registered options principal

2. A college graduate has $1,000 in savings and owes $15,000 on college tuition loans to be paid over the next ten years. What type of mutual fund investment would you recommend to him?

   A. Open an account in an income fund with $1,000 and invest periodically using dollar cost averaging.
   B. Invest $1,000 in a capital appreciation fund.
   C. Invest $1,000 in any fund; because he is young, he can absorb any losses.
   D. Defer investment of the $1,000 until he has enough money accumulated to allow investment without adversely affecting his ability to meet emergency expenses.

3. To open a new account, the registered representative must obtain information about the client's

   I. financial needs
   II. investment objectives
   III. financial condition

   A. I and II only
   B. I and III only
   C. II and III only
   D. I, II and III

4. A registered representative has a new client who has just received a $25,000 inheritance. The client wishes to use the money to purchase 8 1/4% Kelptek industrial development bonds selling at an 8.45% yield. The $1 million bond issue is due in 15 years and is rated Ba. All of the following factors would result in your recommending *against* such a purchase EXCEPT that

   A. the client is in the 18% tax bracket
   B. this would be the client's only investment
   C. the client is willing to accept a moderate amount of risk
   D. the client's job is not secure

5. Which of the following characteristics best define(s) the term "growth"?

   A. Value of the investment increasing over time
   B. Increasing principal and accumulating interest and dividends over time
   C. Investments that appreciate tax deferred
   D. All of the above

6. Which of the following investments is least appropriate for a client who is primarily concerned with liquidity?

   A. Preferred stock
   B. Municipal bond mutual funds
   C. Bank savings accounts
   D. Direct participation programs

7. When deciding on the suitability of a particular investment for a client, that client's need for liquidity is

   A. not necessary to be determined
   B. only necessary to be determined if the individual is planning on retirement
   C. an important element to be considered when determining the suitability of an investment
   D. only important if the client has no other liquid investments

◆ Answers & Rationale

1. **A.** Any recommendation that implies that a gain can be made must be followed by a statement of the attendant risks of the transaction.

(Page 61)

2. **D.** Without knowing more about the graduate's financial situation, you should tell him that he is better off deferring the investment of $1,000 at this time. Should he invest the full $1,000 in any of the mutual funds described in the question, and should an emergency occur, he would most likely have to liquidate his investment. However, if one of the choices were a money market fund, the $1,000 could be considered an emergency fund and this type of investment would be appropriate.

(Page 61)

3. **D.** Under Rule 405 (the NYSE "Know Your Customer" Rule), all of this information is considered essential before opening an account.

(Page 61)

4. **C.** A "Ba" rating is consistent with the client's willingness to accept moderate risk. The client's tax bracket might be too low to take full advantage of the bond's tax-exempt feature. The bonds would also not be very liquid because only 1,000 bonds were issued. If the client lost her job and needed cash, the bonds might be difficult to sell.

(Page 62)

5. **A.** "Growth" refers to an increase in the value of an investment over time.

(Page 63)

6. **D.** An investment is liquid if an investor can sell it quickly at face value or at a fair market price without losing significant principal. Direct participation programs (DPPs) are considered very illiquid because there does not exist a ready secondary market for them.

(Page 64)

7. **C.** Liquidity is very important when determining suitability for a client.

(Page 64)

17 Investment Company Offerings Exam

1. All of the following are advantages of mutual fund investment EXCEPT

   A. the investor retains personal control of her investment in the fund portfolio
   B. exchange privileges within a family of funds managed by the same management company
   C. the ability to invest almost any amount at any time
   D. the ability to qualify for reduced sales loads based on accumulation of investment within the fund

2. Face-amount certificate companies can include any or all of the following conditions in their contracts EXCEPT

   A. require the payment of a stated sum of money on a fixed date by the issuer
   B. require the payment of stated sums by the purchaser at fixed intervals
   C. provide a return that varies daily based on market fluctuation
   D. provide a fixed rate of return during periods of prolonged market decline

3. A typical unit investment trust has

   A. no investment adviser
   B. listed securities
   C. securities representing a divided interest in a unit of specified securities
   D. a board of directors

4. Which of the following statements is(are) FALSE regarding a unit investment trust?

   A. It invests according to stated objectives.
   B. It charges no management fee.
   C. Overall responsibility for the fund rests with the board of directors.
   D. The transfer agent may limit sales to current unit holders.

5. A unit investment trust is an

   A. investment contract that represents an obligation on the part of the issuer to pay a determinable sum at a fixed date more than 24 months after the date of issue
   B. investment company that issues redeemable securities, each of which represents an undivided interest in a portfolio's securities, which are professionally selected
   C. issuer who acquires investment securities exceeding 40% of the value of the issuer's total assets
   D. account established and managed by an insurance company under which income, gains and losses (whether or not realized) are credited to or charged against such account

6. The Investment Company Act of 1940 requires a unit investment trust to issue

   A. shares redeemable for a stated amount on a stated maturity date
   B. shares redeemable for their net asset value upon the shareholder's demand
   C. shares whose selling price is based on market demand rather than on net asset value
   D. shares that are sold at net asset value, with no added sales charge

7. Which of the following would be classified as an investment company?

   I.   Closed-end company
   II. Open-end company
   III. Qualified plan company
   IV. Nonqualified plan company
   V.   Fixed annuity company

   A. I and II
   B. I, II and V
   C. II
   D. III, IV and V

8. Under the definition of a management company, all of the following would qualify EXCEPT

   I.   face-amount certificate companies
   II. unit investment trusts
   III. closed-end investment companies
   IV. open-end investment companies

   A. I
   B. I and II
   C. I, II and III
   D. III and IV

9. Which of the following statements is NOT true of a closed-end investment company?

   A. It can buy back its own shares.
   B. It can be described as a type of management company.
   C. Its shares are sold at the market price plus a commission.
   D. It may be referred to as a mutual fund.

10. Under the Investment Company Act of 1940, which of the following would NOT be required to issue redeemable securities?

    I.   Open-end investment company
    II. Closed-end investment company
    III. Unit investment trust
    IV. Business development company

    A. I and II
    B. I and III
    C. II and III
    D. II and IV

11. The price of closed-end investment company shares is determined by

    A. supply and demand
    B. the New York Stock Exchange
    C. the board of directors
    D. the net asset value plus the sales charge

12. Customers could pay a commission, rather than a sales charge, for shares of a(n)

    A. no-load fund
    B. mutual fund
    C. open-end investment company
    D. closed-end investment company

13. Closed-end investment company shares may be bought and sold by a customer

    I.   in the secondary marketplace, including the exchanges and OTC markets
    II. only in the OTC primary market
    III. by the closed-end investment company
    IV. by an open-end investment company that has not suspended or closed trading in its shares

    A. I
    B. I and III
    C. II
    D. III and IV

14. Where can open-end investment company shares be purchased and sold?

    A. In the secondary marketplace
    B. From the open-end company
    C. In the primary market
    D. All of the above

15. Which of the following statements describe(s) an open-end investment company?

I.   It can sell new shares in any quantity at any time.
II. It must redeem shares in any quantity within seven days of request.
III. It provides for mutual ownership of portfolio assets by shareholders.

A. I and II only
B. II
C. II and III only
D. I, II and III

16. Under the Investment Company Act of 1940, which of the following statements is NOT true regarding shares of mutual funds?

A. They must be redeemed at their net asset value upon shareholder demand.
B. They are issued by open-end investment companies.
C. Their net asset value must be calculated each business day.
D. Their sales price may be greater or less than their net asset value.

17. Any of the following could be considered a redeemable security under the Investment Company Act of 1940 EXCEPT a(n)

A. security that pays out each investor's proportionate share of the company's assets
B. security that can be sold on an exchange at the fair market price the buyers and sellers have established
C. investment company security issued as common stock
D. security issued by an open-end investment company

18. Which of the following statements describe an open-end investment company?

I.   The company may sell new shares in any quantity at any time.
II. The company must sell new shares in any quantity at any time.
III. The company may redeem shares in any quantity at any time but may restrict the redemption of shares at the discretion of the board of directors.
IV. The company must redeem shares in any quantity at any time except that it may suspend the redemption of shares with SEC approval.

A. I and III
B. I and IV
C. II and III
D. II and IV

19. All of the following statements concerning investment companies are true EXCEPT

A. a nondiversified company is any management company not classified as a diversified company
B. to be considered a diversified investment company, the company must invest at least 75% of its total assets in cash and/or securities
C. an investment company that invests the majority of its assets in one company or industry is considered a nondiversified company
D. a diversified company can be only an open-end investment company

20. An investment company qualifies as diversified under the Investment Company Act of 1940 if it restricts its portfolio to what percentage of the voting securities of any one issuer?

A. 10%
B. 20%
C. 25%
D. 50%

21. In order to qualify as a diversified investment company, a company must

    A. invest at least 75% of its assets
    B. not invest more than 5% of its total assets in the securities of any one issuer
    C. not invest in securities that represent more than 10% of the outstanding voting securities of an issuer
    D. adhere to the 75/5/10 limits established by the act of 1940 for diversified investment companies

22. GEM Fund, a diversified open-end investment company, invested 5% of its total assets in Dohspils Pharmaceuticals. The market soared and, because of Dohspils's phenomenal appreciation, Dohspils securities now make up 8% of the GEM Fund's total assets. GEM Fund

    A. must sell enough of Dohspils securities to reduce its holdings in Dohspils to 5% of its total assets
    B. must sell out its holdings in Dohspils completely
    C. must sell Dohspils shares only if the 8% investment represents more than 10% of Dohspils's outstanding voting securities
    D. does not have to sell Dohspils shares, but cannot buy more Dohspils shares and still advertise itself as a diversified company

23. A diversified investment company must invest at least ____ of its assets such that no more than ____ of its assets are in any one company and each investment may represent no more than ____ of the voting securities of the target company.

    A. 50%—10%—5%
    B. 75%—5%—10%
    C. 75%—10%—5%
    D. 100%—5%—15%

24. The ArGood Fund, a diversified investment company, has a net asset value of $225 million. ArGood wishes to invest in General Gizmonics, Inc. GIZ stock is selling at $30 a share, and there are 100,000 shares outstanding. The maximum number of GIZ shares that ArGood Fund could buy and still be diversified is

    A. 5,000
    B. 10,000
    C. $11,250,000 worth
    D. $12,500,000 worth

25. A regulated, diversified investment company cannot own more than what percentage of the outstanding shares of any one company?

    A. 2%
    B. 5%
    C. 8%
    D. 10%

◆ Answers & Rationale

1. **A.**   The control of the investment is given over to the investment manager. All of the other items mentioned are considered advantages.
(Page 73)

2. **C.**   Face-amount certificate companies pay a fixed return.   (Page 74)

3. **A.**   Unit investment trusts issue redeemable securities that are traded by the issuer only (the issuer must maintain a second market); the securities are not listed on an exchange. The shares (units) of a UIT evidence an undivided interest in a portfolio of securities that is not actively managed. A UIT has neither an investment adviser nor a board of directors.   (Page 75)

4. **C.**   A unit investment trust has no board of directors. Answers A and B are true: a UIT must follow a stated investment objective (as must any investment company); and it does not charge a management fee because it is not a managed portfolio.   (Page 75)

5. **B.**   A unit investment trust issues redeemable securities representing an undivided interest in a portfolio of securities that have been professionally selected. A UIT does not actively manage its portfolio. Answer A refers to face-amount certificate companies (FACs). Answer C defines investment companies in general. Answer D describes a separate account but, because the portfolio is managed, the account is set up as a management investment company, not as a UIT.
(Page 75)

6. **B.**   Like mutual fund shares, shares in a unit investment trust are redeemable for their NAV upon the shareholder's request.   (Page 75)

7. **A.**   Open- and closed-end funds are classified as investment companies. Plan companies offer plans in which an investment company may be selected as an investment vehicle, but are not investment companies themselves. Fixed annuities are offered by insurance companies only.
(Page 75)

8. **B.**   As defined in the act of 1940, closed-end and open-end funds are subclassifications of management companies (actively managed portfolios). Face-amount certificate companies and unit trusts are separate investment company classifications under the act.   (Page 75)

9. **D.**   Only open-end funds can be referred to as "mutual funds." Although closed-end fund shares are bought and sold in the secondary market after the initial distribution, nothing prevents a closed-end fund from buying back its shares.
(Page 75)

10. **D.**   The stock of closed-end investment companies is traded on an exchange or over the counter. Business development companies are not required to issue redeemable securities.
(Page 75)

11. **A.**   Closed-end investment company shares trade in the secondary market; hence, price is determined by supply and demand.   (Page 76)

12. **D.**   Sales charges could be paid on all types of open-end funds, while commissions are paid on securities traded in the secondary market, such as a closed-end company.   (Page 76)

13. **A.**   Once a closed-end investment company has distributed all of its authorized shares, those shares are traded in the secondary market—both OTC and through exchanges.   (Page 76)

14. **B.**   Open-end company shares are bought and sold from the investment company. (Page 76)

15. **D.**   An open-end investment company can sell any quantity of new shares, redeem shares within seven days and provide for mutual ownership of portfolio assets by shareholders.
(Page 76)

16. **D.**   Mutual fund shares must be sold at NAV plus any sales charge; therefore, the sales price of

a mutual fund share may be equal to or greater than its NAV, but it may not be less. The other statements are true: the shares must be redeemable upon demand; "mutual fund" is the common name for an open-end investment company; and the NAV must be calculated each business day.   (Page 76)

17. **B.**   A redeemable security is one that is purchased from and redeemed with the issuer of the security. If the security can be traded on a secondary market, it is not considered a redeemable security. Open-end shares are redeemable securities; closed-end shares are not.   (Page 76)

18. **B.**   Under the Investment Company Act of 1940, an investment company selling mutual funds is not required to continuously offer new shares for sale; in fact, a fund will often suspend sales to new investors when it grows too large to adequately meet its investment objective. The act of 1940 does require the fund to continuously offer to redeem shares, and this redemption privilege may be suspended only during nonbusiness days or with the approval of the SEC.   (Page 76)

19. **D.**   A diversified company could be either a closed-end company or an open-end company.
(Page 77)

20. **A.**   By definition, a diversified company must invest at least 75% of its assets, have no more than 5% of its assets concentrated in any one company and own no more than 10% of any single company's voting securities.   (Page 77)

21. **D.**   Answers A, B and C are all correct, but are only partial answers.   (Page 77)

22. **D.**   A fund will not lose its diversified status because of market movement. While this fund may not purchase more Dohspils shares, it is not required to sell off any part of its Dohspils holdings.
(Page 77)

23. **B.**   A management company must be at least 75% invested, its investments must be diversified so that no more than 5% of its assets are in any one company and no single investment can represent more than 10% of the voting securities of another company.   (Page 77)

24. **B.**   A diversified investment company has at least 75% of its assets invested so that no more than 5% of its assets own more than 10% of a company's stock. In this question, 5% of ArGood Fund's assets could purchase the entire General Gizmonics company. Therefore, the ArGood Fund is limited to only 10% of GIZ stock, or 10,000 shares.
(Page 77)

25. **D.**   To be considered a diversified investment company, the fund's portfolio must be invested to at least 75% so that no more than 5% of the *assets* own no more than 10% of a company's outstanding *stock*. Remember: 75% invested, 5% assets, 10% stock.   (Page 77)

18   Characteristics of Mutual Funds Exam

1. Mutual fund shares represent an undivided interest in the fund, which means that

   A. investors can purchase only full shares
   B. the fund can hold securities of only certain companies
   C. the number of shares outstanding is limited to a predetermined maximum
   D. each investor owns a proportional part of every security in the portfolio

2. Lotta Leveridge owns 150 shares of American Conservative Equity Fund. Which of the following statements are true?

   I. When a dividend is declared by the fund, she will receive a cash dividend for each share owned.
   II. She will have difficulty liquidating her shares.
   III. The amount of her dividend will reflect her proportional interest in the value of the fund portfolio on the record date.
   IV. She will receive dividends from only 150 shares of stock held in the fund portfolio.

   A. I, II and IV
   B. I and III
   C. II and III
   D. II, III and IV

3. All the following are advantages of mutual fund investment EXCEPT

   A. the investor retains personal control of her investment in the mutual fund portfolio
   B. exchange privileges within a family of funds managed by the same management company
   C. the ability to invest almost any amount at any time
   D. the ability to qualify for reduced sales loads based on accumulation of investment within the fund

4. Although alternatives are available to a mutual fund issuer regarding the details of redemption procedures, the issuer must, by law

   A. make payment for shares within seven days of tender
   B. inform the investor of his loss or profit
   C. redeem shares at the POP
   D. redeem shares at the net asset value minus the sales charge

5. In a mutual fund, after opening an account an investor can generally make additional periodic investments in minimum amounts of

   A. $50
   B. $100
   C. $500
   D. The amount varies from fund to fund.

6. In a mutual fund, a shareholder who elected not to receive share certificates can liquidate all or a portion of his holdings and receive payment from the fund if the fund receives which of the following?

   I. Written request from the shareholder
   II. Signed stock power from the shareholder
   III. Signature guarantee from the shareholder

   A. I
   B. I and II
   C. I and III
   D. II and III

7. In order to get cash for an emergency that arose, Armand A. Legge redeemed his shares in a mutual fund that offered reinstatement privileges. Within how many days of redemption could he reinvest in the same fund without having to pay additional sales charges?

   A. 7
   B. 30
   C. 45
   D. 60

8. August Polar has $800 to invest in the Amusement Technology Fund. If the shares are currently priced at $21.22 each, August will be able to purchase

   A. no shares because the minimum trading unit is 100 shares
   B. 37 shares and $14.85 in change
   C. 37.7 shares
   D. 38 shares

9. The investment policy of a mutual fund can be changed by a majority vote of the

   A. board of directors
   B. fund's managers
   C. SEC investment committee
   D. outstanding shares

10. The portfolio of a diversified common stock fund would MOST likely consist of

    A. all growth stocks within one particular industry
    B. stocks of many companies in many different industries
    C. convertible bonds and other debt instruments
    D. bargain stocks

11. An investor is in a low tax bracket and wishes to invest a moderate sum in an investment that will provide him with some protection from inflation. Which of the following would you recommend?

    A. Municipal unit investment trust
    B. Growth stock mutual fund
    C. Money-market mutual fund
    D. Ginnie Mae fund

12. During an inflationary period, would a customer who seeks to limit purchasing power risk expect more protection from a growth fund or from a balanced fund?

    A. Growth fund, because its objective is to grow regardless of the economic environment.
    B. Balanced fund, because the bonds and other debt securities held by a balanced fund would provide downside protection.
    C. Growth fund, because stocks of growth companies typically fare well during inflationary periods.
    D. Balanced fund, because any convertible securities held by a balanced fund would increase.

13. The ZBest Invest Fund is a mutual fund that has as its primary objective the payment of dividends, regardless of the current state of the market; preservation of capital and capital growth are secondary objectives. Which of the following industry groups would be appropriate for the ZBest Invest Fund's portfolio?

    A. Aerospace
    B. Public utilities
    C. Computer technology
    D. Consumer appliances

14. ABC Fund invests all of its assets in municipal bonds. This means that

    I. shareholders do not pay federal taxes on dividend distributions
    II. the fund is not subject to federal tax on any interest earnings it retains
    III. shareholders pay all taxes at the preferential capital gains rate

    A. I and II only
    B. I and III only
    C. II and III only
    D. I, II and III

15. ZBest Invest Fund pays regular dividends, offers a high degree of safety of principal and especially appeals to investors seeking tax advantages. ZBest Invest is a(n)

    A. corporate bond fund
    B. money-market fund
    C. aggressive growth fund
    D. municipal bond fund

16. A tax-exempt bond fund may invest in

    A. corporate bonds
    B. short-term money-market instruments
    C. common stock
    D. municipal bonds

17. Max Leveridge believes that the electronics industry will be very successful in the next ten years. If he wants to invest in the industry but does not want to limit his investments to only a few companies, he should invest in a

    A. bond fund
    B. money-market fund
    C. hedge fund
    D. specialized fund

18. Which of the following investments would provide high appreciation potential together with high risk?

    A. Balanced fund
    B. Bond fund
    C. Income fund
    D. Sector fund

19. During a recessionary period, will a growth fund or a balanced fund perform better?

    A. The growth fund will do better because its objective is to grow regardless of the economic environment.
    B. The balanced fund will do better because of the downside protection that the bonds and other debt securities held by the fund will provide.
    C. The growth fund will do better because stocks of growth companies typically fare well during recessionary periods.
    D. The balanced fund will do better because any convertible securities held by the fund will increase.

20. Last year the bond market was very profitable, and ZBest Invest Fund had 70% of its assets in bonds. Next year the fund's managers expect the stock market to do well, and they adjust the fund's portfolio so that 60% will be invested in stock. ZBest Invest is probably what type of fund?

    A. Balanced
    B. Hedge
    C. Specialized
    D. Aggressive growth

21. A 45-year-old woman wants the greatest possible monthly income. Preservation and stability of capital are important, although secondary, objectives. Which of the following investments would you recommend?

    A. Money-market mutual fund
    B. High-grade bond fund
    C. Growth mutual fund
    D. Combination fund

22. Which of the following would probably be found in the portfolio of a money-market fund?

    I. T bills
    II. T bonds with a short time to maturity
    III. Bank certificates of deposit
    IV. Common stock

    A. I
    B. I and II
    C. I, II and III
    D. II, III and IV

23. Which of the following is(are) characteristic of money-market funds?

    I. Portfolio of short-term debt instruments
    II. High beta
    III. Offered without a sales load
    IV. Fixed NAV

    A. I
    B. I, II and IV
    C. I, III and IV
    D. II, III and IV

24. Randy Bear, age 65, will receive a lump-sum distribution from his pension plan. He had invested the money in a growth fund in the pension plan. Randy is reconsidering his investment options; he doesn't want to commit the funds for at least eight or nine months. What would you recommend?

    A. Reinvest the money in a growth fund to match his previous objectives until he decides what he wants to do.
    B. Reinvest the money in a one-year CD to preserve capital.
    C. Reinvest the money in a money-market mutual fund.
    D. Hold onto the check from the pension plan until he decides what he wants.

25. All of the following characteristics are typical of a money-market fund EXCEPT that

    A. the underlying portfolio normally is made up of short-term debt instruments
    B. it is offered as a no-load investment
    C. it has a high beta and is safest in periods of low market volatility
    D. its net asset value normally remains unchanged

26. All of the following statements are true of money-market funds EXCEPT that

    A. investors pay a management fee
    B. interest is computed daily and credited to the investor's account monthly
    C. investors can buy and sell shares quickly and easily
    D. high interest rates are guaranteed

27. Which of the following are money-market instruments?

    I. Repurchase agreements
    II. Treasury bills
    III. Commercial paper
    IV. Treasury bonds maturing in six months

    A. I and II only
    B. I, II and III only
    C. II, III and IV only
    D. I, II, III and IV

28. Your client asks whether he should invest in a particular investment company. You should tell him to check the investment company's

    I.   investment policy
    II. track record
    III. portfolio
    IV. sales load

    A. I, II and III only
    B. I and IV only
    C. III only
    D. I, II, III and IV

29. Which of the following statements is true of the expense ratio of an open-end investment company?

    A. It is computed exclusive of the management fee.
    B. It is computed inclusive of the management fee.
    C. It is computed taking into account the management fee only.
    D. It shows the extent of leverage in the fund.

30. A mutual fund's expense ratio is its

    A. expenses divided by average net assets
    B. expenses divided by public offering price
    C. expenses divided by income
    D. expenses divided by dividends

◆ Answers & Rationale

1. **D.** A mutual fund shareholder owns an undivided interest in the portfolio of the investment company. Because each share represents one class of voting stock, the investor's interest in the fund reflects the number of shares owned.   (Page 79)

2. **B.** A mutual fund share represents an undivided interest in the fund's portfolio. If a dividend is declared, the shareholder receives a dividend for each mutual fund share held. Dividends are paid in cash unless the investor elects to reinvest the cash distribution for the purchase of more fund shares.
(Page 79)

3. **A.** Control of the investment is given over to the investment manager. All of the other items mentioned are considered advantages.   (Page 79)

4. **A.** The Investment Company Act of 1940 requires an open-end investment company to redeem shares upon request within seven days from receipt of the request.   (Page 79)

5. **D.** Minimum amounts are different from fund to fund, and a registered rep must refer to the prospectus for each fund.   (Page 79)

6. **C.** Orders for redemption without a certificate being issued requires a written request and a signature guarantee. A signed stock power would be required if the shareholder had possession of the mutual fund certificates.   (Page 79)

7. **B.** Funds offering the reinstatement privilege allow the investor to redeem and reinvest shares within 30 days without an additional sales charge. The privilege can be used only once, and only the amount withdrawn can be reinstated.
(Page 79)

8. **C.** August will be able to purchase 37.7 shares. Mutual fund shares may be sold in full or fractional amounts and do not trade in round lots of 100 shares.   (Page 79)

9. **D.** Any changes in a mutual fund's investment policies must be made by a majority vote of the fund's outstanding shares.   (Page 80)

10. **B.** A diversified common stock fund will have stocks from many companies and many industries.   (Page 81)

11. **B.** A growth fund will give the investor some protection from inflation. Historically, common stock is a better inflation hedge than fixed-income instruments. The other three answers are income-oriented funds.   (Page 81)

12. **C.** Growth stocks fare well during periods of inflation because their returns respond to the expanding demand. By contrast, the objective of a balanced fund is to offer *stability* of return, usually by investing in both common stock and debt securities; in periods of inflation, the increased return of the stock is tempered by a decline in the value of the debt securities.

A convertible security's value is linked to the value of the common stock into which it can be converted; again, in times of inflation, its upside potential is tempered by its decline in value as a debt instrument.   (Page 81)

13. **B.** Utilities belong to the group known as *defensive industries*, as compared to the other types mentioned. They more consistently produce dividends, although their relative growth potential is limited.   (Page 81)

14. **A.** A municipal bond fund derives its income from interest paid from the municipal bonds held, which is exempt from federal income tax.
(Page 82)

15. **D.** Municipal bonds are considered second only to U.S. government securities in terms of safety. Also, interest received from the bonds is exempt from federal income tax.   (Page 82)

16. **D.** The fund will distribute taxable income or dividends unless it invests in municipal bonds. Because the fund's stated investment objective is to provide tax-exempt income, it must invest in

instruments that enable it to achieve this objective.
(Page 82)

17. **D.**   A specialized or sector fund invests all of its assets in a particular type of security or a particular industry.   (Page 82)

18. **D.**   A sector or specialized fund offers a higher appreciation potential (coupled with higher risk) than an income-oriented fund.   (Page 82)

19. **B.**   A balanced fund's objective is to offer stability of return. Typically, a balanced fund is invested in both common stock and debt securities. During market advances, the common stock portion of the portfolio will show superior returns. During down markets, the debt portion of the portfolio will offer returns that are greater than those of common stock. The value of convertible securities is linked in part to the value of the common stock into which the security can be converted. As a result, the convertible security offers some downside protection but not as much as would a straight-debt instrument.   (Page 83)

20. **A.**   This fund is invested in both stock and bonds; it is likely to be a balanced fund. The percentage invested in the two types of securities will be adjusted to maximize the yield that can be obtained. The percentages are seldom fixed.
(Page 83)

21. **B.**   A high-grade bond fund would provide income that is greater than that provided by a money-market fund while still offering stability and preservation of capital. Many bond funds provide for monthly payment of interest income, whereas stock funds typically offer distributions only on a quarterly or less frequent basis. The objective of a growth fund typically is not to offer income distributions; rather, the objective is appreciation. A combination fund invests in growth and income stocks and attempts to provide both growth and current income; however, the NAV can fluctuate widely.   (Page 83)

22. **C.**   Money-market instruments are considered short-term, very liquid debt instruments. Be-

cause common stock is equity, it would not be in a money-market fund.   (Page 83)

23. **C.**   Money-market mutual funds invest in portfolios of short-term debt instruments such as T bills, commercial paper and repos. They are offered without a sales load or charge. The principal objective of such funds is to generate current interest income, and generally the NAV does not appreciate.   (Page 83)

24. **C.**   Randy wants to park the money from his pension plan distribution for a short period of time so he requires a short-term investment vehicle. The money market fund is best suited to meet his needs. The CD has a maturity that exceeds Randy's time horizon. The growth fund would be likely to entail a load. To do nothing prevents Randy from earning any money during his decision period.   (Page 83)

25. **C.**   A money-market fund has no price volatility; the rate of interest fluctuates in line with that of the instruments underlying the original money-market certificates.   (Page 83)

26. **D.**   Money-market instruments earn high interest rates but the rates are not guaranteed. Money-market funds are typically no-load funds with no redemption fee, but investors do pay a management fee. The interest earned on an investor's shares is computed every day and credited to the account at month end. An advantage of money-market funds is the ease with which shares can be purchased and sold.   (Page 83)

27. **D.**   Money markets are made up of short-term high-yield debt issues. All of the items listed are considered short term—even the bonds because they will mature in less than one year.   (Page 83)

28. **D.**   All of these elements should be checked when assessing a fund.   (Page 84)

29. **B.**   The expense ratio includes the expenses of operating the fund compared to fund assets. Expenses included in the ratio are management fees, administrative fees, brokerage fees and taxes.
(Page 85)

30. **A.** By dividing a mutual fund's expenses by its average net assets, you can calculate the fund's expense ratio.   (Page 85)

19 Investment Company Registration Exam

1. According to the Investment Company Act of 1940

   I. a company must have $1,000,000 in assets before it may begin operations
   II. at least 40% of the board of directors may not be affiliated or hold a position with the fund
   III. the fund must have at least 100 shareholders
   IV. the fund may not borrow more than 33 1/3% of its asset value

   A. I and III only
   B. II, III and IV only
   C. II and IV only
   D. I, II, III and IV

2. In order to make a public offering, a registered investment company must have a minimum net worth of

   A. $100,000
   B. $1,000,000
   C. $10,000,000
   D. $100,000,000

3. An open-end investment company must maintain what percentage of net assets to debt?

   A. 33 1/3%
   B. 50%
   C. 100%
   D. 300%

4. An investment company must register with the SEC, and in doing so must provide all of the following information EXCEPT its

   A. intention to borrow money
   B. intended trading practices
   C. present or future plans to issue senior securities
   D. intention to concentrate its investments in a single industry

5. Each of the following is considered an investment company EXCEPT a

   A. face-amount certificate company
   B. company that has invested 65% of its assets in securities
   C. bank investment advisory account
   D. company that issues redeemable securities

6. Which of the following are NOT excluded from the definition of "investment company" under the Investment Company Act of 1940?

   I. Real estate investment trust
   II. Insurance company separate account
   III. Investment adviser

   A. I and II only
   B. I and III only
   C. II and III only
   D. I, II and III

7. An investment company must file a new prospectus to replace its existing prospectus within how many months from the date of the existing prospectus?

A. 6
B. 12
C. 13
D. 16

8. A prospectus must be delivered to the purchaser of a unit investment trust

A. prior to the purchase
B. with the first confirmation
C. with each confirmation
D. between 45 days and 18 months following the initial deposit

9. All of the following would be violations of NASD rules EXCEPT

A. sending a prospect a prospectus and sales literature at the same time
B. selling a mutual fund without first distributing a prospectus
C. selling a mutual fund with sales literature that is not a prospectus describing the fund's performance over a ten-year period
D. sending a customer sales literature that represents performance history for five years for a fund that has been in existence for ten years

10. Which Federal Reserve Board regulation prohibits brokers and dealers from extending credit for the purchase of open-end investment company shares?

A. Regulation A
B. Regulation G
C. Regulation U
D. Regulation T

11. A prospectus for an individual variable annuity contract

I. must provide full and fair disclosure
II. is required by the Securities Act of 1933
III. must be filed with the SEC
IV. must precede or accompany every sales presentation

A. I only
B. I, III and IV only
C. II and III only
D. I, II, III and IV

12. Which of the following are required of investment companies under the Securities Act of 1933?

I. Filing a registration statement with the SEC
II. Providing a prospectus to potential purchasers
III. Publishing a tombstone advertisment giving the name of the issuer and a brief description of the issuer's type of business
IV. Obtaining the SEC's approval of the truthfulness of the information in the prospectus

A. I and II only
B. I, II and III only
C. II and IV only
D. I, II, III and IV

13. An investment company offering securities registered under the act of 1933 may make which of the following statements?

  I. "The SEC has passed on the merits of these securities as an investment."
  II. "The SEC has passed on the adequacy of the information in our prospectus."
  III. "The SEC has passed on the accuracy of the information in our prospectus."
  IV. "These securities have been approved for retirement accounts and institutional clients by the SEC."

  A. I
  B. I and II
  C. II, III and IV
  D. None of the above

14. A member firm can be sued for damages if an investor purchases an open-end fund and

  I. receives no prospectus
  II. is told an untrue statement by the member or by a person associated with the member
  III. is given a prospectus that omits a material fact
  IV. loses 20% or more in the investment within the first 30 days after the initial purchase

  A. I
  B. I, II and III
  C. II and III
  D. II, III and IV

15. An investor must be provided with a "Statement of Additional Information" about a mutual fund

  A. annually
  B. in addition to the prospectus
  C. upon request
  D. included in the prospectus

16. All of the following transactions are permitted in a mutual fund's portfolio EXCEPT

  A. buying index options
  B. buying junk bonds
  C. buying shares of other mutual funds
  D. buying stock on margin

17. When the NavCo Fund, an open-end investment company, issues and sells new shares, it must comply with the requirements of the

  I. Securities Act of 1933
  II. Securities Exchange Act of 1934
  III. Investment Company Act of 1940

  A. I and II only
  B. I and III only
  C. II and III only
  D. I, II and III

18. Which of the following actions is permissible if the investment company receives the approval of a majority of its voting shares?

  A. Participating in a joint trading account
  B. Lending money to other corporations for use as venture capital
  C. Selling portfolio securities short
  D. Purchasing government bonds on margin

19. In a regulated, diversified open-end investment company, which of the following functions are performed by the investment adviser?

    I. Changing investment objectives as he believes is in the best interest of the investors

    II. Investigating the tax status of potential investments

    III. Ensuring that the fund invests in such a manner as to retain its diversified status

    IV. Attempting to fulfill the fund's investment objective by means of careful investing

    A. I and III
    B. I, III and IV
    C. II, III and IV
    D. II and IV

20. The shareholders of an investment company must vote to approve a change

    I. from a diversified company to a nondiversified company

    II. from an open-end company to a closed-end company

    III. in operations that would cause the firm to cease business as an investment company

    IV. in the objectives of the fund

    A. I and IV only
    B. II and III only
    C. II, III and IV only
    D. I, II, III and IV

21. An open-end investment company wishes to change its investment objective. It may do so only with a

    A. majority vote of the outstanding shares
    B. majority vote of the outstanding shareholders
    C. two-thirds vote of the outstanding shareholders
    D. unanimous vote of the board of directors

◆ Answers & Rationale

1. **B.** A company must have commitments for at least $100,000 in assets before it begins. All of the other items are true.   (Page 87)

2. **A.** No investment company may register an offering with the SEC unless it has a minimum net worth of $100,000 (or will have within 90 days).   (Page 87)

3. **D.** The Investment Company Act of 1940 prohibits a mutual fund from borrowing more than one-third of its net asset value. In other words, the fund must maintain at least 300% assets to debt.   (Page 87)

4. **B.** Investment companies do not need to outline their trading practices. However, the registration statement is required to describe any intent to borrow money or issue senior securities. A company's concentration of investments would be part of its required investment policy description.   (Page 87)

5. **C.** A bank advisory account is specifically exempted from the definition of an investment company.   (Page 88)

6. **C.** Because real estate is not a security, real estate investment trusts are excluded from the definition of "investment company." Other exclusions are banks, S&Ls, broker-dealers, underwriters and issuers whose securities are owned by less than 100 persons. Also excluded are insurance company general accounts; but insurance company separate accounts and investment advisers are not excluded.   (Page 88)

7. **C.** Investment companies must be audited annually, and must file prospectuses no less frequently than every 13 months. Mutual fund shareholders must be sent reports at least semiannually.   (Page 88)

8. **B.** Purchasers of newly issued securities must receive a prospectus no later than with receipt of the confirmation of their purchase.   (Page 88)

9. **A.** Any solicitation for sale must be preceded or accompanied by a prospectus that meets the guidelines put forth by the Securities Act of 1933.   (Page 88)

10. **D.** Regulation T regulates the extension of credit by brokers and dealers for investment company shares.   (Page 88)

11. **D.** A variable annuity is a security and therefore must be registered with the SEC. As part of the registration requirements, a prospectus must be filed and distributed to prospective investors prior to or during any solicitation for sale.   (Page 88)

12. **A.** The Securities Act of 1933 sets forth the registration and prospectus requirements for all companies contemplating the issuance of securities. There is no requirement to publish a tombstone; and the SEC does not approve, pass on the adequacy of, or pass on the completeness of an offering.   (Page 89)

13. **D.** The SEC neither approves nor disapproves of an issue, nor does it pass on the adequacy, accuracy or completeness of the information presented in a prospectus.   (Page 89)

14. **B.** Federal securities laws require that purchasers of newly issued securities be given a full disclosure of material information concerning the issuer and the security. Choice I states that the purchaser received no disclosures. Choices II and III imply a measure of fraud or improper disclosure, and in each of these cases the purchaser could sue to recover damages and costs. A drop in an investment's value (choice IV) is not grounds for suit—unless the loss was directly related to improper disclosure by the company.   (Page 89)

15. **C.** The "Statement of Additional Information" may be obtained by the investor upon request from the fund. The prospectus contains information on the fund's objective, investment policies, sales

charges and management expenses, services offered and a 10-year history of per share capital changes. The "Statement of Additional Information" typically contains the fund's consolidated financial statements including the balance sheet, statement of operations, income statement and portfolio list at the time the statement was compiled. (Page 89)

16. **D.** Mutual funds may not purchase securities on margin because, in the event of a margin call, they have no recourse to investors' funds. A fund is not prohibited from buying options, low-quality bonds and other mutual funds. (Page 89)

17. **D.** A mutual fund issuing shares must comply with the Securities Act of 1933 (registration) and the Investment Company Act of 1940 (one class of security, type of investment company). The Securities Exchange Act of 1934 deals with the people who sell the shares and the markets in which the shares are sold but also details anti-fraud requirements that must be observed by investment companies. (Page 89)

18. **B.** Mutual funds may never participate in joint accounts, sell short or buy securities on margin, regardless of approval by a majority vote. An investment company may lend money as long as the practice conforms to the company's investment policy. (Page 89)

19. **C.** The investment adviser cannot change the fund's investment objectives. Changing the objectives can be done only after approval by the board of directors and the shareholders. The other three choices are all functions of the adviser. (Page 90)

20. **D.** Any substantive change in the form, structure, investment objectives or business operations of an investment company must be approved by a majority vote of the outstanding shares. (Page 90)

21. **A.** The Investment Company Act of 1940 requires the fund to have a clearly defined investment objective. The only action that can be taken to change the investment objective is a majority vote of the outstanding shares (shares vote, not shareholders). (Page 90)

20 Management of Investment Companies Exam

1. Mutual funds are like other types of corporations in that

   I. they may issue equity and debt
   II. the board of directors makes policy decisions
   III. shareholders have ownership rights

   A. I and III only
   B. II only
   C. II and III only
   D. I, II and III

2. Which of the following are functions of an investment company's custodian bank?

   I. Safekeeping of portfolio securities and cash
   II. Providing portfolio advice regarding transactions
   III. Maintaining books and records for accumulation plans
   IV. Safekeeping of customer securities

   A. I and III only
   B. I, III and IV only
   C. II and IV only
   D. I, II, III and IV

3. A management investment company must do all of the following EXCEPT

   A. hold all portfolio securities in a custodian bank
   B. hold all cash in a custodian bank
   C. maintain a bond for persons who have access to monies or securities
   D. investigate the employment record of the officers of the custodian bank

4. The transfer agent of a mutual fund

   I. redeems shares
   II. sells shares
   III. holds custody of fund securities
   IV. handles name changes of mutual fund ownership

   A. I and III
   B. I and IV
   C. II and III
   D. II and IV

5. The transfer agent for a mutual fund is paid a fee, which is

    I.   deducted from the assets of the fund
    II. deducted from the shareholder's net asset value upon share purchase or redemption
    III. included in the fund's expense ratio
    IV. excluded from the fund's expense ratio

    A. I and III
    B. I and IV
    C. II and III
    D. II and IV

6. The principal underwriter of an open-end investment company is also known as the

    A. sponsor
    B. dealer
    C. trustee
    D. registrar

7. An NASD broker-dealer trading in shares of an open-end investment company is prohibited from buying shares of the fund

    A. to cover existing orders
    B. for the firm's own investment purposes
    C. at a discount
    D. for the purpose of resale at a later date

8. June Polar wants to buy $1,000 worth of an open-end investment company. She may buy shares through

    I.   the sponsor of the fund
    II. a brokerage firm
    III. the custodian of the fund
    IV. a bank acting as dealer

    A. I and II
    B. I, II and IV
    C. II
    D. III and IV

9. If a registered representative uses a prospectus as a sales aid, what must accompany the prospectus in her presentation?

    A. All sales literature describing the investment
    B. All advertising describing the investment
    C. The company's balance sheet
    D. No other information is required unless requested.

10. A mutual fund must at a minimum provide which of the following periodic reports to shareholders?

    I.   Audited annual reports
    II. Unaudited annual reports
    III. Audited semiannual reports
    IV. Unaudited semiannual reports

    A. I and III
    B. I and IV
    C. II and III
    D. II and IV

11. Under regulations established by the Investment Company Act of 1940, investment companies must be audited

    A. monthly
    B. quarterly
    C. semiannually
    D. annually

◆ Answers & Rationale

1. **C.** Mutual funds may issue only one class of voting stock. Like corporate stockholders, mutual fund shareholders do have various rights, one of which is the right to elect the board of directors, which sets policies for the fund.   (Page 91)

2. **A.** The custodian bank performs bookkeeping and clerical functions and, principally, retains the fund's cash and securities for safekeeping. The adviser offers portfolio advice and management services. The custodian does not provide for safekeeping of investors' securities.   (Page 92)

3. **D.** The investment company is not required (and would probably find it difficult) to investigate the employment records of the officers of its custodian bank. The Investment Company Act of 1940 requires only that investment companies keep all cash and securities with a custodian bank and maintain a bond.   (Page 92)

4. **B.** The transfer agent redeems shares of a mutual fund at the price next calculated after receiving a request for redemption. The transfer agent also handles transfer of account ownership for such transactions as an inheritance or gift. The fund custodian holds custody of fund securities. A fund underwriter or the fund itself sells shares; the transfer agent then records ownership.   (Page 92)

5. **A.** The fee paid to the transfer agent is a charge against the assets of the fund and is included in calculating the fund's expense ratio. Some funds may charge a nominal redemption fee for share transfers or liquidation; however, this fee would be in addition to payments made to the transfer agent.   (Page 92)

6. **A.** The term "sponsor" is synonymous with the term "underwriter."   (Page 92)

7. **D.** A broker-dealer may purchase shares only to fulfill existing orders or for its own investment account, not for inventory.   (Page 93)

8. **A.** The custodian does not sell the shares, but holds them for safekeeping. A bank cannot be a member of the NASD and therefore cannot act as a dealer (although subsidiaries independent of the bank may be set up as broker-dealers).   (Page 93)

9. **D.** Although the prospectus is required prior to or during any solicitation for sale, no other literature or documentation is required. (Page 93)

10. **B.** An investment company is required to send unaudited reports to shareholders at least semiannually, and an audited report of its financial condition at least annually.   (Page 94)

11. **D.** Investment companies must submit an audited annual statement to the SEC.   (Page 94)

 **21** Mutual Fund Marketing, Pricing and Valuation Exam

1. Typically, no-load mutual funds are sold to the public in which of the following ways?

   A. The fund sells directly to the investor.
   B. The fund sells to a plan company, which in turn sells to the investor.
   C. The fund sells to a dealer, who in turn sells to the investor.
   D. The fund sells to investors through federal banks.

2. An investment company share that is purchased at its net asset value and can be redeemed later at the then current net asset value is a share issued by a(n)

   A. open-end investment company
   B. closed-end investment company
   C. front-end load company
   D. no-load open-end investment company

3. According to the NASD Rules of Fair Practice, a member firm may give certain selling concessions to

   A. the general public
   B. other NASD member firms
   C. nonmember broker-dealers
   D. all of the above

4. The NAV of an open-end investment company

   I. is calculated seven days a week
   II. is calculated as stipulated in the prospectus
   III. takes into account cash held by the fund but not invested
   IV. when divided by the number of shares outstanding equals the net asset value per share

   A. I and IV
   B. II, III and IV
   C. II and IV
   D. IV

5. When comparing definitions in the stock market and mutual funds, the bid price is similar to the NAV, and the ask price is similar to

   A. the net asset value
   B. the sales load
   C. the public offering price
   D. none of the above

6. If the value of securities held in a fund's portfolio increases and the amount of liabilities stays the same, the net assets of the fund will

   A. increase
   B. decrease
   C. stay the same
   D. be more liquid

7. The net asset value per share of a mutual fund will fluctuate in value relative to the

   A. value of the fund's portfolio
   B. law of supply and demand
   C. number of shareholders
   D. S&P 500 market index

8. The net asset value per share will

   I. increase if the assets of the fund appreciate in value
   II. decrease if the fund distributes a dividend to shareholders
   III. decrease when shares are redeemed
   IV. increase if shareholders reinvest dividend and capital gains distributions

   A. I and II
   B. I and III
   C. II and III
   D. II and IV

9. The ArGood Mutual Fund experienced an unrealized loss last month. This loss will result in

   I. a lower NAV per share
   II. lower dividend payments to the shareholders
   III. a reduction in the proceeds payable to shareholders who liquidate their shares

   A. I and II only
   B. I and III only
   C. II and III only
   D. I, II and III

10. Which of the following statements about sales charges is(are) true?

    I. Under NASD rules, mutual fund sales charges may not exceed 8.5% of the offering price.
    II. Under NASD rules, mutual fund sales charges may not exceed 8.5% of the share's net asset value.
    III. An investment company must offer rights of accumulation, breakpoints and reinvestment of dividends at NAV in order to charge an 8.5% sales charge.
    IV. Under the Investment Company Act of 1940, the maximum sales charge for purchases of mutual fund shares under a contractual plan is 9%.

    A. I
    B. I and III
    C. I, III and IV
    D. II, III and IV

11. A 12b-1 asset based fee must be disclosed

    A. in the prospectus
    B. on the share certificate
    C. on the application for investment
    D. on all of the above

12. The NASD allows maximum sales charges of

    A. 9% on mutual funds and variable annuities
    B. 9% on mutual funds and contractual plans
    C. 8 1/2% on mutual funds and contractual plans
    D. 8 1/2% on mutual funds and variable annuities

13. A "sales load" is defined as the

    A. difference between the public offering price and the net asset value
    B. commissions paid on the purchase or sale of securities
    C. fee paid to the investment adviser
    D. concessions allowed on the purchase or sale of securities

14. How often are 12b-1 fees paid?

    A. Monthly
    B. Quarterly
    C. Semiannually
    D. Annually

15. The maximum fee that can be charged under a 12b-1 plan is

    A. an amount equal to the share's net asset value
    B. the difference between the share's POP and NAV
    C. an amount that is reasonable in light of the distribution services offered and described in the plan
    D. 9% over the life of the plan

16. What is the maximum sales charge on a 12b-1 in the first year?

    A. 50%
    B. 20%
    C. 9%
    D. 8.5%

17. A mutual fund collects 12b-1 fees. Which of the following statements are true?

    I. The fund may use the money to pay for mailing sales literature.
    II. Advertising materials may state that the fund is no-load.
    III. The fund may use the money to pay for commissions on securities transactions.
    IV. The fund's prospectus is required to disclose the fee.

    A. I and II only
    B. I and IV only
    C. II and III only
    D. I, II, III and IV

18. In order for a registered investment company to implement a 12b-1 plan, the plan must be approved by a majority of the

    I. outstanding voting shares of the company
    II. board of directors
    III. uninterested members of the board of directors
    IV. investment advisory board

    A. I
    B. I and II
    C. I, II and III
    D. II, III and IV

19. In order for a registered investment company to terminate its 12b-1 plan, the termination must be approved by a majority of the

    I. outstanding voting shares of the company
    II. board of directors
    III. uninterested members of the board of directors
    IV. investment advisory board

    A. I and II
    B. I, II and III
    C. I and III
    D. II, III and IV

20. Your firm is the underwriter of a new mutual fund organized under a 12b-1 plan. Which of the following statements may you make in any mailings or phone calls to your clients?

    A. "The fund has the added advantage of being a no-load investment."
    B. "You will not have to pay any sales charges with this fund because we're buying it as a long-term investment."
    C. "Investments in no-load funds of this type do have some risks, and you will want to review the prospectus carefully."
    D. None of the above

21. Class A shares of a mutual fund have a

    A. back-end load
    B. level load
    C. front-end load
    D. asset-based fee

22. A mutual fund has an NAV of $13.37. An investor was charged a 4% sales charge on a lump-sum purchase of $50,000. How many shares were purchased?

    A. 3,422
    B. 3,564
    C. 3,589
    D. 3,595

23. The net asset value of a mutual fund is $9.30. If its sales charge is 7%, its offering price is

    A. $9.95
    B. $9.97
    C. $10
    D. $10.70

24. An investor purchasing 1,000 shares of a mutual fund that has a maximum sales charge of 8 1/2% and an NAV of $10.30 at the time of purchase will pay a total sales charge (rounded to the nearest dollar) of

    A. $88
    B. $96
    C. $875
    D. $957

25. If a mutual fund charges an 8 1/2% sales charge, all of the following must be offered by the fund EXCEPT

    A. exchange privileges
    B. breakpoints
    C. rights of accumulation
    D. dividend reinvestment at NAV

26. If an investment company offers rights of accumulation and an investor wishes to get a reduced sales charge, the client must deposit sufficient funds within

    A. 45 days
    B. 13 months
    C. There is no time limit.
    D. Each fund may have its own requirements.

27. A customer indicates that she wishes to invest $50,000 in mutual funds. The investments are to be split into three different funds, each with its own management company and all of which are growth-oriented health care funds. The registered representative should advise the customer that

    A. this is an excellent idea because it spreads the risk of investing even more
    B. she will pay greater commissions on the investment when the money is split between three funds than if she put the money into only one fund
    C. she will be able to exchange shares from one fund to another as conditions change without incurring a new sales charge
    D. she should buy individual stocks because mutual funds are only for smaller investors

28. To qualify for the quantity discount, which of the following could NOT be joined together under the definition of "any person"?

    I. Father and his 35-year-old son investing in separate accounts
    II. Husband and wife investing in a joint account
    III. Husband and wife investing in a separate account
    IV. Trust officer working on behalf of a single trust account

    A. I
    B. II, III and IV
    C. II and IV
    D. III and IV

29. Which of the following describes a qualified investor eligible for a quantity discount?

  I. Pension plan trustee
  II. Investor in an individual retirement account
  III. Investment club
  IV. Woman and her husband in a joint account

  A. I and II only
  B. I, II and IV only
  C. II and IV only
  D. I, II, III and IV

30. Amusement Technology Fund permits rights of accumulation. Adam Grizzly has invested $9,000 and has signed a letter of intent for a $15,000 investment. His reinvested dividends during the 13 months total $720. How much money must Adam contribute to fulfill the letter of intent?

  A. $5,280
  B. $6,000
  C. $9,000
  D. $15,000

31. Lotta Leveridge signed a letter of intent stating that she would purchase $25,000 worth of ACE Fund over the next 9 months. After 13 months, she had invested only $12,000. What will be the effect of her actions?

  A. Her entire investment will be charged an 8 1/2% sales charge.
  B. She qualifies for the second breakpoint only, and will be charged 8%.
  C. The entire amount is still due because she signed a binding contract when she signed the letter of intent.
  D. Nothing; she will be charged whatever sales charge she is entitled to for the actual amount she invested.

32. A letter of intent for a mutual fund does NOT contain which of the following provisions?

  A. The time limit is 13 months.
  B. The letter can be backdated 90 days to include a previous deposit.
  C. The fund can halt redemption during the period of time the letter of intent is in effect.
  D. The fund might keep some of the initially issued shares in an escrow account to ensure full payment of the full spread.

33. Joe Kuhl invests $3,000 in open-end investment company shares. After 60 days, he signs a letter of intent for a $10,000 breakpoint and backdates the letter two months. Six months later, he deposits $10,000 into the fund. He will receive a reduced sales charge on

  A. the $3,000 investment only
  B. $7,000 of the investment only
  C. the $10,000 investment only
  D. the entire $13,000 investment

34. Letters of intent can be backdated up to how many days?

  A. 30
  B. 60
  C. 90
  D. 120

35. The quantity of securities an investor owns for purposes of rights of accumulation could be based on the

  I. current net asset value of the securities
  II. current public offering price of the securities
  III. total purchases of shares at the actual offering prices
  IV. current value of all redeemable securities owned by the investor within the same family of funds

  A. I and III only
  B. II only
  C. III only
  D. I, II, III and IV

36. Porter Stout opened an account about twelve years ago with the ABC Mutual Fund. Today his NAV is $20,000. The ABC Fund offers rights of accumulation. Its breakpoints are as follows:

$1 to $24,999	8%
$25,000 to $49,999	6%
$50,000 to $99,999	4%

Porter wishes to deposit $6,000 in the account today. Which of the following would represent his sales charge?

A. $1,000 at 8%, and $5,000 at 6%
B. $4,999 at 8%, and $1,001 at 6%
C. The full $6,000 at 6%
D. The full $6,000 at 8%

37. A registered representative is seeking to sell shares in an investment company to a client. Which of the following statements would be accurate and permissible for him to say regarding his recommendation?

I. "When you redeem your shares, you will not know immediately the dollar value of your redeemed shares."
II. "If you purchase the shares of two or more funds in the same family of funds, you may be entitled to a reduced sales charge."
III. "If you invest just before the dividend distribution, you can benefit by receiving the added value of that dividend."

A. I and II only
B. I and III only
C. II and III only
D. I, II and III

38. A sale of securities in a dollar amount just below the point at which an investor could take advantage of a lower sales charge by making a larger purchase

I. is called a breakpoint sale
II. would not be a conflict of interest
III. is contrary to just and equitable principles of trade
IV. requires the approval of the District Business Conduct Committee

A. I
B. I and III
C. I and IV
D. II

39. The exchange privilege offered by some mutual funds that are in a family of funds managed by the same company refers to the right of the shareholder to

A. convert mutual fund shares to securities listed on the New York Stock Exchange
B. reinvest dividends and capital gains without a sales charge
C. convert shares to a different investment company within the family of funds on a dollar-for-dollar basis
D. switch shares to an investment company within the family of funds and defer the taxes on any capital gains due to the exchange

◆ Answers & Rationale

1. **A.** No-load funds sell directly to the investor through their own sales force. (Page 96)

2. **D.** A share purchased at its NAV and sold at its NAV is a no-load fund. NAV plus the sales charge equals the POP; if there is no sales charge, the NAV equals the POP. (Page 96)

3. **B.** Members may give other members concessions, but must deal with the public and non-members at the public offering price. (Page 96)

4. **B.** NAV must be calculated at least every business day but not on weekends or holidays. It takes into account all of the fund's assets and is arrived at by totaling the assets and dividing that amount by the number of shares outstanding. (Page 97)

5. **C.** Bid and NAV are similar in that they are both the price at which the customer sells shares. The ask price is similar to the public offering price (POP) because this is the price the customer pays for the purchase of shares. (Page 97)

6. **A.** An appreciation in value of fund assets without an attendant increase in liabilities would lead to an increase in the fund's net asset value (assets − liabilities = NAV). (Page 97)

7. **A.** Share prices fluctuate in relation to the assets held in the fund's portfolio. (Page 97)

8. **A.** Share prices will increase when assets in the portfolio increase in value. Share prices decrease when the fund distributes a dividend because the shareholder will receive either cash or additional shares. Redeeming or purchasing shares does not affect share prices, only total assets. Reinvesting dividends or capital gains has no effect on share prices either. (Page 97)

9. **B.** An unrealized loss is the same as a depreciation in asset value, which results in a lower NAV per share. An investor would receive less at redemption than he would have received if the redemption had taken place prior to the depreciation of the asset. (Page 97)

10. **C.** The NASD limits sales charges to 8.5% of the POP as a maximum. If the fund does not allow for breakpoints, reinvestment of dividends at net or rights of accumulation, the maximum is less than 8.5%. Under the Investment Company Act of 1940, the maximum sales charge on mutual funds is deferred to the NASD rules, while a contractual plan specifically may charge 9% over the life of the plan. (Page 98)

11. **A.** The 12b-1 fee must be fully disclosed in the prospectus that is used as the offering document for the mutual fund. (Page 98)

12. **D.** The NASD's maximum allowable sales charges are: contractual plans (periodic pay unit trusts), 9%; mutual funds, 8 1/2%; variable annuities, 8 1/2%. (Page 98)

13. **A.** A sales load is the difference between the public offering price and the amount actually added to the investment company's portfolio (at the current NAV). Commissions, concessions and allowances are part of the sales load. (Page 98)

14. **B.** A 12b-1 fee is a percent of the annual average net assets of the fund. The fee is typically paid in quarterly installments. (Page 99)

15. **C.** The maximum charged under a 12b-1 plan must bear a relationship to the distribution services offered and must be reasonable. The fee charged may pay only for those distribution, selling and promotional expenses specifically described in the plan. Shares offered under a 12b-1 fund are sold at net asset value; there is no POP. The 9% maximum refers to shares sold under contractual plan agreements. (Page 99)

16. **D.** The maximum sales charge on open-end investment companies under NASD rules is 8.5% of the public offering price. For 12b-1 funds, the annual fee cannot exceed on a per-share basis what could have been charged on a load fund with a

12b-1 asset-based fee. This maximum applies unless the fund can prove the 12b-1 charge is reasonable for the promotional, distribution and sales services provided.   (Page 99)

17. **B.** 12b-1 fees may be used only to cover promotional expenses for funds that act as distributors of their own shares. The amount of the fee must be disclosed in the prospectus, and the fund may not use the term "no-load" in any communications with the public.   (Page 99)

18. **C.** A 12b-1 plan must be approved by a majority vote of the shareholders, board of directors and uninterested members of the board of directors. The fee must be reapproved annually.
(Page 100)

19. **C.** In order to terminate a 12b-1 charge, the termination must be approved by a majority vote of the shareholders or a majority of the uninterested members of the board of directors. Approval by the full board of directors is not required. (Page 100)

20. **D.** Any statement or reference to a mutual fund offered under a 12b-1 fund that implies that the fund is a no-load fund is considered misleading and a violation of the Rules of Fair Practice.
(Page 100)

21. **C.** Class A shares have a front-end load; Class B shares have a back-end load; and Class C shares have a level load that is an asset-based fee.
(Page 100)

22. **C.** The first step is to determine the complement of the sales charge percentage ($100 - 4\% = 96\%$); then divide the NAV by the complement ($\$13.37 \div 96\% = \$13.93$). The final step is to divide the invested amount by the purchase price ($\$50,000 \div \$13.93 = 3,589$), and this is the number of shares purchased.   (Page 101)

23. **C.** To determine the selling price of the shares when given the NAV, you must divide the NAV by 100% minus the sales load:

$$\frac{\text{NAV}}{100\% - \text{SL}\%} = \text{Selling price}$$

In this case,

$$\frac{\$9.35}{100\% - 7\%} = \$10$$

(Page 101)

24. **D.** The 1,000 shares have a net asset value of $10,300. Divide that amount by the complement of 8 1/2% (91 1/2%). The result is $11,257, which is the amount of the current offering price. The difference is $957.   (Page 101)

25. **A.** Funds charging the full 8 1/2% sales load must offer breakpoints, rights of accumulation and dividend reinvestment at NAV. Exchange privileges are the exception.   (Page 102)

26. **C.** Rights of accumulation are good for not less than ten years, while the letter of intent has a 13-month limit.   (Page 102)

27. **B.** Because the funds are under separate management, the load charged on each separate investment will most likely be at the maximum. If the customer invested the entire sum within one fund or a family of funds, a reduced sales charge may have been available.   (Page 102)

28. **A.** For the purpose of qualifying for breakpoints, the definition of "person" includes family units—but only minor children, not someone 35 years old.   (Page 102)

29. **B.** The NASD defines a "person" as: any individual; a joint account held by any combination of an individual, spouse or children; or a trustee purchasing for a single account. It allows quantity discounts to any of these. Investment clubs do not qualify under the definition, nor do groups of individuals who form a business or organization for the sole purpose of investment.   (Page 102)

30. **B.** Adam must put in the full $15,000, an additional $6,000. Reinvested dividends and changes in the NAV do not affect the amount required.   (Page 103)

31. **D.** An LOI is not a binding contract, so the customer is not required to deposit the rest of the money. She will be entitled to whatever breakpoint her $12,000 investment qualifies for.   (Page 103)

32. **C.** A letter of intent is not binding on the client in any way. Should the client decide to liquidate the account prior to completion of the letter, the company may reduce the redemption only by the amount of shares held in escrow.   (Page 103)

33. **D.** The entire investment qualifies for the reduced load. A letter of intent covers purchases within a 13-month period and may be backdated 90 days. Joe Kuhl actually had eleven months in which to make the additional investment.   (Page 103)

34. **C.** The time limit for a letter of intent (LOI) is 13 months, but the letter can be backdated by up to 90 days from the date it was filed.   (Page 103)

35. **D.** All of the methods listed are permitted. The choice is up to the investment company; however, it must disclose the method it chooses. (Generally the greater of choices I or III is the option offered.)   (Page 104)

36. **C.** Under rights of accumulation, if an additional investment plus the client's current account value (or money invested) puts the client's account value over a breakpoint, the entire additional investment qualifies for the reduced sales charge. In this case, Porter's additional investment of $6,000 plus his account value of $20,000 puts his account value over the $25,000 breakpoint. The entire $6,000 investment qualifies for the 6% sales charge.   (Page 104)

37. **A.** Purchase of two funds in the same family of funds may qualify an investor for combination privileges. At redemption, he will receive the next price calculated (forward pricing), which is not yet known. Purchase of a mutual fund just prior to a dividend distribution is a detriment: the distribution about to be paid is included in the purchase price and, when received by the investor, will be treated as ordinary income—even though he is essentially being returned a portion of his investment.   (Page 104)

38. **B.** This is called a "breakpoint sale" and is contrary to just and equitable principles of trade.   (Page 105)

39. **C.** The exchange privilege allows a shareholder to exchange shares from one fund to another within a family of funds under the same management without paying an additional sales charge (dollar for dollar). The shareholder is liable for any tax on gains as a result of the exchange.   (Page 105)

40. **B.** Because the bond fund shares were held for less than twelve months, the gain is short term. An exchange privilege does not exempt the transfer of funds from taxation. The exchange is a taxable event.   (Page 105)

41. **D.** The exchange, or conversion, privilege allows an investor to exchange shares of one fund for another fund under the same management without paying an additional sales charge (although the exchange is still a taxable event).   (Page 105)

42. **C.** Orders for redemption without a certificate being issued require a written request and signature guarantee.   (Page 105)

43. **A.** The seven-day redemption guideline is law and may be suspended only with SEC permission or if the NYSE is closed on a day other than customary holidays and weekends.   (Page 105)

44. **B.** Funds offering the reinstatement privilege allow the investor to redeem and reinvest shares within 30 days without an additional sales charge. The privilege can be used only once, and only the amount withdrawn can be reinstated.   (Page 105)

45. **A.** Purchase or redemption of mutual fund shares may occur at the net asset value next calculated after the order is received; this is known as *forward pricing*.   (Page 105)

46. **C.** The price for mutual fund shares is the next price calculated by the fund after receipt of the request. Answer B describes a repurchase transaction.   (Page 106)

47. **D.** Mutual funds use forward pricing. You will pay the offering price calculated at 5:00 pm. (Page 106)

48. **A.** Adam will receive $12.50 per share less a redemption fee of 1%; $12.50 times 100 shares is $12,500. A 1% redemption fee is $125, so Adam receives $12,375. (Page 106)

49. **A.** Always redeem at NAV (bid): 1,000 shares × 11 = $11,000. Next, determine the redemption fee: $11,000 × .005 (a 1/2% redemption fee) = $55. Finally, subtract the fee from the gross redemption proceeds: $11,000 − $55 = $10,945. A shortcut alternative to the last two steps is to multiply the gross redemption proceeds by the complement of the redemption fee: $11,000 × .995 = $10,945. (Page 106)

22 Taxation and Mutual Fund Distributions Exam

1. A customer owns 10M of 7% U.S. Treasury bonds. She is in the 28% federal tax bracket and the 10% state tax bracket. What is her annual tax liability on these bonds?

   A. $70
   B. $98
   C. $196
   D. $266

2. An individual calculating taxable income received from a municipal bond fund investment for this year would consider that

   A. part of the income distribution received as a dividend is taxable at ordinary income tax rates
   B. all of the income distribution received as a dividend is taxable at ordinary income tax rates
   C. any capital gains distributions received from the fund are taxable at ordinary income tax rates
   D. all distributions received from the fund, both income and gains, are exempt from federal income tax

3. Greta Guernsey invested $10,000 in the ACE Fund in February. Greta sold the shares the following January for $9,000. The result is a

   A. capital loss in the year of sale
   B. capital gain in the year of sale
   C. capital loss in the year of purchase
   D. capital gain in the year of purchase

4. An investor in a 28% tax bracket has a $5,000 loss after netting all capital gains and losses realized. How much may the investor deduct from income that year?

   A. $0
   B. $2,500
   C. $3,000
   D. $5,000

5. An investor in a 28% tax bracket has a $5,000 loss after netting all capital gains and losses realized. The following year this investor has a $1,000 capital gain. After netting his gains and losses, what will be his tax situation that second year?

   A. He will have a $1,000 gain.
   B. He will have a $1,000 loss to carry over to the next year.
   C. He will offset $1,000 ordinary income this year.
   D. There will be no tax consequences.

6. Mini Leveridge has not followed your investment advice and now has net capital losses of $10,000 for the year. How much of these losses can she offset against her nonpassive income for the year?

   A. $1,500
   B. $3,000
   C. $6,000
   D. $10,000

7. An investor has effected the following transactions in her account:

> Bought 100 TIP at 40 on June 15, 1995.
>
> Bought 100 TIP at 32 on November 30, 1995.
>
> Sold 100 TIP at 35 on December 20, 1995.

What is the tax consequence of these transactions?

A. Loss of $100
B. Gain of $300
C. Loss of $500
D. No gain or loss

8. The Investment Company Act of 1940 requires that mutual funds pay dividends from their

A. capital gains
B. net income
C. gross income
D. portfolio earnings

9. Which of the following makes up the net investment income of an open-end investment company?

A. Net gains on sales of securities
B. Dividends, interest and unrealized gains
C. Income from dividends and interest paid by securities held by the fund minus the operating expenses
D. Ninety percent of the net asset value of the fund

10. Which of the following are true of mutual fund dividend distributions?

I. The fund pays dividends from net income.
II. A single taxpayer may exclude $100 worth of dividend income from taxes annually.
III. An investor is liable for taxes on distributions whether the dividend is a cash distribution or reinvested in the fund.
IV. An investor is liable for taxes only if the distribution is received in cash.

A. I and II
B. I, II and III
C. I and III
D. II and IV

11. NavCo Fund has incurred the following on a per share basis: dividend income of $1.10, interest income of $.90, long-term gains of $1.00, management fees of $.50. What is the maximum dividend the fund can distribute per share?

A. $1.50
B. $2.00
C. $2.50
D. $3.00

12. Which of the following costs cannot be deducted as an expense from the investment income of an open-end investment company?

A. Custodial fees
B. Auditing fees
C. Advertising fees
D. Accounting fees

13. A mutual fund paid $.30 in dividends and $.75 in capital gains during the year. The offering price at the end of the year is $6.50. The fund's current yield for the year is

A. 4.6%
B. 6.9%
C. 11.5%
D. 16.2%

14. Capital gains distributions may be combined with income distributions to calculate annual yield on mutual fund shares

    A. when the income distribution contains short-term capital gains
    B. when both distributions are accompanied by a source of distribution statement
    C. when both distributions resulted from activities occurring within the same year
    D. under no circumstances

15. Under what conditions does the Investment Company Act of 1940 require a written statement disclosing the source of dividend payments?

    A. Whenever a dividend is paid
    B. Whenever net income is part of the dividend
    C. Whenever all or part of the dividend payment comes from a source other than current income or accumulated undistributed net income
    D. The Investment Company Act of 1940 does not require disclosure, only the Internal Revenue Code requires disclosure of the amount of the dividend.

16. The ex-dividend date for shares of a mutual fund is

    A. two business days prior to the record date
    B. seven days prior to the record date
    C. the same day as the record date
    D. the day following the record date

17. Investment companies are prohibited from distributing capital gains to their shareholders more frequently than

    A. monthly
    B. quarterly
    C. semiannually
    D. annually

18. A client wants to purchase mutual fund shares just before the ex-dividend date. You should tell him that this is

    A. not advisable under any circumstances
    B. not advisable because of the tax consequences.
    C. advisable because the client will receive a dividend.
    D. advisable because it will allow the client to pay more per share, thus increasing his chance of getting to the breakpoint and receiving a lower sales charge

19. Your client has asked about automatic dividend reinvestment offered by the ACE Fund. In describing the differences between dividend reinvestment and receiving distributions in cash, you can say

    I. one benefit of dividend reinvestment is that distributions reinvested are tax deferred, whereas dividends received in cash are taxable in the year received
    II. the taxation of the dividend distribution is not affected by your choice to reinvest or receive the dividend in cash
    III. the shareholder's proportionate ownership in the ACE Fund will decline if she elects to receive dividend distributions in cash
    IV. the shareholder's proportionate ownership in the ACE Fund is guaranteed to increase if dividend reinvestment is elected

    A. I and III
    B. I and IV
    C. II and III
    D. II and IV

20. Randy Bear purchased $2,000 of ACE Income Mutual Fund shares in January and paid the maximum sales charge of 8.5%. ACE declares a quarterly dividend of $0.20 per share on February 15th, payable to shareholders of record March 15th. Randy can reinvest his dividend distribution if he requests that dividends be reinvested

   I.   at the time he purchased his ACE Income shares
   II.   by February 15th
   III.   at least 10 days prior to the record date of the dividend distribution
   IV.   at least the business day before the record date for the dividend distribution

   A.   I
   B.   I and II
   C.   I, II and III
   D.   II and IV

21. Belle Charolais's Form 1099B from a mutual fund investment listed her earnings for last year as follows:

Reinvested capital gains	$5,000
Undistributed capital gains	3,000
Reinvested dividends	7,000

If she filed a separate return and had no other dividend income, what would be Belle's taxable income from this investment?

   A. $10,100
   B. $10,200
   C. $14,900
   D. $15,000

22. The document that must accompany each distribution an investment company pays out to its mutual fund shareholders is a

   A.   Form 1099B IC/VC
   B.   prospectus
   C.   W-2 statement
   D.   statement as to the source of the distribution

23. Unrealized gain in a mutual fund portfolio

   I.   affects the value of fund shares
   II.   represents the growth in market value of securities held in the portfolio
   III.   is realized by shareholders only when they redeem their shares

   A.   I and II only
   B.   I and III only
   C.   II and III only
   D.   I, II and III

24. As the owner of mutual fund shares, you will pay no tax on

   A.   dividends that are reinvested in the fund
   B.   unrealized capital gains
   C.   capital gains that are issued as additional shares
   D.   dividends that do not qualify for the $100 dividend exclusion

25. The conduit theory of taxation means that the

   I.   fund is not taxed on earnings it distributes
   II.   retained earnings are taxed as regular corporate income
   III.   earnings distributed by a regulated mutual fund are taxed twice

   A.   I and II only
   B.   I and III only
   C.   II and III only
   D.   I, II and III

26. ATF, an open-end investment company, has the following financial information:

Dividend income	$2,000
Interest income	900
Short-term gains	1,000
Long-term gains	1,000
Expenses	900

In order to qualify as a regulated investment company, ATF must distribute what amount to its investors?

A. $1,800
B. $2,700
C. $3,510
D. $3,600

27. If you invest in a regulated investment company, any dividend you receive from that investment will be taxed

A. as long-term capital gains
B. as long-term or short-term capital gains, depending on how long you have been an investor
C. to you as ordinary income but will not be taxed at the fund's level
D. to you as capital gains but will not be taxed at the corporate level

28. On January 10th, 1987, Barry Kodiak purchased 1,000 shares of the ArGood open-end investment company. On January 22nd, 1987, ArGood sells 25,000 shares of TCB at a profit. ArGood originally purchased the TCB on June 24th, 1984. On February 15th, 1987, ArGood distributes the gain from the sale of TCB to shareholders. How will Barry be taxed on this distribution?

A. The income will be taxed as a long-term gain taxable as ordinary income.
B. The income will be taxed as a long-term gain qualifying for the 60% exclusion.
C. If Barry is using automatic reinvestment, he will not be taxed at all.
D. Barry will not be taxed because he did not sell the TCB; ArGood is liable for all taxes.

29. Which of the following is the usual source of a mutual fund's capital gains distribution?

A. Net long-term gains resulting from the sale of the company's mutual fund shares
B. Net short-term gains resulting from the sale of the company's mutual fund shares
C. Net long-term gains resulting from the sale of securities in the fund's investment portfolio
D. Net short-term gains resulting from the sale of securities in the fund's investment portfolio

30. Three months after you have purchased 100 shares of an open-end investment company, the company pays a $.32 per share capital gain distribution. On your tax return you will

A. report the distribution as ordinary income
B. report the distribution as a capital gain
C. claim the distribution under your $200 dividend exclusion if you itemize
D. report your registered rep for selling dividends

31. The ACE Fund in which Max and Lotta Leveridge have invested paid $62 in taxes on their share of retained capital gains. How would they report this?

A. They would claim the $62 paid by ACE as a credit against taxes they owe.
B. They would exclude an additional $62 from dividend income.
C. They would pay an additional $62 in taxes and have to refund the $62 paid by the fund.
D. Their tax liability is not affected by the $62 paid by ACE.

32. An investor purchased 200 shares of the ACE Fund when the POP was $11.60 and the NAV was $10.60. The current POP of the ACE Fund is $12.50, and the current NAV is $11.50. If the investor liquidates her 200 shares now, she will have a

    A. loss of $200
    B. loss of $20
    C. gain of $20
    D. gain of $200

33. Three years ago, Bea Kuhl purchased 300 shares of ACE Fund. She sold the shares on August 15th, for a loss of $400. On September 4th of the same year, she repurchased the shares. How would she record the loss for tax purposes?

    A. Forty percent of the loss is deductible.
    B. Fifty percent of the loss is deductible.
    C. Sixty percent of the loss is deductible.
    D. The loss is not deductible.

34. Tex Longhorn uses the FIFO method to determine his capital gains. What does this mean?

    A. The IRS will assume a liquidation of the first shares that were acquired.
    B. Tex will indicate the specific shares that were redeemed without regard to when they were purchased.
    C. The last shares purchased are the first shares to be redeemed.
    D. None of the above apply in this case.

35. Failure by a shareholder to provide or verify her Social Security number to the investment company will result in which of the following taxes?

    A. Surtax
    B. Alternative minimum tax
    C. Noncertification tax
    D. Withholding tax

36. When you inherit a mutual fund upon the death of the owner, what is your cost basis in the shares?

    A. The market value of the shares upon the decedent's death
    B. The same cost basis as the decedent's
    C. The cost basis of the decedent plus the final distribution made by the fund
    D. The market value of the shares twelve months from the date of death

37. Porter Stout originally invested $20,000 into the ACE Fund and has reinvested dividends and gains of $8,000. His shares in ACE are now worth $40,000. He converts his investment in ACE to the ATF Fund, which is under the same management as ACE. Which of the following statements is true?

    A. He retains his cost basis of $28,000 in the ATF Fund.
    B. He must declare $12,000 as a taxable gain upon conversion into the ATF Fund.
    C. He retains a $20,000 cost basis in the ATF Fund because of the conversion privilege.
    D. He is not liable for taxes in the current year because he did not have constructive receipt of the money at conversion.

38. The ACE Tax Free Money Market Fund advertises itself as a triple tax-free investment for purchasers residing in New York City. This means ACE's portfolio

   I.   most likely holds City of New York short-term notes or similar city income tax-exempt securities
   II. is invested so that more than 10% of its assets hold a single issue of City of New York short-term notes
   III. has an average maturity of 90 days or less
   IV. has at least 95% of the securities held rated in the top investment grade for money-market instruments

   A. I and IV only
   B. II and III only
   C. III only
   D. I, II, III and IV

◆ Answers & Rationale

1. **C.** $10,000 times 7% equals $700 annual interest per bond. The $700 annual interest is taxable only by the federal government. $700 × 28% = $196 tax liability.   (Page 107)

2. **C.** Interest in the form of dividends paid from a municipal bond fund would be exempt from federal income tax. Gains from the sale of portfolio securities would be subject to ordinary income tax.   (Page 107)

3. **A.** A gain or loss is claimed in the year of sale, not in the year of purchase.   (Page 108)

4. **C.** The maximum deduction of capital losses in any one year is $3,000. Any remaining losses can be carried forward into the next year.   (Page 109)

5. **C.** The losses carried forward from the previous year are $2,000. These losses are netted against the gain of $1,000 for a net loss of $1,000. That $1,000 loss can be used to offset $1,000 of ordinary income. In other words, the net $1,000 loss is deducted from the investor's income. No further loss remains to carry forward. (Page 109)

6. **B.** Net capital losses are deductible against earned (nonpassive) income to a maximum of $3,000 per year. The balance of such losses can be carried forward to the next year.   (Page 109)

7. **D.** The 30-day wash sale rule of the IRS states that the purchase of substantially identical securities within 30 days of a securities transaction at a loss will result in the loss being disallowed for tax purposes. The 30-day time period is considered to be either before or after the sale date. The wash sale rule supersedes the investor's ability to identify the specific securities sold. The purchase of 100 shares of TIP on November 30, 1995, is within 30 days of the sale on December 20, 1995.   (Page 109)

8. **B.** Dividends are paid from net income (interest plus dividends plus short-term gains when identified minus expenses).   (Page 110)

9. **C.** Dividends and interest paid on the securities held in the portfolio make up investment income. From this the fund's expenses are paid before it becomes net investment income.   (Page 110)

10. **C.** Funds pay dividends from net income, and the investor is liable for taxes on all distributions.   (Page 110)

11. **A.** A mutual fund may distribute net investment income as a dividend. Net investment income is defined as interest and dividends (and short-term gains if identified) less fees. Long-term gains must be distributed separately and no more often than annually. Therefore, dividend income of $1.10 plus interest income of $0.90 minus expenses of $0.50 equals a maximum $1.50 per share dividend distribution.   (Page 110)

12. **C.** Advertising costs are an expense of the underwriter and are paid from the sales charge collected on the sale of investment company shares.   (Page 110)

13. **A.** Current yield of a mutual fund is current income ($.30 dividend in this case) divided by the net asset value ($6.50). Gains are not included in calculation of current yield; they are accounted for separately.   (Page 110)

14. **D.** Capital gains distributions may never be combined with income distributions for this purpose.   (Page 110)

15. **C.** The Investment Company Act of 1940 requires disclosure when all or part of the dividend payment comes from a source other than current income or accumulated undistributed net income.   (Page 110)

16. **D.** Mutual fund record dates are set by the fund's board of directors. Since funds use forward pricing and transactions occur the day an order is received, an investor would be a shareholder of

record if the transaction is completed by the time the fund prices its shares. Corporate stocks in the secondary market have the ex-dividend date of two business days before the record date.   (Page 110)

17. **D.** Under the act of 1940, investment companies are prohibited from distributing capital gains more frequently than once per year. This does not require gains to be distributed, as the fund may retain gains for reinvestment.   (Page 110)

18. **B.** The value of shares will drop by the amount of the dividend on the ex-dividend date. This loss will not be made up by the dividend as the dividend is subject to ordinary income tax. A person in the 28% tax bracket stands to lose 28% of the value of the dividend.   (Page 111)

19. **C.** Dividend reinvestment does not defer taxation of the distribution. Whether the dividend is received in cash or reinvested, the distribution is still taxable in the year paid. An investor electing to receive distributions in cash will see his interest in the fund decline if others are reinvesting. However, reinvestment of distributions does not guarantee an investor will increase his proportionate interest in the fund.   (Page 111)

20. **C.** Dividend reinvestment must be made available to any one making such request if made at least 10 days prior to the distribution's record date. As a result, if the request was made by the date of purchase, the declaration date or 10 days prior to the record date, Randy could reinvest the dividend distribution. Funds may exclude this right to certain individuals with balances of less than $1,200.   (Page 111)

21. **D.** Under the Tax Reform Act of 1986, income and gains distributions are taxable at ordinary income tax rates. The capital gains exclusion has been repealed, as has the dividend exclusion. Undistributed gains are still taxable to the shareholder. The taxes paid by the fund on the retained gain are credited to the shareholder.   (Page 111)

22. **D.** A statement as to the source of the distribution must accompany the distribution of dividends if the source of the dividend is from other than retained or current net income. The 1099B form is sent after the close of the year and details tax information related to distributions for the year.   (Page 112)

23. **D.** Unrealized gains in portfolio securities are the result of the asset's appreciation in value. This appreciation in value will be reflected in an appreciation of the mutual fund shares themselves. An investor wanting to cash in on this appreciation can do so only by selling the shares (realizing the gain).   (Page 112)

24. **B.** A gain is not taxable until it is realized or sold.   (Page 112)

25. **D.** By qualifying as a regulated investment company (the conduit, or pipeline, tax theory), the fund is liable for taxes only on the income retained. The investor benefits because the income is taxed only twice (at the corporate level and at the individual level) and not three times (also at the fund level).   (Page 112)

26. **A.** To qualify as a regulated investment company, at least 90% of net investment income (without regard to gains) must be distributed. Net investment income would equal dividend income ($2,000 in this case) plus interest income ($900) minus expenses ($900), to equal $2,000. Ninety percent of $2,000 is $1,800.   (Page 112)

27. **C.** A mutual fund qualifying as a regulated investment company distributes at least 90% of its net investment income as a dividend to shareholders. Because the company has qualified, the fund pays no tax on the income distributed. However, the shareholders are taxed at their ordinary income tax rate on the distribution.   (Page 112)

28. **A.** Barry owned shares of the mutual fund when it distributed the gain, and he is liable for the taxes. This is considered a long-term gain, which is currently taxed as ordinary income. (Page 113)

29. **C.** Capital gains come from the sale of securities held in the company's portfolio. Most of these gains will be the sale of securities held for long periods of time.   (Page 113)

30. **B.** If a fund makes a capital gains distribution, shareholders are required to report it as capital gain on their individual tax returns (the investment company will provide both the shareholder and the IRS with a 1099B form reflecting the distribution). The distribution is a capital gain taxed at ordinary rates. The dividend exclusion has been repealed by the Tax Reform Act of 1986.   (Page 113)

31. **A.** If a fund realizes a gain but declines to distribute it to shareholders, the gain is still taxable to the investor. The fund will pay taxes on the gain on behalf of the shareholders (similar to a withholding tax) and will issue as part of the 1099B a statement showing their share of taxes paid. In this question, that share equalled $62. The Leveridges can elect to use that share as a credit against their tax liability or can elect to have it refunded. The basis of the shares is increased by the amount of the undistributed gain included in income, less the taxes paid by the fund.   (Page 113)

32. **B.** The investor's cost base in the shares is $11.60. If she liquidates, she will receive the net asset value of $11.50, resulting in a loss of $.10 per share. Liquidating 200 shares, therefore, results in a total loss of $20 (200 × $.10).   (Page 113)

33. **D.** The customer repurchased the shares within 30 days of the loss transaction, and the loss is disallowed (a wash sale).   (Page 113)

34. **A.** FIFO means "first in, first out." Answer C describes LIFO (last in, first out); answer B describes share identification.   (Page 114)

35. **D.** Failure to provide a Social Security or federal tax identification number results in an automatic withholding tax of 20% on the account.   (Page 114)

36. **A.** The basis of property inherited is either stepped up (or down) to its fair market value (FMV) at the date of the decedent's death. No adjustment of basis is necessary for a period prior to the death of the decedent.   (Page 114)

37. **B.** The exchange privilege offers exchange without an additional sales charge, but the exchange is still taxable. Porter is taxed on the gain of $12,000 ($40,000 − $28,000).   (Page 114)

38. **A.** Nontaxable money-market funds come under the same restrictions (Rule 2a-7 of the Investment Company Act of 1940) as taxable money-market funds. However, tax-exempt money-market funds are excluded from the 90-day-or-less average maturity restriction. Finally, a triple tax-exempt fund would most likely have City of New York issues in its portfolio as well as State of New York issues.   (Page 114)

23 Mutual Fund Purchase and Withdrawal Plans Exam

1. June Polar and Joe Kuhl each have open accounts in the ArGood Mutual Fund. June has decided to receive all distributions in cash, while Joe is automatically reinvesting all distributions. How do their decisions affect their investments?

   I. Receiving cash distributions may reduce June's proportional interest in the fund.
   II. June may use the cash distributions to purchase shares later at NAV.
   III. Joe's reinvestments purchase additional shares at NAV rather than at the offering price.

   A. I and II only
   B. I and III only
   C. II and III only
   D. I, II and III

2. Which of the following are characteristic of a mutual fund voluntary accumulation plan?

   I. Minimum initial purchase
   II. Minimum optional additional purchases
   III. Declining sales charges on new investment as money accumulates
   IV. Obligatory purchase goal

   A. I and II only
   B. I, II and III only
   C. II and IV only
   D. I, II, III and IV

3. June Polar has just invested a lump sum in the ACE Fund. If she wishes to purchase additional shares by reinvesting all dividends and capital gains, she can set up a(n)

   A. accumulation plan
   B. regular plan
   C. dollar cost averaging plan
   D. lump-sum plan

4. Which of the following characteristics describe a contractual planholder?

   I. Receives a plan certificate
   II. Owns a specific portion of the underlying mutual fund shares
   III. Owns specific shares in the underlying portfolio
   IV. Must complete the contractual plan

   A. I and II
   B. I and III
   C. II and IV
   D. III and IV

5. A customer has a contractual plan. The customer's daughter is in college and needs money for expenses. The customer has been investing $150 per month into the contractual plan. What would you recommend she do to provide her daughter with expense money?

   A. Give the daughter $100 per month, and invest $50 per month instead of $150 per month into the contractual plan.
   B. Liquidate the plan.
   C. Continue to invest, and make periodic withdrawals from the plan.
   D. Set up a systematic withdrawal plan, and continue to make investments.

6. Which of the following violate(s) provisions of the Investment Company Act of 1940 concerning periodic payment plans?

   I. Sales charge exceeding 9% over the plan's life
   II. Sales charge exceeding 50% in the plan's first year
   III. Sales charge that is disproportionately greater in the last six months than over the plan's life
   IV. First payment requirement of $20 and subsequent payments of $10

   A. I only
   B. I, II and III only
   C. II only
   D. I, II, III and IV

7. After a client makes an initial investment under a new periodic payment plan, he will be making deposits of at least how much for the remaining installments?

   A. $10
   B. $20
   C. $25
   D. $50

8. Bea Kuhl is participating in a periodic payment plan. Fifty percent of her first year's payments are taken as a sales charge. What is the maximum the sales charge can average over the life of the plan?

   A. 8.5%
   B. 9%
   C. 16%
   D. 20%

9. The maximum sales charge on a unit investment trust using mutual funds for its underlying investment is

   A. 7%
   B. 8%
   C. 8 1/2%
   D. 9%

10. Under the spread-load plan provision of the 1970 amendments to the Investment Company Act of 1940, an investor may have no more than what percentage deducted from any one payment?

   A. 8 1/2%
   B. 9%
   C. 16%
   D. 20%

11. The average sales charge on a spread-load contractual plan over the plan's first four years can be no more than

   A. 9%
   B. 16%
   C. 20%
   D. 50%

12. The maximum annual sales charge on a spread-load periodic payment plan certificate is

   A. 8 1/2%
   B. 9%
   C. 20%
   D. 50%

13. An individual has periodically invested $24,000 in a unit investment trust over ten years. What is the maximum sales charge?

   A. $2,040
   B. $2,160
   C. $4,800
   D. $12,000

14. A customer canceling a contractual plan will have all of his sales charge refunded if he cancels the plan within

   A. 15 days of receiving the notice by the custodian bank
   B. 30 days of the mailing of the notice by the custodian bank
   C. 45 days of the mailing of the notice by the custodian bank
   D. 18 months of receiving the notice from the custodian bank

15. June Polar has signed up for a mutual fund contractual plan with a 50% front-end load and $300 monthly payments. She has decided to cancel the plan after her second payment but within 45 days. If her current NAV is $340, how much will she get back from the plan?

   A. $340
   B. $550
   C. $600
   D. $640

16. Klaus Bruin has decided to terminate his contractual plan one month after opening it. At the time he opened the account, the NAV was $11.50, and it is now $11.80. He has acquired 212 shares and has paid sales charges of $930. What will Klaus's refund be?

   A. The total NAV for his shares at the time of their purchase plus 50% of the sales charges
   B. The current NAV of his shares plus all sales charges
   C. Only the current NAV of his shares
   D. The current NAV of his shares plus sales charges that exceed 15% of gross payments

17. A participant in a periodic payment plan fails to make a payment for three months. Which of the following actions must the broker-dealer take?

   A. Cancel the account and return the entire account value.
   B. Liquidate the account and return the NAV and all sales charges.
   C. Notify the participant that he may request a return of all sales charges less 15% of his total deposits plus the value of the account.
   D. Begin court action to collect the delinquent amount.

18. A customer purchased a front-end load periodic payment plan last year. The investment company stopped receiving payments from her after six months. Because she hasn't been heard from for the last four months, the investment company

A. must recalculate the deposits, retain its 50% sales charge and return the balance from the escrow account
B. must send a notice to the customer informing her of both the value of the account and the refund to which she is entitled if she decides to cancel the plan
C. must refund all sales charges in excess of 15% of the deposits and return the net asset value of her investment
D. may sue the customer for the past due payment(s)

19. An investor in a spread-load plan wants to withdraw after investing $150 a month for eight months. The plan has taken $240 in sales charges. If the NAV has not changed, how much refund will the investor receive?

A. $600
B. $960
C. $1,020
D. $1,200

20. A customer canceling a front load contractual plan will have all or part of his sales charge refunded if he cancels the plan within

A. 8 months
B. 18 months
C. 28 months
D. 38 months

21. If the holder of a front-end load contractual plan misses three payments during the first year, the investment company will

A. notify the holder that she may cancel the plan and receive a refund equal to the investment's NAV plus 100% of the sales charge
B. terminate the plan and send the holder the total deposit less any sales charge
C. notify the holder that she may cancel the plan and receive a refund equal to the investment's NAV plus 15% of the sales charge
D. notify the holder that she may cancel the plan and receive a refund equal to the investment's NAV plus all of the sales charge in excess of 15% of the gross deposits

22. The result of a client investing the same amount of money into a mutual fund at regular intervals over a long period of time is a lower

A. price per share than cost per share
B. cost per share than price per share
C. dollar amount invested
D. return on the cost basis

23. Adam Grizzly has been investing $100 a month in the Amusement Technology Fund over the past five months. His purchases are as follows:

Month	Price/Share	Quantity
1	10	10
2	20	5
3	25	4
4	5	20
5	10	10

What is the difference between Adam's average cost and the average price he paid for the shares?

A. $3.80
B. $7.14
C. $10.20
D. $14

24. An advantage of dollar cost averaging during a bull market is that it will result in an average cost per share that is *less* than the cost of the stock on any given day, assuming that

   I. the price of the underlying shares fluctuates
   II. a set number of shares is purchased regularly
   III. a set dollar amount is invested regularly
   IV. a set dollar amount of investments is maintained

   A. I and II
   B. I and III
   C. II and III
   D. III and IV

25. Which of the following withdrawal plans offered by the ArGood Mutual Fund will pay the client a fixed monthly payment?

   I. Fixed-dollar withdrawal
   II. Fixed-percentage withdrawal
   III. Fixed-share withdrawal
   IV. Liquidation over a fixed period of time

   A. I only
   B. II and III only
   C. II, III and IV only
   D. I, II, III and IV

26. Concerning a fixed-time withdrawal plan offered by a mutual fund

   I. the amount received each month by the client may vary
   II. a fixed number of shares will be liquidated each month
   III. not all funds offer this type of withdrawal
   IV. this plan is self-exhausting

   A. I
   B. I and II
   C. I, III and IV
   D. II, III and IV

27. Bud Charolais has a large investment in the ATF open-end investment company. He has selected a fixed-time withdrawal plan. The computation for the withdrawal plan will be based on the

   A. NAV each period
   B. NAV at the first payment
   C. POP each period
   D. POP at the first payment

28. One risk of a withdrawal plan is that the

   A. sales charge for the service will be high
   B. cost basis of the shares will be high
   C. plan is illegal in many states
   D. principal value will fluctuate

29. A client is receiving funds from an open-end investment company under the provisions of a withdrawal plan. This means

   A. the client must continue to make investments into the fund
   B. the client will generally be discouraged from making further investments into the fund
   C. the client will always exhaust the plan within a predetermined period of time
   D. that if the client withdraws only dividend and gains distributions, the principal amount of the investment will always remain intact

◆ Answers & Rationale

1. **B.** By electing to receive distributions in cash while others are purchasing shares through reinvestment, the customer's proportional interest in the fund will decline. Most funds allow reinvestment of dividends at net asset value. Cash invested is considered a new purchase, and the shares will be purchased at the public offering price, not NAV. (Page 115)

2. **B.** A voluntary accumulation plan is voluntary, not binding. The company may require that the initial investment meet a certain minimum dollar amount. It may also specify that any additions meet set minimums (for example, $50). The sales charge is level, and the plan may qualify for breakpoints based on the accumulated value. (Page 115)

3. **A.** The customer can elect to reinvest fund distributions through an accumulation plan. (Page 115)

4. **A.** A contractual planholder receives a certificate evidencing ownership of shares held in trust by the plan company. Remember, plan companies are unit investment trusts that invest in shares of mutual funds. The plan participant holds units in the trust, not specific shares of the mutual fund. (Page 115)

5. **A.** The best choice is to reduce the contractual plan payments to $50 per month and give the daughter $100 per month (allowed by most plans). By doing so, the contractual plan remains intact (although the time necessary to accumulate the plan's stated investment is extended). By liquidating, or withdrawing from the plan, the customer is using money that has been subject to heavy sales charges (50% or 20% loads). Clearly, using money reduced by heavy sales charges is not in the best interest of the customer. (Page 115)

6. **D.** Mutual funds and variable annuity contracts are limited to a maximum sales charge of 8 1/2%; periodic payment plans and contractual plans are limited to 9%. Front-end load contractual plans may deduct no more than 50% of the first year's deposits as sales charges, and spread-load plans may deduct no more than 20% during the first year. A periodic payment plan must charge at least $20 for the first installment and no less than $10 for subsequent installments. (Page 116)

7. **A.** The minimum initial investment for a contractual plan is $20, and remaining installments must be at least $10. (Page 116)

8. **B.** The maximum sales charge on a contractual plan whether front-end load or spread load is 9% over the life of the plan. (Page 117)

9. **D.** A UIT investing in mutual fund shares is most likely a contractual plan operating under the Investment Company Act of 1940 or the 1970 act amendments. The maximum sales load permissible under either type of plan (front-end load or spread-load) is 9% over the life of the plan. (Page 117)

10. **D.** Under the Investment Company Act Amendments of 1970, a spread-load plan cannot take more than 20% of any plan payment in the first year as a sales charge. Therefore, total sales charges cannot exceed 20% in the first year and cannot average more than 16% over the first four years of the plan. A maximum sales charge of 9% is permitted over the life of the plan; 8 1/2% is the maximum sales charge permitted by the NASD for single pay unit trusts and investment company open accounts. (Page 117)

11. **B.** The Investment Company Act Amendments of 1970 states that a spread-load plan cannot take more than 20% of any plan payment as a sales charge and the sales charge cannot exceed an average of more than 16% over the first four years of the plan investment. (Page 117)

12. **C.** A spread-load plan has a maximum annual sales charge of 20% in the first year. All contractual plans are limited to a maximum sales charge of 9% over the life of the contract. Mutual funds and variable annuities can charge a maximum of 8 1/2%. (Page 117)

13. **B.** First, the method of investment describes a contractual plan (i.e., a periodic investment into a unit investment trust over a period of time). The maximum sales charge over the life of a contractual plan is 9%. In this case, 9% of $24,000 equals $2,160. (Page 118)

14. **C.** Under the Investment Company Act of 1940, contractual planholders must be allowed a full refund if they return their shares within 45 days of the mailing of the notice by the custodian bank. (Page 118)

15. **D.** Under the Investment Company Act of 1940, an investor terminating a plan within 45 days is entitled to a refund of all sales charges plus the current value of the account. Because the customer has made two payments of $300 each, a total of $600 was invested. From that $600, 50% ($300) was deducted as a sales charge. The current value of the account is $340, so the customer will receive $640 as a refund. (Page 118)

16. **B.** Termination of a contractual plan within 45 days results in a refund of all sales charges plus the current value of the account. (Page 118)

17. **C.** Plan participants who miss three or more payments within the first 18 months of the contract, or one or more payments between the 15th and the 18th month, must be notified of their rights of withdrawal. If they request that their contract be canceled, the company must send them the current net asset value of their account plus any sales charges deducted from their payments that are in excess of 15% of total deposits. (Page 118)

18. **B.** Purchasers of front-end load plans have surrender rights for 18 months after their initial investment. The purchaser must be officially notified of these rights if she misses any three payments within the first 15 months or misses one or more payments between the 15th and the 18th month. Under these rights, the purchaser will be refunded some (but not all) of the sales charges as well as the current value of the account. (Page 119)

19. **B.** Refunds from a spread-load plan that has been in effect for more than 45 days are limited to a return of net asset value only. The investor would receive the difference between the amount invested (NAV remains the same) and the sales charges deducted. In this case, a total investment of $1,200 minus the sales charge of $240 equals a refund of $960. (Page 119)

20. **B.** Purchasers of front load plans have surrender rights for 18 months after their initial investment. Under the Investment Company Act of 1940, an investor terminating a plan within 18 months is entitled to a refund of all sales charges in excess of 15% of the total (gross) payments made to date, plus the current value of the investment, which is liquidated at current NAV (and may result in a profit or loss). (Page 119)

21. **D.** Under the Investment Company Act of 1940, an investor in a contractual plan who misses three payments within the first 18 months must be advised of her redemption privileges: a refund of the current net asset value of the investment plus all sales charges in excess of 15% of the gross deposits. (Page 119)

22. **B.** By investing a predetermined amount of money periodically for a long period of time, the investor is investing using the concept of *dollar cost averaging*. The result is to reduce the cost per share compared to the average market price. (Page 120)

23. **A.** Adam paid a total of $500 for 49 shares of stock, or $10.20 per share. The average price of the shares during this time was the total of the share prices ($70) divided by the number of investment periods (5), or $14. The difference between the two is $3.80. (Page 120)

24. **B.** Dollar cost averaging will result in a lower average cost per share as long as the price of the shares fluctuates, the general trend of the stock price is up, and the same number of dollars is invested during each interval. (Page 120)

25. **A.** In a withdrawal plan, if one variable is fixed, such as fixed dollar, all other aspects of the payment will vary. If a client is receiving a fixed-

dollar payment, the plan must be a fixed-dollar plan.   (Page 121)

26. **C.** A fixed-time withdrawal plan is considered self-liquidating. Only the time is fixed; the number of shares liquidated, the amount of money received and the percentage of the account liquidated will vary from period to period. Funds may or may not offer withdrawal plans. If they do, the prospectus will describe information concerning the plans.   (Page 121)

27. **A.** At first, withdrawal of funds will be based on the NAV. Subsequently, it will be determined each time a payment is made.   (Page 121)

28. **D.** Withdrawal plans have no guarantee of payment. The investor's account value is at the mercy of market fluctuations.   (Page 121)

29. **B.** Taking money out of a fund at the same time a person is putting money into the fund is generally discouraged.   (Page 121)

24   New Accounts Exam

1. August Polar wishes to open a cash account with you. You are the registered rep and Chip Bullock is the branch manager of your office. Who must sign the new account form in order to open this account?

   A. Mr. Polar only
   B. You only
   C. Mr. Bullock and you only
   D. Mr. Polar, Mr. Bullock, and you

2. When a client opens an account, which of the following pieces of information will need to be noted on the application?

   I. Client's name and Social Security number
   II. Whether the client is employed by an NASD member firm
   III. Signature of the registered rep
   IV. Signature of the office manager, partner or other designated principal
   V. Statement that the client understands the risks involved

   A. I only
   B. I, II, III and IV only
   C. II and IV only
   D. I, II, III, IV and V

3. A customer wishes to open a new account but declines to provide all of the financial information requested by the member firm. In this case the member firm may

   I. not open an account
   II. open the account if it determines by other means that the customer has the financial resources to carry the account and determines that trading is suitable
   III. not recommend uncovered option writing transactions unless they are suitable for the customer

   A. I
   B. II
   C. II and III
   D. III

4. A change in which of the following should be indicated in a customer's file?

   I. Name or address
   II. Marital status
   III. Objectives

   A. I only
   B. I and II only
   C. III only
   D. I, II and III

5. A lawyer with power of attorney over one of your client's accounts trades for the account because the client is currently residing in the Near East. The lawyer requests that all statements and trade confirmations be sent to his office. Which of the following statements is(are) true?

   A. The lawyer needs approval of the NYSE for such a discretionary account.
   B. You must continue to send statements and trade confirmations to the client's official permanent residence.
   C. The lawyer's orders must be followed because he has power of attorney.
   D. The client must approve each trade, regardless of where he is currently residing.

6. A client is going on a trip and wishes to have his brokerage firm stop sending mail. The firm can do all of the following EXCEPT

   A. if he is traveling domestically, hold the mail for two months
   B. if he is traveling internationally, hold the mail for three months
   C. send the mail to a post office box
   D. send the mail to the office of the client's registered rep

7. A registered rep must follow special rules when opening an account for

   A. the six-year-old child of a clerical employee of a competitive brokerage firm
   B. the wife of an operations manager at another brokerage firm
   C. a registered rep at an affiliated brokerage firm that is owned by the same financial holding company
   D. any of the above

8. If a partner of a member firm wishes to open an account with another member firm, the

   I. account may not be opened under any circumstances due to the privileged information to which the partner has access
   II. account may be opened, but the partner may not engage in any transactions in securities recommended by his own firm
   III. member firm opening the account must send duplicate confirmations or statements to the employing member firm, if requested to do so
   IV. member firm opening the account is required to give notice to the employing member firm

   A. I
   B. II and III
   C. II and IV
   D. III and IV

9. A registered representative of an NASD member firm wishes to open an account with another member firm. The executing member shall take all the following actions EXCEPT

   A. notify the employer member in writing prior to the execution of the transaction of the intention to open or maintain the account for the representative
   B. immediately transmit to the employer member duplicate copies of confirmations or other statements with respect to the representative's account
   C. transmit duplicate copies of confirmations or other statements with respect to the representative's account upon request of the employer member
   D. notify the registered representative of the executing member's intent to notify the employer member

◆ Answers & Rationale

1. **C.** The signature of the customer is not required to open a cash account. To open a margin account, the customers signature must be obtained on the margin agreement. For all accounts, the registered rep must sign the new account form, indicating that the information on the form is true and complete. The branch manager serves as the principal, and must review and accept the new account by signing the form prior to opening the account. (Page 123)

2. **D.** When opening an account, the minimum information needed is the name of the client, whether the client is employed with another NASD firm and the client's tax identification number. Additionally, the registered representative must have discussed the risks of the investment with the client and must sign the appropriate forms. All accounts will be reviewed by a supervisor (principal of the firm). (Page 124)

3. **C.** If a customer refuses to provide financial information, the member firm must use whatever information it has available to decide whether to open the account. Any recommendation made to a customer must be suitable, taking into account the customer's investment objectives, financial situation and any other relevant information. (Page 124)

4. **D.** All information that could affect recommendations or the financial situation of a customer must be noted immediately in the file. (Page 124)

5. **B.** You must continue to send statements and trade confirmations to the client's official permanent residence unless the client instructs you in writing to discontinue this service. (Page 124)

6. **D.** Client mail may not be sent to the office of the client's registered rep. This could provide a way for the rep to withhold information from the client. (Page 124)

7. **D.** The NYSE, NASD and MSRB all have rules which require broker-dealers to give special attention to accounts opened by certain individuals. This special attention typically involves permission from, or written notification to, some other broker-dealer regarding establishment of the account. Accounts opened by the following individuals fall within these rules:

- all employees of broker-dealers; and
- all spouses or minor children of employees of broker-dealers.

(Page 126)

8. **D.** The member firm at which the account is being opened must give notice to the employing firm, and the employing firm must receive duplicate copies of all trade confirmations if it requests them. (Page 126)

9. **B.** When an employee opens an account with another member, the employee will be notified by the executing member that the employing member will be notified that the account is to be opened, and copies of confirmations and other reports will be available upon request. (Page 126)

1. Hugh and Bambi Heifer are tenants in common in a joint account. Which of the following statements is(are) true?

   I.   If one of them dies, the survivor will not automatically assume full ownership.

   II.   They need not have equal interest in the account.

   III.   They have an undivided interest in the property in the account.

   A.   I only
   B.   I and II only
   C.   II and III only
   D.   I, II and III

2. Joe and his wife Bea own shares in the ACE Fund as joint tenants with rights of survivorship. If Joe dies, what happens to the shares in the account?

   A.   One half of the shares would belong to Bea, and the remaining half would be distributed to Joe's estate.
   B.   Bea would own all the shares.
   C.   Ownership of the shares would have to be determined by probate court.
   D.   None of the above would occur.

3. A woman wishes to open a cash account in her name only, and allow her husband to make purchases and receive checks in his name only. She must instruct her broker-dealer to open a

   A.   margin account
   B.   cash account with limited power of attorney
   C.   cash account with full power of attorney
   D.   cash account

4. Which of the following constitutes a discretionary account?

   A.   Trading account of the registered representative
   B.   Trading account of the broker-dealer
   C.   Account where the investor gives the broker-dealer the authority to buy or sell securities in the customer's account
   D.   Mutual fund account allowing periodic withdrawals

5. Which of the following is(are) discretionary order(s) under the Rules of Fair Practice?

    I.   A customer gives a member firm a check for $25,000 and instructs the firm to purchase bank and insurance company stocks when the price appears favorable.
    II.   A customer instructs a registered representative to buy 1,000 shares of ACME Corporation at a time and price that the representative determines.
    III. A customer instructs a registered representative to purchase as many shares of XYZ Corporation as the rep deems appropriate.
    IV.   A customer instructs a registered representative to sell 300 shares of ABC Company that are long in the account when the rep thinks the time and price appropriate.

    A. I and III only
    B. II and IV only
    C. III only
    D. I, II, III and IV

6. Persons wishing to give a broker the right to make investment decisions for them should do so by

    A. providing a letter from an attorney
    B. providing a letter giving discretionary powers
    C. calling the broker each time such an order is to be placed
    D. calling the broker once to advise her to use her own judgment in investment decisions

7. Which of the following statements is true of a limited power of attorney that a customer gives his rep?

    A. The rep needs written permission from the customer for each trade.
    B. The customer must renew the power of attorney every year.
    C. The customer can still enter independent orders.
    D. The branch manager must initial each order before it is entered.

◆ Answers & Rationale

1. **D.** Under tenants in common, owners may have a fractional interest in the undivided ownership of an asset. The interest passes to the decedent's estate at death unlike JTWROS, wherein the survivor succeeds to the interest.   (Page 127)

2. **B.** In a JTWROS account, securities pass to the surviving owner.   (Page 127)

3. **C.** In order for a person other than the person in whose name an account is held to enter trades and withdraw assets, a full power of attorney is required. A limited power of attorney enables someone other than the account owner to enter trades, but not to withdraw assets.   (Page 128)

4. **C.** A discretionary account is an account where a representative has been given authority to select the amount and type of investment for a client. The authorization must be written.
(Page 128)

5. **A.** Discretion is given when the broker chooses the stock, the amount of shares or whether to buy or sell. Time and price are not considered discretionary decisions.   (Page 128)

6. **B.** Discretionary accounts always require prior written authorization from the customer in the form of a limited power of attorney.   (Page 129)

7. **C.** The registered rep must have prior written authority from the client and have received approval from a supervisory person before accepting discretionary authority. While a designated principal must frequently review the account, the branch manager need not initial each order before it is entered.   (Page 129)

26 Uniform Gifts to Minors Act Accounts Exam

1. Max Leveridge wants to open an UGMA account for his son Tiny. He may do all of the following EXCEPT

   I. contribute an unlimited amount of securities and cash
   II. contribute no more than $10,000 worth of securities and cash
   III. keep the account in his name until Tiny reaches the age of majority
   IV. list his son as the beneficial owner of the account

   A. I and III
   B. I and IV
   C. II and III
   D. II and IV

2. Under the Uniform Gifts to Minors Act, you can

   I. give an unlimited amount of cash
   II. give securities
   III. give up to $10,000 cash
   IV. revoke a gift

   A. I
   B. I and II
   C. I, II and IV
   D. II and III

3. Under the Uniform Gifts to Minors Act, the beneficial owner of the securities held in the account is the

   A. custodian
   B. minor
   C. parent of the minor
   D. donor of the securities

4. Under the provisions of an UGMA account, when the minor reaches the age of majority

   A. the account should be turned over to the donee
   B. the account should be turned over to the donor
   C. the account remains as an UGMA account
   D. any securities in the account must be converted to cash

5. A gift given to a minor may be revoked under UGMA

   A. at any time before the minor reaches majority
   B. if the minor dies before reaching majority
   C. if the custodian dies before the minor reaches majority
   D. under no circumstances

6. A woman has given securities to her ten-year-old niece under the Uniform Gifts to Minors Act and is acting as custodian. The aunt may do which of the following?

   I. Pay for the niece's support and education out of the niece's funds.
   II. Donate bearer securities to the account.
   III. Buy and sell securities in the custodian account.
   IV. Withhold a reasonable amount of dividends and interest earned in the account as reimbursement for expenses.

   A. I and II
   B. I, II and III
   C. II and III
   D. III and IV

7. A woman wishes to make a gift of securities to her niece's account under the Uniform Gifts to Minors Act. The niece's guardian is opposed to the gift. Under these circumstances, the woman may give the securities

   A. only if the niece approves
   B. as she desires
   C. only with the written approval of the guardian
   D. only after obtaining the permission of the court

8. Under the Uniform Gifts to Minors Act, which of the following is allowable?

   A. A gift from one donor to one child with both parents named as custodian
   B. A gift from two donors to more than one child jointly
   C. A gift from one donor to more than one child jointly
   D. A gift from one donor to one child

9. What information must be included on the application certificate for an UGMA account?

   A. Customer's name and Social Security number, and minor's name
   B. Minor's and customer's names
   C. Guardian's name, and minor's name and Social Security number
   D. Customer's name, minor's name and Social Security number, and state of registration

10. The Social Security number of which of the following persons is used when opening a custodial account?

    A. Minor's parent or guardian
    B. Minor
    C. Custodian
    D. Any of the above

11. Klaus Bruin is appointed custodian for Adam Grizzly, a minor. Certificates will be registered as

    A. Klaus Bruin and Sandy Bruin as custodians for Adam Grizzly
    B. Klaus Bruin as custodian for Adam Grizzly
    C. Adam Grizzly
    D. Adam Grizzly as custodian for Klaus Bruin

12. Which of the following statements is(are) true of a custodial account in which an individual is custodian for his or her son under UGMA?

    I.   If the stock is held at a broker-dealer's firm, it may be registered in the name of the custodian or in street name.
    II. The securities will be registered in the parent's name until the son reaches the age of majority.
    III. The custodial relationship is terminated when the son reaches majority.
    IV. The parent's Social Security number is used for purposes of reporting and paying taxes.

    A. II and III only
    B. II and IV only
    C. III only
    D. I, II, III and IV

13. Under the Uniform Gifts to Minors Act, a custodian may invest in all of the following EXCEPT

    A. variable annuities
    B. commodity futures
    C. blue chip stocks
    D. corporate bonds

14. In general, a registered representative could have power of attorney for accounts of each of the following EXCEPT a(n)

    A. corporation
    B. individual
    C. partnership
    D. custodian

◆ Answers & Rationale

1.   **C.**   Max may contribute an unlimited amount of cash and securities, and he must put the account in the custodian's name, listing his son as the beneficial owner.   (Page 130)

2.   **B.**   There is no limit to the size of the gift that may be transferred under a Uniform Gifts to Minors Act account. The $10,000 is the gift tax exclusion and relates only to the amount of the gift that may be subject to tax.   (Page 130)

3.   **B.**   The minor is the beneficial owner of the securities in an UGMA account while they are held in the name of the custodian.   (Page 130)

4.   **A.**   Under the terms of the Uniform Gifts to Minors Act. when a minor reaches the age of majority the proceeds must be handed over to the child (donee).   (Page 130)

5.   **D.**   The Uniform Gifts to Minors Act states that all gifts to minors are irrevocable. (Page 130)

6.   **B.**   A custodian may use custodial property for the support, education and general use and benefit of the minor. A custodian is empowered to collect, hold, manage, sell, exchange or dispose of the property as she deems advisable. However, a donor may not designate herself custodian of bearer securities unless the gift is accompanied by a deed of gift. A custodian may be compensated for reasonable services and reimbursed for necessary expenses if she is not the donor.   (Page 131)

7.   **B.**   In a custodian account, any adult, whether related or unrelated, can make gifts. All gifts, however, are irrevocable.   (Page 131)

8.   **D.**   Under UGMA, an unlimited amount of money or securities may be given by a donor to *one child* with *one* entity named as *custodian*.   (Page 131)

9.   **D.**   The Uniform Gifts to Minors Act is a uniform act accepted in the majority of states. As such, each account set up under UGMA must include the state of registration, the minor's name and Social Security number, as well as the name of the customer setting up the account.   (Page 131)

10.   **B.**   When a custodial account is opened, the minor's Social Security number is used because it is the minor's account, and it is the minor who pays taxes in the account.   (Page 131)

11.   **B.**   The certificates will be registered as Klaus Bruin as custodian for Adam Grizzly. There can only be one custodian for one minor per account.   (Page 131)

12.   **C.**   When a minor reaches the age of majority, a custodial account must be reregistered in his or her name. Securities held in a custodial account cannot be kept at the brokerage firm in street name; the securities are registered, for example, "Robert Jones as Custodian for Billy Jones," not in the name of the parents; and it is the minor's Social Security number that is used.   (Page 131)

13.   **B.**   Commodity futures cannot be purchased in a custodial account because commodity futures are purchased on margin. Margin transactions are prohibited in a custodial account.   (Page 131)

14.   **D.**   A custodian for an UGMA account cannot grant trading authority to a third party.
(Page 131)

27 Annuity Plans Exam

1. Which of the following represent rights of investors who have purchased variable annuity units?

   I. Right to vote on proposed changes in investment policy
   II. Right to approve changes in the plan portfolio
   III. Right to vote for the investment adviser
   IV. Right to make additional purchases at no sales charge

   A. I and III
   B. I and IV
   C. II and III
   D. II and IV

2. The difference between a fixed annuity and a variable annuity is that the variable annuity

   I. offers a guaranteed return
   II. offers a payment that may vary in amount
   III. will always pay out more money than the fixed annuity
   IV. attempts to offer protection to the annuitant from inflation

   A. I and III
   B. I and IV
   C. II and III
   D. II and IV

3. A mutual fund and a variable annuity's separate account are similar in that

   I. the investment portfolio is professionally managed
   II. the client may vote for the board of directors or board of managers
   III. the client assumes the investment risk
   IV. payout plans guarantee the client income for life

   A. I, II and III only
   B. II and IV only
   C. III and IV only
   D. I, II, III and IV

4. Lotta Leveridge assumes the risk involved with her variable annuity. What does this mean?

   I. She is not assured of the return of her invested principal.
   II. The underlying portfolio is primarily common stocks, which have no guaranteed return.
   III. As an investor, she can be held liable for the debts incurred by the insurance company.

   A. I and II only
   B. II and III only
   C. III only
   D. I, II and III

5. For a retiring investor, which of the following is the MOST important factor in determining the suitability of a variable annuity investment?

A. The fact that the annuity payment may go up or down
B. Whether the investor is married
C. Whether the investor has concerns about taxes
D. The fact that the periodic payments into the contract may go up or down

6. A variable annuity's separate account is

I. used for the investment of monies paid by variable annuity contract holders
II. separate from the general investments of the insurance company
III. operated in a manner similar to an investment company
IV. as much a security as it is an insurance product

A. I only
B. I and II only
C. II and III only
D. I, II, III and IV

7. The value of a variable annuity separate account fluctuates in relationship to the

A. general account maintained by the insurance company
B. value of the separate account portfolio
C. Consumer Price Index
D. S&P 500 market index

8. Your client is 68 years old, retired and in good health. She is concerned about budgeting funds. She needs funds for day-to-day living expenses starting now. As her representative, you might suggest that she purchase

A. all the whole life insurance that she can afford
B. a periodic-payment deferred variable annuity
C. a single-payment deferred variable annuity
D. an immediate annuity

9. According to the NASD, the maximum sales charge on a variable annuity contract is

A. 8.5% of the total amount invested
B. 8.5% of the net amount invested
C. 9% of the total amount invested
D. unlimited

10. At age 65, Chip Bullock purchased an immediate variable annuity contract. Chip made a lump-sum $100,000 initial payment and selected a life income with ten-year period certain payment option. Chip lived until age 88. The insurance company made payments to Chip

A. until his initial payment of $100,000 was exhausted
B. for ten years
C. for 23 years
D. at a fixed rate for ten years and at a variable rate up until his death

11. If a customer, age 35, invests $100 a month in a variable annuity for seven years and suddenly dies

A. the customer's beneficiaries will not receive any money until the year in which the customer would have turned 59 1/2
B. the insurance company gets to keep all the contributions made to date because the contract was not annuitized
C. the customer's beneficiaries will receive only the amount contributed
D. if the contract were insured, the customer's beneficiaries would receive the greater of the contributions or current value of the account

12. A joint life with last survivor annuity

    I. covers more than one person
    II. continues payments as long as one annuitant is alive
    III. continues payments as long as all annuitants are alive
    IV. guarantees payments will be made for a certain period of time

    A. I and II
    B. I and III
    C. I and IV
    D. II and IV

13. In calculating the investment performance of a separate account, you would take into account

    A. realized capital gains
    B. unrealized capital gains
    C. dividend income
    D. all of the above

14. In a variable annuity, total accumulation units are equal to

    A. the investor's bookkeeping value
    B. the investor's percentage of ownership of the separate account
    C. reinvested dividends
    D. the offering price

15. An investor begins to receive the payout on a variable annuity. Which of the following statements is true?

    A. Accumulation units are converted to annuity units.
    B. Annuity units are converted to accumulation units.
    C. The value of the annuity unit is fixed.
    D. The amount of each payment is fixed.

16. Which of the following factors may determine the amount of payout from a variable annuity?

    I. Mortality experience of the company
    II. Age and sex of the annuitant
    III. Insurability of the annuitant
    IV. Rate of return of the separate account

    A. I, II and IV only
    B. II only
    C. III and IV only
    D. I, II, III and IV

17. All of the following are true statements concerning the assumed interest rate EXCEPT that the

    A. AIR is used in projecting earnings for variable annuities
    B. higher the AIR, the lower the assumed payment
    C. higher the AIR, the higher the initial payment
    D. more conservative the AIR, the more likely the target payment will be achieved

18. If a variable annuity has an assumed investment rate of 5% and the annualized return of the separate account is 4%, what are the consequences?

    I. The value of the accumulation unit will rise.
    II. The value of the annuity unit will rise.
    III. The value of the accumulation unit will fall.
    IV. The value of the annuity unit will fall.

    A. I and II
    B. I and IV
    C. II and III
    D. III and IV

19. Gordy Guernsey owns a variable annuity contract, and the AIR stated in the contract is 5%. In January the realized rate of return in the separate account was 7%, and Gordy received a check based on this return for $200. In February the rate of return was 10%, and Gordy received a check for $210. To maintain the same payment Gordy received in February, what rate of return would the separate account have to earn in March?

    A. 3%
    B. 5%
    C. 7%
    D. 10%

20. A teacher has placed money into a tax-qualified variable annuity over the past twelve years. The teacher has contributed $26,000, and the value of the annuity today is $36,000. If the teacher withdraws $15,000 today, what are the tax consequences if the teacher is in the 30% tax bracket?

    A. $1,500
    B. $3,000
    C. $4,500
    D. There are no taxes due on this withdrawal.

21. June Polar is 65. She had payroll deduction contributions into a nonqualified tax-deferred annuity. Her contributions totaled $10,000, and the current value of her account is $16,000. For tax purposes, what is June's cost basis?

    A. $0
    B. $10,000
    C. $16,000
    D. $6,000

22. Under the Tax Reform Act of 1986, all of the following investments offer either full or partially tax-deductible contributions to individuals who meet eligibility requirements EXCEPT

    A. IRAs
    B. Keogh plans
    C. variable annuities
    D. defined contribution plans

23. If a customer, age 52, cashes in her annuity contract before payout begins, she will

    I.   be taxed at the ordinary income tax rate on earnings in excess of cost base
    II. be taxed at ordinary rates on the amount withdrawn that represents cost base, and will be taxed at capital gains rates on the amount withdrawn that exceeds cost base
    III. have to pay a 5% penalty on the amount withdrawn that exceeds cost base
    IV. have to pay a 10% penalty on the amount withdrawn that exceeds cost base

    A. I
    B. I and III
    C. I and IV
    D. II and III

◆ Answers & Rationale

1. **A.** Owners of variable annuities, like owners of mutual fund shares, have the right to vote on changes in investment policy and the right to vote for the investment adviser every two years. They also have the benefit of enjoying reduced sales charges for large dollar purchases.   (Page 141)

2. **D.** Variable annuities differ from fixed because the payments vary and they are designed to offer the annuitant protection against inflation.   (Page 142)

3. **A.** Both a mutual fund and a variable annuity offer professional management and a board of managers or directors, and the client assumes the investment risk. Only variable annuities have payout plans that guarantee the client income for life.   (Page 142)

4. **A.** The annuitant bears the investment risk in a variable annuity. The portfolio is not guaranteed to return a specified rate, and the principal invested will also fluctuate in value according to the securities held in the separate account portfolio.   (Page 142)

5. **A.** The most important consideration in purchasing a variable annuity is that benefit payments will fluctuate with the investment performance of the separate account. Answer D is not a consideration because normally the payments into an annuity are level or in a lump sum. (Page 142)

6. **D.** The separate account is used for the moneys invested in variable annuities. It is kept separate from the general account and operated very much like an investment company. It is considered both an insurance product and an investment product.   (Page 142)

7. **B.** The value of the separate account fluctuates in relation to the securities held in the account.   (Page 142)

8. **D.** Your client needs immediate income. Of the options listed, only the immediate annuity offers this.   (Page 144)

9. **A.** NASD rules allow a maximum sales charge on a variable annuity contract of 8 1/2%.   (Page 144)

10. **C.** An annuity with life and ten-year certain will pay for the greater of ten years or the life of the annuitant. Chip lived for 23 more years, which is more than the ten certain.   (Page 146)

11. **D.** The client's beneficiaries would receive the current market value, but if the contract were insured, they would receive the greater of the amount invested or the current market value.   (Page 146)

12. **A.** A joint life with last survivor contract covers multiple annuitants and ceases payments at the death of the last surviving annuitant. A period certain contract guarantees payments for a certain amount of time.   (Page 146)

13. **D.** Performance of a separate account will depend on increases and decreases of the securities held in the portfolio. Whether gains are realized or unrealized, the account will reflect the gain or loss.   (Page 147)

14. **B.** Accumulation units are an accounting measure that represent an investor's share of ownership in the account.   (Page 147)

15. **A.** To determine the amount of the payment, accumulation units are converted to annuity units. In a variable annuity, neither the value of the annuity unit nor the amount of the monthly payment can be fixed.   (Page 147)

16. **A.** Mortality experience, age, sex and rate of return all have a bearing on the size of payout. The insurability of the annuitant has no bearing.   (Page 147)

17. **B.** The level of the AIR alone does not determine the payment.   (Page 147)

18. **B.** The accumulation unit will increase in value because the portfolio earned 4%; however, the annuity unit value will decrease because actual return of the portfolio (4%) was less than the assumed interest rate of 5% necessary to maintain payments.   (Page 148)

19. **B.** If the actual rate of return equals the assumed interest rate, the check will stay the same. Recall that the payout is based on an accumulated value to be distributed over the life of the annuitant (like compounding). Therefore, for Gordy to receive the $210 in March, the account must earn 5%.   (Page 148)

20. **C.** Contributions to a tax-qualified annuity are taxable when withdrawn at ordinary income tax rates. Because in this case the teacher is withdrawing $15,000, that amount is subject to tax. Thirty percent of $15,000 equals a tax liability of $4,500.   (Page 149)

21. **B.** Contributions to a nonqualified annuity are made aftertax. The growth of the annuity is deferred, representing ordinary income when withdrawn. Cost basis is $10,000.   (Page 149)

22. **C.** Contributions to a variable annuity are not tax-deductible. Contributions to an IRA or a Keogh may be tax-deductible, depending on the individual's earnings and his access to company-sponsored retirement plans.   (Page 149)

23. **C.** Cashing in an annuity will cause the client taxation at the ordinary income tax rate on all earnings in excess of the cost base. Any withdrawal prior to age 59 1/2 is subject to a 10% penalty unless it is for death or disability, or if the contract has been annuitized for a period of five years or life, whichever is greater.   (Page 149)

1. A variable life insurance policy is defined as any policy that provides for a death benefit that varies according to the

   A. investment experience of the life insurance company's general account
   B. amount of the premium invested into the insurance company's general account
   C. investment experience of the life insurance company's separate account
   D. investment experience of the variable annuity set up to provide for retirement benefits

2. Which of the following statements can an agent use to describe the scheduled premium VLI product offered by his life insurance company?

   A. The variable life policy is a life insurance policy providing for variable death benefit, cash values and premium payments depending on the performance of investments held in an insurance company's separate account.
   B. The variable life policy is a fixed-premium life insurance policy providing for variable death benefit and cash values depending on the performance of investments held in an insurance company's separate account.
   C. The variable life policy is a fixed-premium life insurance policy providing for a fixed death benefit and cash values that fluctuate depending on the performance of investments held in the insurance company's separate account.
   D. None of the above can be used.

3. A distinguishing characteristic of scheduled premium VLI is that an increase or a decrease in the value of the separate account used to fund the VLI contract will lead to an increase or a decrease in the

   I.   annual premium payable
   II. death benefit payable exclusive of the minimum guaranteed in the contract
   III. amount of cash value
   IV. number of individuals the insured can name as beneficiaries of the contract

   A. I, II and III only
   B. I and IV only
   C. II and III only
   D. I, II, III and IV

4. Premiums for a scheduled payment variable life policy are

   I.   fixed as to the premium amount
   II. variable as to the premium amount, depending on the face amount of the policy
   III. fixed as to time of payment
   IV. variable as to time of payment

   A. I and III
   B. I and IV
   C. II and III
   D. II and IV

5. The maximum amount that may be deducted for mortality and expense fees is

   A. .5%
   B. .75%
   C. the maximum stated in the contract
   D. dependent on the mortality experience of the insurance company

6. Which of the following fees and expenses may be deducted from the gross premium paid in a variable life insurance contract?

   I.   Mortality risk fee
   II. Administrative fees
   III. Amount to provide for insurance
   IV. Sales expenses including commissions paid to agents

   A. I and II
   B. II and III
   C. II and IV
   D. III and IV

7. Deductions and charges against the variable life insurance separate account may include

   I.   expense and mortality risk fees
   II. sales load
   III. state premium taxes
   IV. cost of insurance

   A. I and III
   B. I and IV
   C. II and III
   D. II and IV

8. Fees such as mortality and risk expenses are deducted from the

   I.   premium payment for flexible premium policies
   II. premium payment for fixed premium policies
   III. benefit base for flexible premium policies
   IV. benefit base for fixed premium policies

   A. I and II
   B. I and IV
   C. II and III
   D. III and IV

9. The variable death benefit provided by the variable life insurance contract is best described as the amount of the death benefit

A. other than incidental benefits payable under a variable life insurance policy dependent upon the investment performance of the separate account, which the insurer pays in excess of the minimum benefit

B. guaranteed by the variable life insurance policy

C. including incidental benefits payable under a variable life insurance policy dependent upon the investment performance of the separate account, which the insurer pays as a minimum guaranteed death benefit

D. other than incidental benefits payable under a variable life insurance policy dependent upon the investment performance of the general account, which the insurer pays as a minimum guaranteed death benefit

10. The separate account of a variable life insurance contract has an assumed interest rate of 4%. Its performance in the past six months has been 3%. The account is now earning 8%. Which of the following statements is true?

A. The death benefit will increase immediately.

B. The death benefit will increase at the next valuation.

C. The death benefit will increase only if the earnings are enough to offset the negative performance of the previous months.

D. The death benefit is fixed at the guaranteed rate.

11. If the assumed interest rate of the variable life insurance policy is 4% and the separate account earns 6%, the policyholder would expect the

I. cash value to increase
II. cash value to decrease
III. death benefit to increase
IV. death benefit to decrease

A. I and III
B. I and IV
C. II and III
D. II and IV

12. A distinguishing characteristic of fixed premium VLI is that an increase or a decrease in the value of the separate account used to fund the VLI contract will lead to an increase or a decrease in the

I. death benefit payable exclusive of the minimum guaranteed in the contract
II. annual premium payable
III. number of individuals the insured can name as beneficiaries of the contract
IV. amount of cash value

A. I, II and III only
B. I and IV only
C. II and III only
D. I, II, III and IV

13. If an individual purchases a flexible premium policy and the separate account earned 3%, assuming the individual has paid sufficient premiums to fund the contract's face amount and expenses, the contract's cash value would

A. increase
B. decrease
C. stay the same
D. not be affected by separate account performance

14. The cash value of a variable life contract for a policyholder does NOT have to be determined daily if

    I.   changes in the value of the separate account do not affect the contract's cash value
    II. no request for redemption or payment is made to the separate account by the policyholder
    III. the day is a regularly scheduled holiday
    IV. the contract's cash value is calculated at least monthly by the insurance company

    A. I only
    B. I and II only
    C. II and III only
    D. I, II, III and IV

15. A policy loan provision must be offered by the insurer after three years allowing the contract holder to borrow what percentage of cash value?

    A. 75%
    B. 90%
    C. 100%
    D. No policy loan is allowed from a variable life contract.

16. Klaus Bruin purchased a variable life insurance contract on July 3, 1992. On July 29, 1995, Klaus decides to exchange his contract for a fixed-benefit policy offered by the same insurance company. As his agent, you tell Klaus that

    A. his new policy will have the same contract date and age as his VLI policy
    B. his new policy will include the same riders as his VLI policy
    C. he will not require new evidence of insurability
    D. None of the above statements is true.

17. According to federal law, an insurance company must allow a variable life policyholder the option to convert the policy into a whole life contract for a period of

    A. 45 days
    B. 12 months
    C. 18 months
    D. 24 months

18. The maximum sales charge that can be deducted on a variable life contract is limited to 9% of

    A. the first year's premium
    B. each premium collected
    C. the payments to be made over the life of the contract
    D. the policyholder's life expectancy

19. An investor purchases a fixed premium variable life contract on July 1st. Four days after receiving notification of his free-look right, he cancels the policy. The investor would receive

    A. a full refund of all money paid to date
    B. all money invested in the separate account and 30% of the sales charges
    C. 30% of the money invested in the separate account plus all sales charges
    D. no refund of the premium paid

20. What sales charge is refunded in a variable life contract after six months?

    A. No refund is allowed.
    B. All sales charges collected are refunded.
    C. Sales charges exceeding an amount over 30% are refunded.
    D. Sales charges less management fees are refunded.

21. If, within a two-year period, a variable life contract holder terminates the policy, she must receive as a refund the

    A. current cash value of the contract
    B. current cash value of the contract plus 10% of the sales charges deducted
    C. current cash value of the contract plus 30% of the sales charges deducted
    D. current cash value of the contract plus all sales charges deducted in excess of 30% of the premium in the first year and 10% of the premium in the second year

22. Voting rights extended to contract holders of variable life insurance contracts funded by a separate account shall be one vote on company matters for each

    A. contract owned
    B. dollar of cash value credited to the contract
    C. $100 of cash value funded by the insurance company's general account
    D. $100 of cash value funded by the insurance company's separate account

23. The investment objective of a separate account funding variable life insurance may be changed

    A. with a majority vote of shares
    B. by order of the state insurance commissioner
    C. if either A or B occurs
    D. under no circumstances

24. An individual purchasing a flexible premium variable life contract should know that

    I. premiums are discretionary as to timing and amount
    II. the death benefit may equal the contract's face amount
    III. the death benefit may equal the contract's face amount plus cash value
    IV. cash value and duration of the policy are directly affected by the performance of the separate account

    A. I, II and III only
    B. I, III and IV only
    C. IV only
    D. I, II, III and IV

◆ Answers & Rationale

1. **C.** Variable life is any policy that provides for insurance protection that varies according to the investment performance of one or more separate accounts.   (Page 154)

2. **B.** Scheduled premium VLI is a fixed premium contract providing for a minimum guaranteed death benefit. Cash values and death benefit may increase or decrease depending on the investment performance of the separate account. Cash values may decline to zero, but the death benefit may never decline below the minimum guaranteed.   (Page 153)

3. **C.** The separate account performance will affect the cash value or death benefit only. Premiums are fixed and level.   (Page 152)

4. **A.** Scheduled payment VLI contracts have fixed premiums and payment periods. (Page 152)

5. **C.** The maximum fee that may be charged for expenses and mortality costs is stated in the contract. The fee charged may be more or less than the actual costs incurred by the insurance company during the contact period.   (Page 154)

6. **C.** Sales load, administrative fees and a charge for state premium taxes are deducted from the gross premium; expense and mortality risk fees, investment management fees and the cost of insurance are deducted from the separate account.   (Page 154)

7. **B.** Cost of insurance and mortality and expense risk fees are deducted from the separate account. Sales loads and premium taxes are deducted from the premium.   (Page 153)

8. **D.** Expenses are deducted from the benefit base (cash value) for both scheduled and flexible premium VLI contracts.   (Page 153)

9. **A.** The variable death benefit is that amount of insurance above the minimum guaranteed which may increase or decrease depending on the performance of the separate account.   (Page 153)

10. **C.** The account must earn enough to offset previous negative earnings before an increase in the death benefit can occur.   (Page 156)

11. **A.** If the separate account earns at a rate that is greater than the rate assumed, the extra earnings may lead to an increase in the death benefit and cash value.   (Page 156)

12. **B.** The separate account performance will affect the cash value or death benefit only. Premiums are fixed and level.   (Page 153)

13. **A.** With a flexible premium policy, account performance affects the contract directly. Cash value equals the net premium invested, increased or decreased by the change in separate account assets, less charges and expenses. Cash value reflects actual performance of the separate account. If the account earned 3%, cash value would increase (although by very little).   (Page 154)

14. **D.** The separate account must be valued at least once per business day (i.e., the days the NYSE is open for business, which excludes holidays). The cash value of a contract must be calculated at least monthly, but this calculation may be waived if activity in the separate account is such that cash value is not affected.   (Page 154)

15. **A.** Seventy-five percent of cash value is the minimum that must be available in a VLI contract.   (Page 153)

16. **D.** The investor has had the VLI contract for more than 24 months; the exchange privilege option has expired. As a result, he would be required to purchase a new contract if he wanted the new policy (although this is not recommended).   (Page 155)

17. **D.** Although state law may allow for periods other than 24 months, federal law requires a two-year conversion privilege.   (Page 155)

18. **C.** The maximum sales charge is limited to 9% of the contract's life (actual life expectancy or 20 years, whichever is greater).   (Page 155)

19. **A.** According to the act of 1940, if the investor cancels the plan within the free-look period, he will receive all monies paid.   (Page 155)

20. **C.** The refund provisions for variable life contracts extend for two years from issuance of the policy. If, within the two-year period, the contract holder terminates participation in the contract, the insurer must refund from the premium the cash value on the contract (the value calculated after receipt of the redemption notice) *plus* all sales charges deducted in excess of 30% in the first year of the contract and 10% in the second year. After the two-year period has lapsed, only the cash value need be refunded; the insurer retains all sales charges collected to date.   (Page 156)

21. **D.** The law requires a full refund of cash value plus a return of sales charges in excess of 30% in year one and 10% in year two. After two years, only cash value need be refunded.   (Page 156)

22. **D.** Contract holders receive one vote per $100 of cash value funded by the separate account. Additionally, if the insurance company votes the shares, the company must vote according to proxies received from the contract holders.   (Page 156)

23. **C.** The insurance commissioner has the authority to change an investment objective if the objective is in violation of state law; otherwise, the objective may be changed only by majority vote of the separate account's outstanding shares.
(Page 156)

24. **D.** Flexible premium policies allow for the insured to determine the amount and timing of premium payments. Depending on the policy, the death benefit may equal the face value of the contract, a percentage of cash value or a combination of the two. If performance of the separate account is such that cash value drops below an amount necessary to maintain the policy in force, the policy will lapse.   (Page 156)

29 Individual Retirement Accounts Exam

1. You work for the Tippecanoe Ferry Co. and are a participant in its 401K plan. How much can you invest in an IRA?

   A. $0
   B. $2,000
   C. $2,250
   D. Up to 25% of annual compensation

2. All of the following statements concerning IRA contributions are true EXCEPT

   A. between January 1st and April 15th, contributions may be made for the current year, the past year or both
   B. contributions for the past year may be made after April 15th, provided an extension has been filed on a timely basis
   C. if you pay your tax on January 15th, you can still deduct your IRA contribution even if not made until April 15th
   D. contributions can be paid into this year's IRA from January 1st of this year until April 15th of next year

3. A self-employed individual has a Keogh plan. He is also employed part time by a corporation that pays him $8,000 a year. Which of the following statements is true?

   A. He may start an IRA because anyone can open an IRA and contribute 100% of his or her adjusted earnings or $2,000, whichever is less, although the contribution may or may not be tax-deductible.
   B. He may start an IRA but his contribution is limited to 12% or $1,500 of his gross income.
   C. He may not start an IRA because he is employed by a corporation that possibly has a Keogh plan.
   D. He may not start an IRA because he is covered by a Keogh plan.

4. Lotta Leveridge makes $65,000 a year as an advertising executive, and her husband, Tiny, makes $40,000 a year as Lotta's assistant. How much can the Leveridges contribute to IRAs?

   A. They cannot make a contribution because their combined income is too high.
   B. They can contribute up to $2,250 split over both accounts, with no more than $2,000 in either account.
   C. They can each contribute $2,000 to an IRA.
   D. They can each contribute $2,500 to an IRA.

5. Which of the following investors are eligible to establish an IRA?

   I. Independently wealthy individual whose sole source of income is $125,000 per year in dividend and interest income
   II. Law student who earned $1,200 in a part-time job
   III. Woman who earned $3,500 last year selling cosmetics but whose spouse is covered by a company profit-sharing plan

   A. I and II only
   B. I and III only
   C. II and III only
   D. I, II and III

6. A husband and wife are both employed, and each qualifies to open an IRA. To make their maximum allowable contributions, they should open

   A. a joint IRA and deposit $2,000
   B. a joint IRA and deposit $4,000
   C. two separate IRAs and deposit $2,000 each
   D. two separate IRAs and deposit $2,250

7. Which of the following statements is(are) true of spousal IRAs?

   I. Contributions must be distributed equally between the accounts.
   II. Contributions can be greater than in a regular IRA.
   III. Rollover to a new plan is 18 months rather than the one-year rollover allowed in a regular IRA.

   A. I and II
   B. I and III
   C. II
   D. II and III

8. An employee makes a withdrawal from her IRA at age 52. She pays no penalty tax if she

   A. has retired
   B. is disabled
   C. had no earned income that year
   D. transferred her account to another custodian

9. An employee not covered under his company's pension plan has been contributing to an IRA for five years. He now leaves his old job, starts a new job and is covered under the new corporation's pension plan. Which of the following statements is true?

   A. His IRA must be closed.
   B. Nondeductible contributions to his IRA may continue.
   C. The money in his IRA must be combined with any money he will receive from the pension plan.
   D. Contributions to his IRA must stop; the money in the account will be frozen, but interest and dividends can accrue tax-free until he retires.

10. A customer has just started an IRA. She will be vested

   A. immediately
   B. in two years
   C. in five years
   D. at age 70 1/2

11. Excess IRA contributions are subject to a penalty of what percentage annually until they are used up or withdrawn?

   A. 6%
   B. 10%
   C. 12%
   D. 15%

12. Which of the following investment activities are suitable for an individual retirement account?

    I. Writing uncovered calls
    II. Writing covered calls
    III. Buying puts on stock held long
    IV. Writing naked puts

    A. I and II only
    B. I, II and IV only
    C. II and III only
    D. I, II, III and IV

13. Which of the following would be the MOST suitable investment for the IRAs of a young couple with a combined annual income of $42,000?

    A. Stock in a growth fund
    B. Initial public offerings of small companies
    C. Options on blue chip common stock
    D. Partnership interests in an oil and gas drilling program

14. Lotta and Tiny Leveridge are both in their twenties and have been married only a few years. They have asked for your recommendation as to an investment for their IRAs. You should suggest

    A. growth-oriented mutual funds
    B. penny precious metals stocks
    C. oil and gas exploration limited partnerships
    D. index options

15. Which of the following can be rolled over into an IRA?

    I. Another IRA
    II. Corporate pension plan
    III. Corporate profit-sharing plan
    IV. Keogh plan

    A. I and IV only
    B. II and III only
    C. II, III and IV only
    D. I, II, III and IV

16. Chip Bullock received a lump-sum distribution from a 401K plan when he left his job. He may now

    I. roll over his account within 60 days
    II. transfer his account without taking possession of the money
    III. keep the funds and pay ordinary income tax
    IV. invest in a tax-exempt municipal bond fund to avoid paying tax

    A. I and II
    B. I and III
    C. II and IV
    D. III and IV

17. Which of the following statements about SEP-IRAs is true?

    A. They are used primarily by large corporations.
    B. They are used primarily by small businesses.
    C. They are set up by employees.
    D. They are set up by self-employed persons.

18. A tax-free rollover of an IRA may occur once every

    A. 30 days
    B. 60 days
    C. 1 year
    D. 3 years

19. Distributions from an IRA or a Keogh must begin by April 1st of the year following the year in which the participant

    A. reaches age 65
    B. reaches age 68
    C. reaches age 70 1/2
    D. retires

20. When a customer withdraws money from an IRA after age 59 1/2, the

    A. amount withdrawn is subject to a 10% penalty
    B. amount withdrawn is subject to taxes at the capital gains rate
    C. entire amount in the IRA is subject to taxation at the ordinary rate, regardless of the amount withdrawn
    D. amount withdrawn is subject to taxation at ordinary income tax rates

21. Which of the following individuals will NOT be penalized on an IRA withdrawal?

    A. Man who has just become disabled
    B. Woman who turned 59 one month before the withdrawal
    C. Person, age 50, who decides on early retirement
    D. Man in his early 40s who uses the money to buy a house

22. Under IRS rules, IRA distributions upon retirement can go to the

    I. employee only
    II. employee jointly with the employee's spouse
    III. employee, and at the employee's death, to a designated beneficiary
    IV. employer only

    A. I only
    B. I, II and III only
    C. IV only
    D. I, II, III and IV

23. Which of the following is required to establish a SEP?

    A. 50% of the eligible employees must have an IRA.
    B. 75% of the eligible employees must have an IRA.
    C. 100% of the eligible employees must have an IRA.
    D. The employer must establish a separate IRA for each eligible employee.

24. June Polar works for a small business and would like to participate in a SEP. Which of the following statements is true?

    A. June may not participate in a SEP because she has been employed by this company for only five years.
    B. The maximum SEP contribution is higher than the maximum IRA contribution.
    C. June's employer must match her contributions.
    D. Contributions over $2,000 are not tax deductible.

25. The money contributed to a SEP vests

    A. according to a preset schedule
    B. immediately
    C. beginning at the fifth anniversary of establishment
    D. after the employee retires

◆ Answers & Rationale

1. B. The maximum annual contribution to an IRA is $2,000, whether or not the account owner participates in a qualified retirement plan. The full amount of the contribution may not be tax deductible, but all earnings in the account are still tax deferred. (Page 158)

2. B. Contributions can be made to an IRA only until the first tax filing deadline (April 15th) even though you may have filed an extension. Anyone with earned income can make a contribution to an IRA. (Page 158)

3. A. Anyone can open an IRA, whether covered by a pension or Keogh plan. An individual may contribute 100% of earned income up to $2,000 a year. But whether the contribution is tax-deductible depends on many other factors. (Page 158)

4. C. No matter how much an individual or a couple make, IRA contributions can still be made. Each spouse is entitled to contribute 100% of earned income up to $2,000 (insofar as both spouses are working). (Page 158)

5. C. An individual may contribute 100% of earned income up to a maximum of $2,000. Interest and dividend income is passive income, not earned income. (Page 159)

6. C. Each individual with earned income may open an IRA and deposit 100% of this earned income up to $2,000 per year. (Page 159)

7. C. If only one spouse of a married couple works and they file a joint tax return, the couple can open an IRA with a spousal option. The couple can contribute a maximum of $2,250 to the two accounts and can divide it between the accounts in any manner they choose as long as they put no more than $2,000 in either account. (Page 159)

8. B. An IRA account holder may withdraw money before the age of 59 1/2 without incurring a penalty tax only in the case of death or disability.

A transfer between custodians does not constitute a withdrawal from the account. (Page 159)

9. B. An employee covered under a qualified retirement plan may continue to own and contribute to an IRA. The contributions may or may not be fully tax deductible, depending on the amount of compensation earned, but the employee benefits from the tax deferral of IRA earnings. (Page 159)

10. A. Investors are always vested immediately in their IRAs. (Page 159)

11. A. Excess IRA contributions are subject to a yearly penalty of 6% until they are withdrawn or are applied to the following year's contribution limit. (Page 159)

12. C. In a retirement account, investment activities generally strive to seek reasonable income, preserve capital and avoid speculative investments. In regard to options strategies, writing covered calls and buying puts on stock held in the portfolio are considered conservative positions. Writing uncovered calls and puts subject the investor to a high degree of risk and are considered unsuitable. (Page 160)

13. A. The IRA for this couple should be established with an eye towards long-term appreciation. Answers B and C are riskier and are generally considered inappropriate for IRAs. The DPP is inappropriate because tax losses in an IRA cannot be used to offset gains. (Page 160)

14. A. A growth mutual fund is appropriate for a young couple's IRA. All other answers bear a high risk that is not appropriate for a retirement account. (Page 160)

15. D. Only a tax-deferred annuity cannot be rolled over into an IRA. (Page 160)

16. B. If the investor does not roll over the money into an IRA account, it will be taxed as ordinary income. Because he has already received the lump sum, he cannot transfer the account to a new custodian. Any amount he does not roll over will be taxed as income even if he invests it in tax-exempt bonds.   (Page 160)

17.   **B.**   SEP-IRAs are used primarily by small businesses because they are much easier and less expensive to set up than other plans. The employer sets up and administers the SEP-IRA. (Page 160)

18.   **C.**   Rollovers may occur once a year and must be completed within 60 days. Transfers may be effected as often as the account owner desires.
(Page 160)

19.   **C.**   According to the Tax Reform Act of 1986, distributions must begin by April 1st of the year after the year in which the participant turns 70 1/2.   (Page 161)

20.   **D.**   Money withdrawn from an IRA after age 59 1/2 is subject to ordinary taxation on the amount withdrawn, but there is no 10% penalty.
(Page 161)

21.   **A.**   Disability is a legitimate reason for withdrawal before age 59 1/2. The other individuals described will be taxed on the withdrawal because they are under 59 1/2 years of age.   (Page 161)

22.   **B.**   Under IRS rules, when an employee retires IRA payments can be made to the employee or jointly to the employee and spouse. In the event that the account owner dies, payments may continue to be made to a designated beneficiary; a person's rights to accumulated IRA benefits do not stop at the death of that person.   (Page 161)

23.   **C.**   In order for a small business to establish a SEP, each eligible employee must have an IRA. If an employee refuses to establish an IRA, the employer *must* open an IRA in that employee's name.   (Page 163)

24.   **B.**   The contribution limit is 15% of earned income up to $30,000 for a SEP retirement plan, compared to just $2,000 for a regular IRA, and the entire amount is tax deductible. Full-time employees who have been employed for at least three of the immediately preceding five years are automatically eligible to participate. The entire amount of the employer's contribution up to the maximum contribution is tax deductible.   (Page 163)

25.   **B.**   SEP contributions, like IRA contributions, are fully vested immediately.   (Page 163)

30 Keogh (HR-10) Plans Exam

1. Which of the following describe(s) a Keogh plan?

   I.   Retirement fund
   II. Tax-deferred trust
   III. Tax-free trust
   IV. Tax-exempt trust

   A. I
   B. I and II
   C. I and III
   D. IV

2. Hugh Heifer has a salaried, full-time position but his employer does not offer a company retirement plan. Hugh also has his own clock repair business, which earns less than his salaried position. He wants to invest for his retirement. Which of the following investments are options for him?

   A. An IRA if he does not have a Keogh plan
   B. A Keogh plan if he does not have an IRA
   C. Both an IRA and a Keogh plan
   D. An IRA, but not a Keogh plan because his self-employment is not his main source of income

3. Which of the following individuals are entitled to participate in a Keogh plan?

   I.   Doctor
   II. Security analyst who makes $2,000 giving lectures
   III. Engineer of a corporation who earns $5,000 making public speeches
   IV. Executive of a corporation who receives $5,000 in stock options from his company

   A. I
   B. I and II
   C. I, II and III
   D. IV

4. Which two of the following choices qualify an employee for contributions to a Keogh plan?

   I.   Working 800 hours per year
   II. Working 1,250 hours per year
   III. Full-time status
   IV. Part-time or seasonal status

   A. I and III
   B. I and IV
   C. II and III
   D. II and IV

5. Which of the following statements regarding Keogh plans and individual retirement accounts are true?

    I. Contributions to both funds are tax deferred.

    II. The Keogh plan is restricted to persons who are self-employed.

    III. Contributions to both funds are tax exempt.

    IV. The IRA is restricted to persons who have earned income.

    A. I and II
    B. I, II and IV
    C. II, III and IV
    D. III and IV

6. All of the following factors influence the amount of money that can be contributed to a Keogh plan in one year EXCEPT

    A. the rules regarding maximum contributions
    B. whether the plan is qualified or non-qualified
    C. the amount of self-employment income
    D. whether the participant is an employee or a business owner

7. Which of the following people would not be eligible to start her own Keogh, but would be eligible to open an IRA?

    A. College professor who makes $10,000 on the sale of a book and several articles
    B. Corporate officer who earns $40,000 plus an additional $10,000 as a part-time speaker
    C. Doctor who receives $10,000 from a restaurant she owns
    D. Corporate officer who receives a $5,000 bonus

8. If an employer has a Keogh plan, the employer must make contributions for all

    A. employees
    B. full-time employees
    C. full-time employees who have been employed for at least one year
    D. employees selected at the employer's discretion

9. Keogh plans are retirement programs designed for use by nonincorporated businesses. These plans allow the self-employed individual to contribute on a tax-deductible basis

    A. the lesser of 25% of earned income or $30,000
    B. the lesser of 25% of all income or $30,000
    C. the greater of 25% of earned income or $30,000
    D. the greater of 25% of all income or $30,000

10. A doctor has compensation of $160,000. What is the maximum he may contribute to his Keogh plan?

    A. $5,000
    B. $22,000
    C. $28,000
    D. $30,000

11. An individual earned $75,000 in royalties from his writings; $5,000 from interest and dividends; $2,000 from long-term capital gains in the stock market; and $3,000 from rents on two cottages. He could contribute to his Keogh plan

    A. $12,570
    B. $12,750
    C. $15,000
    D. $18,750

12. What are the two consequences when a participant in a Keogh plan makes a contribution in excess of 25% or the $30,000 annual limit?

    I. The contributions are tax-deductible.
    II. The contributions are not tax-deductible.
    III. Interest and dividends accumulate tax-deferred.
    IV. Interest and dividends do not accumulate tax-deferred.

    A. I and III
    B. I and IV
    C. II and III
    D. II and IV

13. If an employer installs a Keogh plan, that plan must include all full-time employees with how many years of service?

    A. One
    B. Three
    C. Five
    D. None of the above

14. Under Keogh plan provisions, a full-time employee would be defined as one working at least how many hours per year?

    A. 100
    B. 500
    C. 800
    D. 1,000

15. An employer makes $75,000 and contributes the maximum to her own Keogh account. She must contribute how much to the Keogh of a full-time employee earning $12,000?

    A. $1,200
    B. $2,400
    C. $3,000
    D. $7,500

16. Which of the following employees need not be included in a Keogh plan if the business owner has a Keogh account?

    I. Waitress who works 30 hours a week for twelve months
    II. Bookkeeper who works full time for eight months of the year
    III. Janitor who works full time for three months of the year
    IV. Clerical assistant who works 20 hours a week for 20 weeks

    A. II and III only
    B. III and IV only
    C. IV only
    D. I, II, III and IV

17. An employee who is covered under a Keogh plan will become fully vested

    A. depending on the vesting schedule chosen by the employer
    B. after one year
    C. after two years
    D. after three years

18. Distribution of funds from a Keogh plan may be made without penalty if the

    A. investor becomes disabled
    B. IRS is notified within 60 days
    C. investor makes a major purchase, such as a car
    D. investments in the account decrease in value

19. Tex Longhorn is 61 years old. He would like to take a lump-sum distribution from his Keogh plan. What would be the tax treatment of this distribution?

    A. It is eligible for five-year income averaging.
    B. It will be taxed at long-term capital gains rates.
    C. There will be a 10% penalty.
    D. There will be a 50% penalty.

20. Your customer, who is 40 years of age, wants to withdraw funds from her Keogh. She asks you about the tax implications of early withdrawal. You should tell her the withdrawal will be taxed as

A. ordinary income
B. ordinary income plus a 10% penalty
C. capital gains
D. capital gains plus a 10% penalty

21. Early withdrawals may be made without penalty from a Keogh plan in all of the following circumstances EXCEPT

A. the account owner's death
B. the account owner's disability
C. from the voluntary, nondeductible contributions
D. from the tax-deductible contributions

22. A nurse had been participating in her employer's Keogh plan. Upon leaving the clinic, she may roll over the distributed Keogh assets into an IRA and defer taxes on these assets if the transaction is completed within

A. 30 days
B. 60 days
C. 90 days
D. 6 months

23. Under a Keogh plan, which of the following would be an acceptable investment?

A. Unit investment trust
B. Variable annuity
C. U.S. government bond
D. All of the above

◆ Answers & Rationale

1. **B.** Keogh plans are personal retirement plans that allow a self-employed individual to set aside income on a tax-deferred basis for withdrawal after retirement. (Page 164)

2. **C.** The investor can start an IRA, assuming that he is under age 70 1/2. How much of his IRA contributions are deductible depends on his income level. He is also eligible to invest in a Keogh plan because he is self-employed, regardless of how much or how little he earns from his self-employment or how those earnings compare to his salary. Investment in an IRA does not affect his eligibility for a Keogh plan. (Page 164)

3. **C.** Stock options, dividends, capital gains and interest are not considered income earned from self-employment. (Page 164)

4. **C.** To qualify for a contribution in a Keogh plan, an employee must work full time and have at least one year's tenure. "Full time" is defined as working more than 1,000 of the average 2,000 working hours in a year. (Page 164)

5. **B.** IRAs and Keoghs are vehicles for the deferment of taxes until retirement; they do not provide tax exemptions. (Page 164)

6. **B.** By definition, Keogh plans are qualified plans. (Page 164)

7. **D.** Anyone can open an IRA; the tax deductibility of a person's contributions will depend on the availability of an employer-sponsored qualified retirement plan and on the person's income. Each of the listed individuals had income earned from self-employment except for the corporate officer receiving a bonus. (Page 164)

8. **C.** Keogh plans must include all full-time employees (working over 1,000 hours a year) who have worked at least one year. (Page 164)

9. **A.** Keogh plans allow contributions for the lesser of 25% of earned income or $30,000. (Page 164)

10. **D.** For an employer, Keogh contributions are limited to the lesser of 25% of after-contribution income (the equivalent of 20% of pretax income) or $30,000. In this case the doctor's $160,000 income times 20% equals $32,000, $2,000 more than the maximum contribution. (Page 164)

11. **C.** Only the royalties count as self-employment income; therefore 20% of $75,000 equals $15,000. (Page 164)

12. **C.** Individuals with Keogh retirement plans are permitted to make nondeductible contributions. The interest and dividends on these contributions will accumulate tax deferred until the owner withdraws them. (Page 165)

13. **A.** Keogh plans must allow for the inclusion of all full-time employees, age 21, with one year of service. (Page 165)

14. **D.** "Full-time" is defined as 1,000 hours or more per year, regardless of the number of days, weeks or months worked. In other words, to be considered full time, a person must work more than 50% of the 2,000 hours a normal employee works in a year. (Page 165)

15. **C.** Because she is self-employed, the employer must calculate her Keogh contribution based on post-contribution income. If she makes her maximum contribution of 25% of her post-contribution income (which is equivalent to 20% of her precontribution income), she will contribute $15,000. Her employee is, by definition, not self-employed; thus the Keogh plan, like other qualified plans, sets a maximum of 25% of total earnings or $30,000. The employer then must contribute 25% of her employee's precontribution income of $12,000, which is $3,000. (Page 165)

16. **B.** An employee must work at least 1,000 hours a year if he is to be included in an employer's Keogh plan. The janitor and the clerical assistant

described here do not meet this requirement.
(Page 165)

17. **A.**   Benefits vest to an employee according to the schedule chosen by the employer, usually over five or seven years.   (Page 165)

18. **A.**   Premature distribution is allowed without penalty if the participant dies or becomes disabled.   (Page 166)

19. **A.**   The distribution would be taxed as ordinary income but would also qualify for five-year income averaging (TRA 1986). A 10% penalty would apply if Tex were under age 59 1/2; the 50% penalty would apply if he did not take the distribution according to his life expectancy by April 1st of the year following the year he turned 70 1/2.
(Page 166)

20. **B.**   An early withdrawal from a Keogh is taxed in the same way as an early withdrawal from an IRA—as ordinary income plus a 10% penalty.
(Page 166)

21. **D.**   A Keogh account owner can always withdraw her own voluntary contributions, and can withdraw tax-deductible contributions in the event of death or disability.   (Page 166)

22. **B.**   Rollovers may take place once a year and must occur within a 60-day period. There are no limits on direct transfers of retirement assets.
(Page 166)

23. **D.**   The only investments that are not permitted in Keoghs are commodities, term life insurance, collectibles and antiques, precious metals (other than U.S.-issued gold and silver coins) and uncovered options.   (Page 166)

31   Corporate Retirement Plans Exam

1. Corporate profit-sharing plans must be in the form of a(n)

   A. trust
   B. conservatorship
   C. administrator
   D. beneficial ownership

2. Under a tax-qualified corporate pension plan, ERISA provisions permit all of the following EXCEPT

   A. allocating contributions according to income
   B. requiring that account money be used only for the participants' benefits
   C. restricting distributions to allowable purposes
   D. ceasing contributions in unprofitable years

3. Under a defined-contribution plan, the

   I. participant is guaranteed a contribution that is based on an agreed-upon percentage or rate
   II. participant's retirement benefits are based on the balance in his individual account
   III. employer may discriminate among employees as to participation

   A. I and II only
   B. I and III only
   C. II and III only
   D. I, II and III

4. In a defined benefit plan

   A. all employees receive the same benefits at retirement
   B. all participating employees are immediately vested
   C. high-income employees who are near retirement will benefit the most
   D. the same amount must be contributed for each eligible employee

5. The amount paid into a defined contribution plan is set by the

   A. ERISA-defined contribution requirements
   B. trust agreement
   C. employer's age
   D. employer's profits

6. Which of the following statements is(are) true about a qualified, noncontributory defined benefit plan?

   I. Contributions are taxable.
   II. Distributions are taxable.
   III. Contributions may vary.

   A. I and II
   B. II
   C. II and III
   D. III

7. When an employee's contribution to an employer-sponsored qualified pension plan is distributed to the employee, it is

A. returned tax-free
B. taxed at a reduced rate
C. taxed at the beneficiary's ordinary tax rate
D. taxed at the current capital gains rate

8. Distributions to an employee from a profit-sharing plan after retirement are made

A. from interest accumulating on the plan's assets
B. only from the profits on the plan's assets
C. from the amount allocated to the individual's account during the employee's participation in the plan
D. only from the amount allocated to the individual's account plus accumulated earnings during the employee's participation in the plan

9. What of the following attributes of 401K thrift plans is NOT allowed in most other retirement plans?

A. Tax-deferred earnings
B. Deductible contributions to the plan
C. Matching employer contributions
D. No penalties for premature distributions

◆ Answers & Rationale

1. **A.** All corporate pension and profit-sharing plans must be set up under a trust agreement. The plan's trustee will have fiduciary responsibility for the plan. (Page 167)

2. **D.** Only a profit-sharing plan may base its contributions on the company's income (or lack of income); employee accounts, including voluntary contributions and vested amounts, are the employee's property—the company has no say in their use or distribution. (Page 167)

3. **A.** Under a defined-contribution plan, contributions may be based on years of service or, more frequently, salary. Benefits are provided based on what the accumulated contributions will provide at retirement. The plan is qualified and may not discriminate. (Page 167)

4. **C.** The rules regarding the maximum amount of contributions are different for defined contribution plans and defined benefit plans. Defined contribution plans set the amount that can be contributed, according to the employee's salary level. Defined benefit plans set the amount of retirement benefits that a retiree will receive as a percentage of the previous several years' salaries, to a maximum of $90,000 per year. For the highly paid individual who is nearing retirement, the defined benefit plan allows a larger contribution in a shorter period of time. (Page 167)

5. **B.** The retirement plan's trust agreement will contain a section explaining the formula(s) used to determine the contributions to a defined contribution plan. (Page 167)

6. **C.** Contributions to a qualified, noncontributory plan are made by the employer, not the employee. Contributions are not taxed until they are received as distributions by the participant. Because the benefits provided by this type of qualified plan may vary (depending upon the participant's age, sex, income, etc.), the contributions made on his behalf will vary. All distributions from the plan are taxed upon receipt by the participant. (Page 168)

7. **A.** All employee contributions to a qualified retirement plan are made with aftertax dollars. Therefore, because the employee already paid taxes on the money, it will be returned tax-free. All earnings attributable to employee contributions as well as all employer-contributed money will be taxed at the employee's ordinary income rate at the time of distribution. (Page 168)

8. **D.** Distributions from a profit-sharing plan are made from the individual's account, reflecting the accrued amount of contributions and earnings on the contributions. Contributions to the plan are normally based on a predetermined percentage of profits. (Page 169)

9. **C.** Thrift or 401K plans allow the employer to match employee contributions up to a stipulated percentage. (Page 169)

32 Qualified Annuity Plans Exam

1. Which of the following people is ineligible for a tax-sheltered annuity?

   A. Professor at a land grant college
   B. Custodian at a municipal public school
   C. Student at a state college
   D. Clerical employee of a county high school

2. Of the following statements describing IRAs, which one is NOT true of TSA qualified plans?

   A. A self-employed person may participate.
   B. Contributions are tax deferred.
   C. Distributions must begin by age 70 1/2.
   D. Distributions after age 59 1/2 will be taxed as ordinary income.

3. Adam Grizzly invests in a tax-qualified variable annuity. What is the tax treatment of the distributions he receives?

   A. Partially tax-free; partially ordinary income
   B. Partially tax-free; partially capital gains
   C. All ordinary income
   D. All capital gains

4. Your customer works as a nurse in a public school. He wants to know more about participating in his school's TSA plan. You should tell him

   I. his contributions are tax deferred
   II. he is not eligible to participate
   III. distributions before age 59 1/2 are normally subject to penalty tax
   IV. mutual funds and CDs are available investment vehicles

   A. I, II and III
   B. I and III
   C. I, III and IV
   D. II

◆ Answers & Rationale

1.   **C.**   The student is the only person listed who does not work for or receive compensation from a school.   (Page 171)

2.   **A.**   Only employees of schools, church organizations and nonprofit organizations are eligible to participate in 403B TSA plans. The provisions for contributions and distributions are the same for IRAs and TSA qualified plans.
(Page 173)

3.   **C.**   In a tax-qualified annuity, the annuitant has no basis unless voluntary aftertax contributions were made. Such aftertax contributions are the exception and are not mentioned in this question.

Because the annuitant has no basis, all payments are considered ordinary income. In a nonqualified annuity, contributions are made with aftertax dollars, which establish the annuitant's basis. Annuity payments from nonqualified annuities are treated as ordinary income to the extent that they exceed the basis.   (Page 173)

4.   **C.**   Because he is employed by a public school system, your customer is eligible to participate in the tax-sheltered annuity plan. Employee contributions to a TSA plan are excluded from gross income in the year in which they are made. Like other retirement plans, a penalty tax is assessed on distributions received before age 59 1/2. A TSA plan may invest in various instruments, including mutual funds, stocks, bonds and CDs, in addition to annuity contracts.   (Page 173)

33 The Regulation of New Issues Exam

1. Which of the following statements are true of the Securities Act of 1933?

    I. The act applies only to listed securities traded over the counter.
    II. One chief purpose of the requirements for registration and prospectuses is to provide full disclosure of pertinent information to the public.
    III. The act is designed to prevent fraud in the sale of newly issued securities.

    A. I and II only
    B. I and III only
    C. II and III only
    D. I, II and III

2. To which securities market does the Securities Act of 1933 apply?

    A. Primary
    B. Secondary
    C. Third
    D. Fourth

3. The Securities Act of 1933 requires that which of the following be offered only by prospectus?

    I. Treasury bonds
    II. Mutual fund shares
    III. Variable annuities
    IV. Unit investment trusts

    A. I and II
    B. II and III
    C. II, III and IV
    D. III and IV

4. The Securities Act of 1933 covers all of the following EXCEPT

    A. due diligence
    B. prospectus requirements
    C. full and fair disclosure
    D. blue-sky laws

5. Which of the following statements about a red herring is FALSE?

    A. A red herring is used to obtain indications of interest from investors.
    B. The final offering price does not appear in a red herring.
    C. Additional information may be added to a red herring at a later date.
    D. A registered rep may send a copy of the company's research report with it.

6. Which of the following is NOT required in a preliminary prospectus?

    A. Written statement in red that the prospectus may be subject to change and amendment and that a final prospectus will be issued
    B. Purpose for which the funds that are being raised will be used
    C. Final offering price
    D. Financial status and history of the company

7. In the sale of open-end investment company shares, the prospectus

   A. is not necessary
   B. must be delivered to the client either before or during the sales solicitation
   C. must be delivered before the sales solicitation
   D. must be delivered at or before the delivery of the fund share certificate

8. Which of the following will NOT be found in a final prospectus?

   A. Underwriting agreements and the underwriters' compensation
   B. Stabilization plans
   C. Date and offering price
   D. Statement that the SEC neither approves nor disapproves of the issue

9. A prospectus for an individual variable annuity contract

   I. must provide full and fair disclosure
   II. is required by the Securities Act of 1933
   III. must be filed with the SEC
   IV. must precede or accompany every sales presentation

   A. I only
   B. I, III and IV only
   C. II and III only
   D. I, II, III and IV

10. Which of the following information must be included in a prospectus describing variable life insurance to clients?

   I. Summary explanation in nontechnical terms of the principal features of the policy
   II. Statement of investment policy of the separate account
   III. Statement of the separate account's net investment return for the past ten years
   IV. Statement of the deductions and charges against the gross premium, including all commissions paid to agents for each policy year the commissions are to be paid

   A. I and II only
   B. I, II and III only
   C. III and IV only
   D. I, II, III and IV

◆ Answers & Rationale

1. **C.** The Securities Act of 1933 applies to all newly issued securities and requires a registration statement and prospectus to be filed with the SEC. The purpose of filing and distributing the prospectus is to provide full disclosure of the offering and thus deter the sale of fraudulent securities.
(Page 181)

2. **A.** The Securities Act of 1933 covers the registration and disclosure requirements regarding new issues. The new issue market is the primary market. The trading markets are covered under the Securities Exchange Act of 1934. (Page 182)

3. **C.** Treasury securities are exempt from registration requirements, as are municipal issues, and do not require a prospectus. (Page 182)

4. **D.** Blue-sky laws are state laws and are not covered under the federal securities act.
(Page 182)

5. **D.** A registered rep is prohibited from sending a research report with either a preliminary or a final prospectus. During the first 90 days of a new issue, printed information discussing the new issue or the company cannot be circulated. (Page 183)

6. **C.** A preliminary prospectus is issued before the price is established, and it does not include the eventual offering date or the spread.
(Page 183)

7. **B.** The sale of mutual fund shares requires that the client receives the prospectus before or during the sales solicitation. (Page 183)

8. **A.** The underwriting agreements (also known as the *agreement among underwriters*) are separate documents and are not included in a prospectus. (Page 184)

9. **D.** A variable annuity is a security and therefore must be registered with the SEC. As part of the registration requirements, a prospectus must be filed and distributed to prospective investors prior to or during any solicitation for sale.
(Page 184)

10. **D.** All of the information listed here must be presented in the prospectus distributed to clients.
(Page 184)

34   The Regulation of Trading Exam

1. Which of the following is(are) regulated or mandated by the Securities Exchange Act of 1934?

    I. Full and fair disclosure on new offerings
    II. Creation of the SEC
    III. Manipulation of the market
    IV. Margin requirements on securities

    A. I
    B. I, II and III
    C. II
    D. II, III and IV

2. The Securities Exchange Act of 1934 covers which of the following?

    I. Trading of government securities
    II. Trading of corporate securities
    III. Issuance of financial reports by corporations
    IV. Issuance of government securities

    A. I, II and III
    B. I, II and IV
    C. I and III
    D. II and IV

3. Which of the following statements describe the Securities Exchange Act of 1934?

    I. It created the SEC.
    II. It requires registration of broker-dealers with the SEC.
    III. It provides for regulation of the over-the-counter market.
    IV. It prohibits inequitable and unfair trade practices.

    A. I and II only
    B. II and III only
    C. II, III and IV only
    D. I, II, III and IV

4. The Securities Exchange Act of 1934 does which of the following?

    I. Requires registration of securities
    II. Requires registration of broker-dealers with the SEC
    III. Prohibits inequitable and unfair trade practices
    IV. Provides for regulation of the over-the-counter market

    A. I only
    B. II and III only
    C. II, III and IV only
    D. I, II, III and IV

5. Corporations are required to issue annual statements (reports) by the

    A. Investment Company Act of 1940
    B. Trust Indenture Act of 1939
    C. Securities Exchange Act of 1934
    D. Securities Act of 1933

◆ Answers & Rationale

1.   **D.**   The Securities Exchange Act of 1934 set up the SEC and regulates the market. The Securities Act of 1933 requires full and fair disclosure.
(Page 186)

2.   **A.**   The Securities Exchange Act of 1934 regulates secondary trading or trading markets, while the Securities Act of 1933 regulates the primary, or new issue, market. Trading of corporates and governments would therefore fall under the 1934 act, as does corporate financial reporting. The 1933 act covers the issuance of new securities. Governments are exempt securities under the 1933 act.
(Page 186)

3.   **D.**   The Securities Act of 1933 requires registration of securities (paper act). The Securities Exchange Act of 1934 (people act) requires registration of people and exchanges transacting securities business in order to prevent manipulative and deceptive practices. The NASD is the SRO of the OTC market, but the SEC has final authority.
(Page 186)

4.   **C.**   The Securities Act of 1933 (paper act) requires registration of securities. The act of 1934 (people act) requires registration of people and exchanges transacting securities business in order to prevent manipulative and deceptive practices. The NASD is the SRO of the OTC market, but the SEC has final authority.
(Page 186)

5.   **C.**   The Securities Exchange Act of 1934 mandates that companies file annual reports with the SEC.
(Page 187)

35 The Investment Advisers Act Exam

1. Which of the following persons meets the definition of "investment adviser" under the Investment Advisers Act of 1940?

    A. Porter provides a range of financial services for a fee; investment advice is included among these services but is not his primary business.
    B. June gives investment tips to friends who work with her at a department store; her friends often make money when they follow her advice.
    C. Karen calls herself a "financial planner"; she helps people budget wisely, pay off their debts, establish savings plans and set financial goals.
    D. Joe is paid to advise clients regarding the purchase of futures contracts.

2. Which of the following are NOT included in the definition of "investment adviser" under the Investment Advisers Act of 1940 if their investment advice is incidental to the practice of their professions?

    A. Publishers of investment newsletters
    B. Pension consultants
    C. Chemical engineers
    D. Members of the clergy

3. Which of the following investment advisers are exempt from registration under the Investment Advisers Act of 1940?

    I. Clara does not hold herself out to the public as an investment adviser and has 14 clients, all of whom are individuals.
    II. All of Joe's customers reside in his home state, and Joe offers no advice on any exchange-listed stocks.
    III. All of Chip's customers are investment companies.

    A. I and II only
    B. I and III only
    C. II and III only
    D. I, II and III

4. A person who renders investment advice solely with respect to securities issued by the U.S. government

    A. is exempt from state registration under the Uniform Securities Act, but must be federally registered under the Investment Advisers Act of 1940
    B. is exempt from both federal and state registration requirements
    C. must be registered with both the SEC and the state
    D. need not be federally registered under the Investment Advisers Act of 1940, but generally must be state registered under the Uniform Securities Act

5.   Which of the following compensation arrangements is NOT allowed under the Investment Advisers Act of 1940?

   A.   Randy waives a client's fee if the client experiences a loss for the year.
   B.   Joe charges a set fee regardless of how long it takes him to generate his recommendation for a given client or how well the recommendation turns out.
   C.   Greta varies her fee according to the amount of time she spends managing the account.
   D.   Belle charges her clients a percentage of assets under management.

6.   Which of the following is NOT exempt from registration as an investment adviser under the act of 1940?

   A.   Bank
   B.   Broker-dealer
   C.   Doctor
   D.   Engineer

7.   The exclusion for providing investment advice that is solely incidental to the practice of a profession is NOT available to which of the following under the Investment Advisers Act of 1940?

   A.   Real estate agents
   B.   Engineers
   C.   Teachers
   D.   Broker-dealers

◆ Answers & Rationale

1.　**A.**　Porter provides investment advice, for compensation, as part of his regular business, which is the definition of "investment adviser"; the fact that the advice is a minor part of Porter's business is irrelevant. June receives no compensation for her investment advice. Karen's services do not include investment advice, and neither do Joe's because futures contracts are not securities.

(Page 188)

2.　**C.**　Engineers qualify for a professional exclusion if the advice they render is solely incidental to the practice of their profession. No exclusion applies to publishers of investment newsletters, pension consultants or members of the clergy.

(Page 188)

3.　**A.**　There are three exemptions from the registration requirement under the Advisers Act: advisers who do not hold themselves out as investment advisers and who have fewer than 15 clients per year, none of which are investment companies (choice I); advisers who render no advice on any exchange-listed security and whose clients are all in one state (choice II); and advisers whose only clients are insurance companies. In choice III, Chip's clients are investment companies.

(Page 188)

4.　**D.**　A person who renders advice solely with respect to securities issued or guaranteed by the U.S. government is exempt from federal registration under the Advisers Act but not from state registration under the Uniform Securities Act.

(Page 189)

5.　**A.**　A fee whereby payment is contingent on investment results is prohibited. Set fees, hourly fees and fees based on the percentage of assets under management are allowed.　(Page 188)

6.　**C.**　Banks, broker-dealers, certain publishers, teachers, lawyers, accountants and engineers whose giving of investment advice is incidental to the practice of their profession are exempt from registration as investment advisers.　(Page 188)

7.　**A.**　A professional exclusion is not available to real estate agents. It is available to engineers, teachers and broker-dealers if the advice rendered is solely incidental to the practice of their professions.

(Page 188)

36 Insider Trading and Securities Fraud Enforcement Act Exam

1. Which of the following statements is NOT true regarding the civil penalties that may be imposed for insider trading violations under the Securities Exchange Act of 1934?

   A. A civil penalty may be imposed only on a person who is registered under a securities act.
   B. The violation for which the penalty may be imposed is defined as "buying or selling securities while in possession of material, nonpublic information."
   C. The SEC may ask a court to impose a penalty of up to three times the loss avoided or profit gained on an illegal transaction.
   D. Improper supervision may cause an investment advisory firm to be liable to pay a penalty for an insider trading violation committed by one of its representatives.

2. Tex Longhorn is in possession of material inside information about General Gizmonics, Inc. He may communicate this information to a customer

   A. if the customer knows it's inside information
   B. the day before the information is made public
   C. if the customer enters an unsolicited order
   D. under no circumstances

3. Under the Securities Exchange Act of 1934, insiders include

   I. the attorney who wrote the offering circular for the company
   II. a bookkeeper in the accounting department of the company
   III. the wife of the president of the company
   IV. a brother of the president of the company

   A. I only
   B. II only
   C. II, III and IV only
   D. I, II, III and IV

4. Who might be defined as an insider regarding access to and profiting from inside information?

   I. Corporate attorney
   II. Corporate research lab technician
   III. Exchange member
   IV. News wire service employee
   V. CPA engaged by the corporation

   A. I, II and III only
   B. I and IV only
   C. II and IV only
   D. I, II, III, IV and V

5. In determining whether a purchase and sale of securities is based on inside information, which of the following factors are considered?

    I.   Whether the individual made a profit on the transaction
    II. Whether other parties were privy to the same information
    III. The method by which the information was released to the public
    IV. The time of the transaction in relation to the time when the information was released to the public

    A. I, II and III only
    B. II, III and IV only
    C. III and IV only
    D. I, II, III and IV

6. Broker-dealers are required to have written supervisory procedures to prevent the misuse of inside information by

    I.   employees of the broker-dealer
    II. associated persons of the broker-dealer
    III. suppliers to the broker-dealer
    IV. disinterested persons

    A. I only
    B. I and II only
    C. II and IV only
    D. I, II, III and IV

◆ Answers & Rationale

1.   **A.**   The penalty may be imposed on anyone who trades on inside information, not just persons registered under the act. The other statements are correct: answer B is the definition of "insider trading;" the penalty is up to three times the profit gained or loss avoided; and an advisory firm may face a penalty for the actions of its representatives.
(Page 190)

2.   **D.**   Inside information may never be discussed until it is made public, at which point it is no longer inside information. Violations may be punished with civil penalties as well as prison sentences.
(Page 190)

3.   **D.**   While the act of 1934 defines an insider as an officer, director or 10% stockholder of the company, the courts have broadened the definition to include anyone who has inside information.
(Page 190)

4.   **D.**   Anybody who has information before it is made available to the public can be considered an insider.
(Page 190)

5.   **D.**   The following would be considered in determining whether a trade was based on inside information: whether a profit was made; how many individuals knew the information; how and when the information was released to the public; and the timing of the trade relative to the release of the information.
(Page 190)

6.   **B.**   All broker-dealers are required to have written supervisory procedures to prevent the misuse of inside information by employees and associated persons of the firm; *associated persons* include lawyers, accountants, and so on.
(Page 190)

37 Securities Investor Protection Corporation Exam

1. Which of the following is protected by the Securities Investor Protection Corporation?

   A. Broker-dealer failure
   B. Fraudulent transaction
   C. Issuer default
   D. Market risk

2. The determination of a broker-dealer's financial failure is made under the provisions of the

   A. Securities Act of 1933
   B. Securities Exchange Act of 1934
   C. Securities Investor Protection Act of 1970
   D. specific determination of the SEC

3. The Securities Investor Protection Act applies to registered broker-dealers that

   A. are members of an exchange
   B. are members of the NASD
   C. are members of both an exchange and the NASD
   D. use the mails or other instruments of interstate commerce

4. Which of the following entities are exempt from membership in SIPC?

   I. Fully disclosed broker-dealers
   II. Broker-dealers dealing exclusively in mutual funds or unit trusts
   III. Investment advisers
   IV. Nonbank municipal dealers

   A. I and II
   B. II and III
   C. II and IV
   D. III and IV

5. A husband and wife have both a joint cash account and a joint margin account. In addition, each has an individual retirement account. SIPC would cover

   A. the joint accounts separately and the retirement accounts as one
   B. the retirement accounts separately and the joint accounts as one
   C. all accounts combined as one
   D. all accounts individually and separately

6. A client has a special cash account with stock valued at $460,000 and $40,000 in cash. The same client also has a joint account with a spouse that has a market value of $320,000 and $180,000 in cash. SIPC coverage would be

A. $460,000 for the special cash account and $320,000 for the joint account
B. $500,000 for the special cash account and $420,000 for the joint account
C. $500,000 for the special cash account and $500,000 for the joint account
D. a total of $1,000,000 for both accounts

7. The insurance limit under SIPC is $500,000 per

A. person
B. separate person
C. account
D. separate customer

8. A medical partnership holds a margin account and one of the partners also has a margin account. For SIPC purposes

A. only the partnership's account is covered
B. only the partner's account is covered
C. both accounts are covered with each account considered a separate person
D. both accounts are covered on an aggregate basis

9. A corporation opens a trading account with ALFA Financial Services. At the same time, a director of the corporation opens an individual trading account with ALFA. According to SIPC rules, how will the accounts be treated?

A. Both accounts will be combined as one separate customer account.
B. The corporation's account will be covered under SIPC, but the director's account will not.
C. The director's account will be covered under SIPC, but the corporation's account will not.
D. Each account will be treated as a separate customer.

10. A customer has a margin account with $300,000 of securities and a $100,000 debit; she also has a separate cash account with no securities positions and a $150,000 free credit balance. The customer's coverage under SIPC is

A. $200,000
B. $300,000
C. $350,000
D. $400,000

◆ Answers & Rationale

1.   **A.**   SIPC protects customer accounts against broker-dealer failure.   (Page 191)

2.   **C.**   The determination of financial failure is made under the Securities Investor Protection Act of 1970.   (Page 191)

3.   **D.**   The Securities Investor Protection Act of 1970 applies to all broker-dealers that use the mails or other instruments of interstate commerce (and, therefore, must register with the SEC).
(Page 191)

4.   **B.**   As a general rule, all broker-dealers registered with the SEC must be members of SIPC. Exceptions are made for: broker-dealers whose business is limited to U.S. government securities, the distribution of mutual fund shares, the sale of variable annuities, the business of insurance, and the sale of unit investment trusts; investment advisers; and banks registered as municipal securities dealers.   (Page 191)

5.   **B.**   SIPC provides up to $500,000 of protection to each separate customer. Multiple accounts held by the same person would be considered as only one customer for SIPC purposes (remember that the definition of "person" can include individuals, groups, companies, and so on). However, there are different elements of beneficial ownership. If a woman has an account in her name, a man has an account in his name and they are joint owners of a third account, SIPC will treat them as three separate customers.   (Page 191)

6.   **B.**   SIPC coverage is $500,000 per customer account, with cash not to exceed $100,000. Thus, in the single-name account, SIPC provides full coverage, while in the joint account SIPC covers the full value of the securities but only $100,000 of the $180,000 in cash. The remaining $80,000 becomes a general debt of the bankrupt broker-dealer.
(Page 191)

7.   **D.**   SIPC is based on the concept of separate customer coverage, which means separate ownership entities. Coverage per separate customer is $500,000 with a $100,000 limit on cash per account.   (Page 191)

8.   **C.**   SIPC looks at the title an account is registered in rather than the type. If any aspect of a title differs between accounts, they are considered separate accounts for insurance purposes.
(Page 191)

9.   **D.**   The corporate account (in corporate name) will be treated as a separate customer from the individual account. (Note that if the director of the corporation were a director of the broker-dealer, the account would not be covered.)   (Page 191)

10.   **B.**   SIPC rules require that in a margin account the securities value covered is, in effect, the equity in the account. Therefore, a margin account with $300,000 worth of market value and $100,000 debit has a securities coverage of $200,000 (the equity in the account). In addition, the customer has a free credit balance of $150,000. Under SIPC, cash balances are covered only up to $100,000. Therefore, the total coverage under SIPC is $200,000 of securities plus $100,000 of the free credit balance.   (Page 192)

38 Registration and Regulation of Broker-Dealers Exam

1. If a registered representative is suspended by a member firm, the member firm must report the suspension to

   A. the appropriate SRO
   B. the state securities commissioner
   C. the SEC
   D. the news media

2. Which of the following brokerage house staff are NOT subject to the mandatory fingerprinting rule?

   A. Associated persons employed as sales representatives
   B. Auditors and accountants in charge of the firm's money and securities accounting records
   C. Officers or partners who supervise the cashiering and accounting departments of the firm in sales production
   D. Associated persons engaged exclusively in securities research

◆ Answers & Rationale

1.   **A.**   If a registered representative is suspended by a member firm, the firm must report the suspension to the exchanges where the firm is a member. Each exchange is a self-regulatory organization.   (Page 193)

2.   **D.**   SEC Rule 17f-2 requires that all officers and employees of a broker-dealer organization be fingerprinted if they (1) engage in the sale of securities, (2) have access to physical securities, cash or accounting records, or (3) directly supervise employees who handle securities, cash or accounting records.   (Page 193)

39 NASD Bylaws Exam

1. The NASD was established to

   I. set and standardize charges and commissions
   II. encourage just and equitable principles of trade
   III. adopt and enforce Rules of Fair Practice among brokers and dealers

   A. I only
   B. II and III only
   C. III only
   D. I, II and III

2. The NASD Uniform Practice Code was established to

   A. require that practices in the investment banking and securities industry be just, reasonable, and nondiscriminatory between investors
   B. eliminate advertising and sales literature that the SEC considers to be in violation of standards
   C. provide a procedure for handling trade complaints from investors
   D. maintain similarity of business practices among member organizations in the securities industry

3. According to the NASD Bylaws, which of the following must be verified for a person who seeks a job that involves handling funds or securities?

   I. Record of arrest or indictment for any crime involving the purchase, sale or delivery of securities
   II. Record of denial of membership in any national securities exchange
   III. Listing of the person's business connections over the past ten years and reasons for leaving each previous position
   IV. Educational institutions attended within the past ten years

   A. I and II only
   B. I, III and IV only
   C. II and III only
   D. I, II, III and IV

4. It is ethical for a broker-dealer to pay commissions under a continuing commission contract to which of the following?

    I.   Retired employee or his widow, for continuing business
    II. Broker-dealership purchased by you for that broker-dealer's continuing business
    III. Retired employee who refers an old neighbor to the broker-dealer
    IV. Retired employee who, in the course of his travels, acquires new business for the broker-dealer

    A. I and II only
    B. II and III only
    C. III and IV only
    D. I, II, III and IV

5. A secretary for a registered representative takes messages from customers regarding the purchase and sale of securities during the rep's absence. The secretary is unregistered. This activity is

    A. a violation of exchange rules and will subject both the secretary and the registered representative to disciplinary proceedings
    B. a violation of exchange rules and will subject the registered representative to disciplinary proceedings
    C. permitted
    D. permitted only if the registered representative reviews the activities of the secretary on a daily basis

6. An employee who is involved in the management of an NASD member's business, particularly in the supervision of business solicitation or in training, would have to be registered as a

    A. broker
    B. dealer
    C. partner
    D. principal

7. Which of the following is a statutory disqualification preventing an individual from participating in the securities business as a registered person of the SEC or other self-regulatory organization?

    I.   The individual has been convicted within 10 years of a securities-related crime.
    II. The individual has willfully violated the provisions of a federal securities act.
    III. The individual has been expelled or suspended from an SRO.
    IV. The individual is subject to an order of the Commission denying, suspending or revoking registration.

    A. I only
    B. I and II only
    C. II and III only
    D. I, II, III and IV

◆ Answers & Rationale

1. **B.** The commissions charged are not set, but must be fair and reasonable for the service provided as enumerated in the NASD Rules of Fair Practice.   (Page 194)

2. **D.** The Uniform Practice Code is designed to standardize the customs, practices and trading techniques employed in the investment banking and securities business.   (Page 196)

3. **D.** Under the NASD Bylaws, a broker must verify all of the choices given.   (Page 196)

4. **A.** A member firm may continue to pay commissions either to a retired employee (or to a retired employee's spouse) or to a broker-dealer purchased by the firm for continuing business, provided that a prior written contract exists.   (Page 197)

5. **C.** As long as the secretary does not solicit or take orders, she can be unregistered. However, the secretary's activities should be supervised by the registered representative.   (Page 198)

6. **D.** Supervision of business solicitation or training requires being registered as a principal.   (Page 198)

7. **D.** Conviction of a securities crime, suspension or expulsion from a self-regulatory organization, infraction of a securities law or suspension by ruling of the SEC represent a statutory disqualification. The term "statutory" means *written in law.* If an individual is found to fall under any of the above categories he or she can be summarily barred from participation in the securities industry.   (Page 200)

40 Ethics in the Securities Industry Exam

1. A registered representative of an NYSE member firm who wishes to work outside the firm after hours would require permission from the

   A. member firm
   B. NASD
   C. NYSE
   D. SEC

2. A registered rep may NOT do which of the following without prior approval from her firm?

   I. Work part-time as piano player
   II. Work part-time as a bartender
   III. Invest passively in a night club
   IV. Receive a salary as a manager and general partner of an apartment building offering investment interests to passive partners

   A. I, II and IV only
   B. II and IV only
   C. III only
   D. I, II, III and IV

3. The NASD Rules of Fair Practice govern the actions of its members. All of the following are considered violations of the rules EXCEPT

   A. churning accounts
   B. the blanket recommending of low-price speculative stocks
   C. using discretionary authority
   D. guaranteeing the customer against loss

4. The term "churning" refers to

   A. excessive trading in a customer's account for the express purpose of generating commissions
   B. the practice of freeriding in more than one customer's account at a time
   C. manipulation of market prices by a firm
   D. making false or misleading statements to a customer for the purpose of inducing the customer to purchase or sell a security

5. A broker-dealer decides to give a $300 bonus to the registered representative from any other member firm who sells the most shares in a joint sales contest. This arrangement is

   I. unacceptable
   II. acceptable if the SEC approves
   III. acceptable if the underwriter is an NASD member
   IV. acceptable as long as it is not considered compensation

   A. I
   B. I and IV
   C. II
   D. II and III

6. NASD rules permit members to

    A. execute an order to sell shares of a customer's securities, knowing that delivery of these shares will be two weeks later
    B. continue to compensate a registered representative for sales that were made while the representative was working for the firm according to a previous contract
    C. arrange for a customer to receive $5,000 worth of credit in order to purchase mutual fund shares
    D. give a selling concession to a nonmember firm because of the large number of shares the nonmember is purchasing

7. To what does the term "selling dividends" refer?

    A. Encouraging mutual fund customers to sell their holdings just before the fund declares a dividend payment
    B. Enticing customers to buy mutual fund shares just before a dividend payment
    C. Withdrawing dividends rather than reinvesting these amounts in additional shares
    D. Encouraging investors to postpone purchases of mutual fund shares until after the ex-date for a dividend distribution

8. Encouraging a customer to purchase mutual fund shares in an amount just under the next dollar volume bracket, which entitles the customer to a reduction in sales charges, or remaining silent on the matter, is called

    A. breakpoint sales
    B. boiler room selling
    C. double-dip selling
    D. low-ball sales

9. According to the Rules of Fair Practice, a member organization must

    A. grant an extension of the settlement date for a purchase made in a special cash account
    B. repurchase from a client any securities offered for sale by the client
    C. quote a quantity discount on lots of more than 100 shares
    D. authorize in writing the sharing of a client's profits or losses by a registered representative

10. Which of the following individuals may not purchase shares of a hot issue of stock?

    A. General partner of a member firm
    B. Spouse of the person who is the managing underwriter of the issue
    C. Senior officer of a bank
    D. All of the above

11. Which of the following situations might fall into the category of a hot issue?

    A. New issue is offered at $30 and immediately appreciates to $35.
    B. New issue is offered at $30 and immediately decreases to $25.
    C. Market maker buys at $17 and immediately sells with a spread of $2.
    D. Broker-dealer sells inventory at $60 three weeks after buying at $30.

◆ Answers & Rationale

1. **A.** A rep would always need to get permission from the firm before working for another firm. (Page 204)

2. **A.** A registered representative may make passive investments for her own account at will. A registered representative may not, without prior notification to and approval from her member, receive compensation for employment outside her regular duties with the member. Additionally, a registered representative is not allowed to participate in private securities transactions without first notifying the member in writing. (Page 204)

3. **C.** Use of discretionary authority is not a violation of the Rules of Fair Practice, but abuse of that authority by excessive trading and the misuse of a customer's funds or securities is. Answers A, B and D are clear violations. Recommendations should be based on the customer's financial status and objectives. Low-priced stocks may result in a higher percentage of commission. Brokers that make a practice of selling low-priced stocks are often called *penny brokers*. (Page 205)

4. **A.** "Churning" describes trading that is excessive in light of a particular customer's circumstances or trading more excessive than what would normally be considered suitable. This is equally true for both discretionary and nondiscretionary accounts. (Page 206)

5. **A.** Gifts in excess of $100 per person per year are not allowed. (Page 206)

6. **B.** Registered reps may continue to be compensated for sales that were made while working for the firm and were in accordance with the contract. (Page 206)

7. **B.** "Selling dividends" is an unethical sales practice in which a seller intentionally or unintentionally misleads customers into believing they will be getting the equivalent of a rebate on their investments because the fund will soon be paying a distribution. The customers suffer out-of-pocket losses because the cash immediately coming back is dividend income, subject to tax. (Page 207)

8. **A.** "Breakpoint sales" are those in which a customer unknowingly buys investment company shares in an amount just under a dollar bracket amount that would qualify the customer's investment for a reduction in sales charges. As a result the customer pays a higher dollar amount in sales charges, which reduces the number of shares purchased and results in a higher cost basis per share. (Page 207)

9. **D.** According to the NASD Rules of Fair Practice, members and persons associated with them are forbidden to:

- guarantee that a customer will not sustain a loss; or
- share in the profits or losses of a customer's account unless the member firm's prior written approval has been obtained and the member shares only to the extent of his prorated equity contribution to the account. (Note that accounts of the immediate family of the associated person or member are exempt from the proportionate share limitation.)

(Page 208)

10. **D.** None of the people listed may purchase hot issues. (Page 209)

11. **A.** When a stock goes up in price dramatically upon issue, it is said to be hot. Although there is no mathematical formula, a rise in price of 1/8th point or more upon issue is generally considered an example of a hot issue. (Page 209)

41   Codes of Procedure and of Arbitration Procedure Exam

1. The Code of Procedure was designed for all of the following purposes EXCEPT settling

   A. when-, as- and if-issued securities transactions between member firms
   B. complaints between or among members
   C. complaints between registered reps and members
   D. complaints made by customers against members

2. Who may assess the penalties on, suspend, or expel a firm or registered representative from NASD membership?

   I. District Business Conduct Committee
   II. NASD Board of Governors
   III. Uniform Practice Committee

   A. I and II
   B. II
   C. II and III
   D. III

3. If a complaint is filed with the NASD charging that a member or associated person violated one or more of the Association's rules, which of the following codes governs the resolution of such matters?

   A. Code of Arbitration
   B. Code of Procedure
   C. Professional Practice Code
   D. Business Conduct Code

4. A charge that an NASD member or associated person violated one of the Rules of Fair Practice or some other body of NASD rules and regulations may be brought by which of the following persons?

   I. Customer against a member or an associated person
   II. Member firm against another member firm or an associated person
   III. NASD-DBCC against a member or an associated person
   IV. NASD Board of Governors against a member or an associated person

   A. I only
   B. I and II only
   C. II, III and IV only
   D. I, II, III and IV

5. What is(are) the responsibilities of a respondent when the party learns that it is involved in an arbitration dispute?

   I. The respondent must file the appropriate forms with the Director of Arbitration within 20 calendar days of the receipt of service.
   II. In its answer, the respondent must put forth all defenses to the statement of claim.
   III. The respondent may set forth a counterclaim, if any, against the initiating party or a third party.

   A. I only
   B. I and II only
   C. III only
   D. I, II and III

6. Which of the following statements apply to the Code of Procedure?

   I. The Board of Governors may review the findings of the District Business Conduct Committee within 45 days.
   II. All answers by respondents must be in writing and must be submitted to the District Business Conduct Committee within 20 calendar days.
   III. All complaints must be in writing.
   IV. The SEC will approve or disapprove the penalty assessed within 60 days.

   A. I and II only
   B. I, II and III only
   C. III and IV only
   D. I, II, III and IV

7. If not appealed to the Board of Governors, findings by a District Business Conduct Committee become effective

   A. immediately
   B. only after review by the SEC
   C. no sooner than 10 days from the date of the decision
   D. no sooner than 45 days from the date of the decision

8. The Board of Governors of the NASD has the authority to

   I. suspend a person, prohibiting him from associating with any exchange
   II. censure a partner of a member firm
   III. suspend or expel a member firm from membership in the NASD
   IV. either suspend or bar a person from further association with a member firm

   A. I and III only
   B. II, III and IV only
   C. II and IV only
   D. I, II, III and IV

9. The NASD may take which of the following actions against members who violate the Rules of Fair Practice?

   I. Expulsion
   II. Censure
   III. Fine
   IV. Suspension

   A. I, II and IV only
   B. I and IV only
   C. II and III only
   D. I, II, III and IV

10. If a registered representative violates NASD rules, the

   A. NASD may only impose a fine
   B. rep may be expelled only by the NASD
   C. NASD may recommend that disciplinary action be taken, but only the SEC can take such action
   D. NASD may fine, censure, suspend or expel the rep

11. Upon making an acceptable offer of settlement to the DBCC, a broker-dealer gives up its right to appeal the decision to the

   I. Board of Governors
   II. SEC
   III. federal district courts

   A. I and II only
   B. I and III only
   C. II only
   D. I, II and III

12. Unless the law directs otherwise, all awards rendered under or proceeding before the arbitration panel shall be

    A. subject to review by the MSRB
    B. subject to review by the SEC
    C. subject to appeal to the federal courts
    D. deemed final and not subject to review or appeal

13. The maximum fine in a summary complaint proceeding is

    A. $1,000
    B. $2,500
    C. $5,000
    D. $10,000

14. The Code of Arbitration is mandatory when there are disputes between a broker-dealer and

    A. the Securities and Exchange Commission
    B. another broker-dealer
    C. the general public
    D. the National Association of Securities Dealers

15. How are disputes between NASD members regarding such things as delivery and payment for securities transactions settled?

    A. By the SEC
    B. Under the provisions of the Code of Arbitration
    C. By the Board of Governors
    D. By the District Business Conduct Committee

16. Which of the following means of settling disputes is attractive to broker-dealers because of its relatively low cost?

    A. Litigation
    B. Coterminous defeasance
    C. Repatriation
    D. Arbitration

17. How long does a client have in which to lodge a complaint against a registered representative or a member firm under the Code of Arbitration?

    A. Six months
    B. One year
    C. Six years
    D. Ten years

18. When initiating an arbitration proceeding, the document filed by the initial party that states the relevant facts of the cases and the remedies sought is called the

    A. submission agreement
    B. statement of claim
    C. official statement
    D. director's brief

19. Arbitration under the NASD Code of Arbitration Procedure is mandatory in which of the following disputes?

    I. Member against a person associated with a member
    II. Member against another member
    III. Member against a public customer
    IV. Public customer against a member

    A. I only
    B. I, II and IV only
    C. II only
    D. I, II, III and IV

20. Findings under the NASD Code of Arbitration Procedure

    A. are binding on members, but not on customers
    B. are binding on all parties involved in the dispute
    C. may be appealed to the NASD's Board of Governors
    D. may be appealed to the SEC

21. The dollar limit for simplified arbitration procedures between members is

    A. $1,000
    B. $2,500
    C. $5,000
    D. $10,000

22. Brought to arbitration is a matter involving a $50,000 complaint or discrepancy. The panel hearing this dispute will consist of

    A. not fewer than three or more than five arbitrators
    B. five arbitrators
    C. seven arbitrators
    D. a number of arbitrators determined by the arbitration committee

◆ Answers & Rationale

1. **A.** The Code of Procedure is a mechanism for settling complaints between or among members or between members and nonmembers. The Uniform Practice Code establishes standard operating procedures for the settlement of transactions.
(Page 211)

2. **A.** Under the NASD Code of Procedure, both the DBCC and the Board of Governors are empowered to penalize, suspend or expel a member firm or an associated person.   (Page 211)

3. **B.** Complaints charging that a member firm or an associated person violated one or more of the NASD's rules are handled under the Code of Procedure. Complaints, which charge that a specific rule was violated, should not be confused with disputes, which tend to deal more with business ethics, failures to perform and misunderstandings. Disputes are submitted for resolution under the NASD's Code of Arbitration.   (Page 211)

4. **D.** Anyone can bring charges of rule violations against a member firm or an associated person, including customers, which is the reason each branch office must maintain library copies of the NASD's Bylaws, Rules of Fair Practice and Code of Procedure.   (Page 211)

5. **D.** The respondent must respond to the notice within 20 calendar days, at which time he may set forth his defense and/or file a counter or addition suit.   (Page 211)

6. **B.** The Board of Governors may review any findings by the DBCC within 45 days if it sees fit. In every instance, charges by complainants and replies by respondents must be in writing. Respondents have 20 calendar days in which to answer a complaint.   (Page 212)

7. **D.** If not appealed, District Business Conduct Committee decisions become final 45 days after the decision date.   (Page 212)

8. **B.** The Board of Governors of the NASD may censure, suspend or expel a member or a person associated with a member. It has no jurisdiction over the exchanges and cannot prohibit any person from associating with them.   (Page 212)

9. **D.** Members or employees of members found to violate the Rules of Fair Practice can be subjected to any penalty in the NASD's arsenal.
(Page 212)

10. **D.** Under the Code of Procedure, a member or its employees may be censured, suspended, expelled or fined for a violation of NASD rules.
(Page 212)

11. **D.** An offer of settlement is the broker-dealer's choice. Once the DBCC accepts the offer, the member cannot back out of the deal.
(Page 212)

12. **D.** All decisions made by the arbitration committee are deemed final and binding.
(Page 212)

13. **B.** The maximum fine in a summary complaint is $2,500, according to the NASD Code of Procedure.   (Page 213)

14. **B.** The Code of Arbitration covers interdealer disputes.   (Page 213)

15. **B.** Disputes regarding the provisions of the Uniform Practice Code (UPC) are handled through the NASD Code of Arbitration. The UPC specifies the mechanics of member-to-member dealings.
(Page 213)

16. **D.** Arbitration is a system for resolving disputes between parties by submitting the disagreement to an impartial panel, consisting of one, three or five people. Arbitration expedites binding decisions involving disputes and avoids costly litigation. The words *coterminous defeasance* are nonsense; taken separately, *coterminous* applies to overlapping debt, while *defeasance* refers to an action taken by a corporation to reduce its debt on its balance sheet. Repatriation has no bearing on the question.   (Page 213)

17. **C.** Under the Code of Arbitration, no dispute or claim is eligible for submission to arbitration six years after the date of occurrence of the dispute. The statute for arbitration does not extend applicable state statutes of limitations (typically two years). (Page 213)

18. **B.** The filing of the claim in a dispute is called the *statement of claim*. (Page 213)

19. **B.** The Code of Arbitration is mandatory in member against member disputes. In a dispute between a member and a public customer, the public customer cannot be forced to arbitrate by the member, but the member can be forced to arbitrate at the customer's request. (Page 213)

20. **B.** Members and associated persons must submit disputes to arbitration. Customers are subject to arbitration only if they agree to submit to arbitration. Findings under the Code of Arbitration are considered binding on all parties involved. (Page 214)

21. **D.** Simplified arbitration procedures are allowed and encouraged between member broker-dealers for complaints or amounts estimated to have a value of less than $10,000. (Page 214)

22. **A.** In disputes involving more than $30,000, the code dictates that there be no fewer than three arbitrators but no more than five arbitrators. (Page 214)

 **42** **Communications with the Public Exam**

1. Which of the following is NOT considered either advertising or sales literature?

   A. Radio advertisement that describes the range of services offered by a firm
   B. Advertisement for the firm published in the telephone directory
   C. Report to a firm's customers on recent changes in the president's economic policies
   D. Market letters sent to a firm's customers

2. Which of the following is(are) subject to NASD rules on advertising and sales literature?

   I. Newspaper advertisements offering an opportunity for employment as a registered representative
   II. Material used in a newspaper or on television
   III. Letters sent to an individual discussing investments relating to his securities portfolio
   IV. Form letters sent to customers

   A. I
   B. I and II
   C. I, II and IV
   D. III and IV

3. Which of the following are included under the terms "advertising" and "sales literature" with respect to mutual funds?

   I. Commercial messages broadcast on radio and television
   II. "Sales ideas" and marketing literature sent by issuers to broker-dealers to be used as internal sales development materials
   III. Sales aids and product literature distributed to broker-dealers by a fund's principal underwriter, such materials to be sent to prospective buyers or displayed for their viewing
   IV. Written communications such as direct mail pieces sent to the general public

   A. I and II only
   B. I, III and IV only
   C. III and IV only
   D. I, II, III and IV

4. All of the following are considered advertising or sales literature EXCEPT

   A. market letters
   B. research reports
   C. prospectuses
   D. telephone directory listings

5. Sales literature and advertising used in connection with the solicitation or sale of variable life products is defined as

I. circulars and leaflets describing the variable life product
II. prepared presentations used at a seminar open to the public
III. newspaper advertising of the benefits of variable life insurance
IV. a letter that is sent to 50 of the agent's present clients describing variable life insurance

A. I and II only
B. I and III only
C. III only
D. I, II, III and IV

6. Which of the following forms of written communication must be approved prior to its use by a branch officer or manager?

A. Letter to a customer offering advice about a stock
B. Letter sent to 30 customers offering advice about a stock
C. Interoffice memorandum
D. Preliminary prospectus

7. Which of the following activities is(are) likely to lead to a charge of rule violation by the NASD and/or the SEC?

I. A featured columnist for a nationally distributed financial newspaper writes a favorable report on a certain company and is invited on an all-expenses-paid vacation sponsored by a market maker in the company's securities.
II. A paid advertisement is placed in a local newspaper by a broker-dealer publicizing the range of investment banking services the firm has provided for locally based corporations.
III. A broker-dealer agrees to fund a major portion of the circulation expenses incurred by the sponsor or publisher of a monthly investment newsletter in exchange for priority placements of news items and research opinions at the direction of the broker-dealer.
IV. A broker-dealer offers sales incentives in the form of higher selling concessions to registered representatives, but only on buy orders for a select list of equity securities in which the firm makes markets.

A. I
B. I and III
C. I, III and IV
D. II, III and IV

8. Recommendations to a customer

A. must be approved in advance by a principal and must be suitable based on the facts disclosed by the customer regarding other holdings and financial situations
B. must be suitable based on the facts disclosed by the customer regarding other holdings and financial situations
C. must be approved in advance by a principal
D. are not covered by NASD rules

9. While recommending the purchase of a security, a registered representative presented material indicating a possible upward move in the price of the recommended security. This recommendation to buy was probably

    I.   fraudulent
    II. in violation of the Rules of Fair Practice
    III. not suitable for all investors
    IV. acceptable if the statements about prices and earnings were clearly labeled as forecasts

    A. I
    B. I and II
    C. III
    D. III and IV

10. All advertisements recommending securities must include the

    I.   fact that the member firm intends to buy or sell the security
    II. price at the time the original recommendation was made
    III. fact that the member firm makes a market in the security if such is the case
    IV. name of the member firm providing the recommendation

    A. I and III only
    B. II and IV only
    C. III only
    D. I, II, III and IV

11. When a member firm refers to its previous recommendations, it must also

    I.   indicate that the market was generally rising if such is the case
    II. show all of its recommendations of the same type of securities made within the previous twelve months
    III. indicate the date and price of the security at the time of recommendation
    IV. give the amount of profit or loss that would have been realized had an individual acted on all of the recommendations

    A. I, II and III only
    B. II and III only
    C. I, II, III and IV
    D. None of the above

12. If ArGood Mutual Funds uses performance charts and return on investment statistics in its sales literature, which of the following NASD policy statements apply?

    I.   Performance charts and similar financial information displays should cover a minimum of ten years (or the life of the fund, if shorter); periods in excess of ten years can be reported in five-year increments.
    II. All earnings and total return figures should provide a separate accounting of dividends and capital gains.
    III. In computing and reporting historical yields and return on investment, the shares' maximum offering price should be used.
    IV. Current yield figures must be based on the fund's income distributions only.

    A. I and II only
    B. II and IV only
    C. III and IV only
    D. I, II, III and IV

13. In a mutual fund, the amount of increases and/or decreases in the NAV over the past years can be reviewed in the

A. official statement
B. customer account form
C. prospectus
D. tombstone

14. When using the annual report as sales literature, the

I. principal of the firm must approve its use as such
II. prospectus must accompany the report
III. figures contained in the report must be as of a specific date
IV. report must contain the complete portfolio list

A. I, II and III only
B. I and IV only
C. II, III and IV only
D. I, II, III and IV

15. A testimonial used by a member firm must state

A. the qualifications of the person giving the testimonial if a specialized or experienced opinion is implied
B. that past performance is not indicative of future performance and that other investors may not obtain comparable results
C. the fact that compensation was paid to the person giving the testimonial if such compensation was paid
D. all of the above

16. General communications by a broker-dealer firm, such as advertising or research reports, must be approved by which of the following?

A. Member
B. Principal of a member
C. Supervisory analyst
D. Certified financial analyst

17. Sales literature and advertising material that have been prepared by the firm's principal underwriter and are to be used by a member firm in connection with the offering of investment company shares must be reviewed by the

I. firm's advertising manager
II. NASD
III. SEC

A. I
B. I and II
C. II
D. II and III

◆ Answers & Rationale

1. **C.** Publications of a general nature (that is, not recommending securities or promoting a firm) are not considered advertising.   (Page 215)

2. **C.** Individual letters to customers of a specific nature are not considered advertisements.
    (Page 215)

3. **B.** The terms "advertising" and "sales literature" refer only to materials prepared for publication or broadcast to a mass audience or investors in general. Materials intended for internal use within a broker-dealer's organization are not considered advertising or sales literature—assuming, of course, that the firm keeps them away from customers.   (Page 215)

4. **C.** Advertising is any communication to the general public. Prospectuses are not considered advertising.   (Page 215)

5. **D.** All of the materials listed are considered as either sales literature or advertising when used in connection with the solicitation of variable life insurance.   (Page 215)

6. **B.** Form letters fall into the category of advertisements and must be approved by the principal or manager prior to use.   (Page 216)

7. **C.** Rule 9a-5 of the act of 1934 and the NASD's Rules of Fair Practice both prohibit the activities and inducements described in all of the choices except choice II. The rules on what is permissible cover promotional materials that are clearly distinguishable as paid advertising.
    (Page 216)

8. **B.** Recommendations made to a customer must be suitable for that customer.   (Page 217)

9. **D.** No investment is suitable for all investors. Statements about future prices and earnings may be used if they are clearly labeled as forecasts.   (Page 217)

10. **D.** All items listed here must be disclosed in advertisements recommending securities: the source of the recommendation, the security's price, any member firm interest in the security or the fact that the member firm is a market maker in the security.   (Page 218)

11. **A.** When referring to past recommendations, a member must show the whole universe of recommendations in the past year, not only the winners. A member must indicate whether the overall market was generally rising and the date and price of the security at the time of recommendation.   (Page 218)

12. **D.** Performance charts should cover a sufficient number of years to allow prospective buyers to evaluate a mutual fund's performance during good times as well as bad, which is why the NASD approves of ten-year performance histories. The NASD also believes that prospective buyers should be alerted as to whether a fund's performance is based on reinvestment of capital gains only or on reinvestment of capital gains and dividends. Further, for purposes of both reporting fairness and statistical consistency, yield and total return figures should be based on the maximum offering price during the period covered.   (Page 218)

13. **C.** Changes in NAV will be found in the prospectus for at least ten years if the fund has existed that long.   (Page 218)

14. **D.** The principal of the firm must approve the use of the annual report as sales literature, and the figures contained must be current and complete. A prospectus is always required.   (Page 218)

15. **D.** Testimonials must state whether the testimonial giver was paid, that the giver's experience may not be indicative of other investors' experience, and the qualifications of the giver if a specialized or experienced opinion is implied.
    (Page 219)

16. **B.** All advertising and other communications made by a broker-dealer must be approved by a qualified principal of the firm.   (Page 220)

17. **C.** All sales literature used in connection with a new offering must be filed for review with the NASD. A principal of the firm must approve its use and is responsible for corrections required by the NASD.   (Page 220)

43 Securities and Markets Exam

1. A company may pay dividends in which of the following ways?

   I. Stock of another company
   II. Cash
   III. Stock
   IV. Product

   A. I only
   B. II and III only
   C. III only
   D. I, II, III and IV

2. Which of the following actions is(are) the responsibility of an investment banker?

   I. Distributing large blocks of stock to the public and to institutions
   II. Buying previously unissued securities from an issuer and selling them to the public
   III. Raising long-term capital for corporations by underwriting new issues of securities
   IV. Lending money to corporate clients that require debt financing

   A. I, II and III only
   B. I, II and IV only
   C. III only
   D. I, II, III and IV

3. Which of the following is(are) the responsibility of an underwriter?

   I. Managing the distribution of large blocks of stock to the public and to institutions
   II. Selling a predetermined share of an offering to its customers
   III. Raising capital for corporations by assisting in the distribution of a corporation's new offering
   IV. Lending money to corporate clients that require debt financing

   A. I, II and III only
   B. I, II and IV only
   C. II only
   D. I, II, III and IV

4. An investment banker performs which of the following functions?

   I. Lending money to corporate clients requiring debt financing
   II. Buying securities from an issuer and reselling them to the public
   III. Raising long-term capital for corporations by underwriting new issues of securities

   A. I and II only
   B. I and III only
   C. II and III only
   D. I, II and III

5. Which of the following activities are characteristic of a primary offering?

    I.   Raising additional capital for the company
    II. Selling previously issued securities
    III. Increasing the number of shares or bonds outstanding

    A. I and II only
    B. I and III only
    C. II and III only
    D. I, II and III

6. When a customer gives a broker-dealer an order to buy securities, the broker-dealer may

    I.   act as the customer's agent by finding a seller and arranging the sale
    II. buy the securities, mark up the price and resell them to the customer on a dealer basis
    III. sell the shares from its own inventory to the customer if it has the security in inventory

    A. I only
    B. I and II only
    C. II and III only
    D. I, II and III

7. Which of the following statements describe a securities exchange?

    I.   The highest bid and the lowest offer prevail.
    II. Only listed securities can be traded.
    III. Minimum prices are established.

    A. I and II only
    B. I and III only
    C. II and III only
    D. I, II and III

8. A customer confirmation must

    I.   contain all relevant information concerning the trade
    II. be sent within 24 hours of the trade
    III. be sent by settlement of the trade
    IV. accompany the delivery of the stock certificate

    A. I
    B. I and III
    C. II
    D. II and IV

9. What is the function of Nasdaq?

    I.   It is a computerized system available to market makers allowing the subscriber to access bid and ask quotations and quotation sizes for all market makers in the OTC market.
    II. It is a computerized system available to market makers allowing them to complete trades in the OTC market.
    III. It is a computerized system allowing OTC market makers to complete transactions on the floor of the NYSE.
    IV. It is a computerized system allowing clients to trade directly with OTC market makers.

    A. I only
    B. II only
    C. II and III only
    D. I, II, III and IV

10. Stock rights (also called *subscription rights*) are

    I.   short-term instruments that become worthless after the expiration date
    II. most commonly offered in connection with debentures to sweeten the offering
    III. issued by a corporation
    IV. traded in the securities market

    A. I and II
    B. I and III
    C. I, III and IV
    D. II, III and IV

11. An owner of common stock has which of the following rights?

   I.   Right to determine when dividends will be issued

   II.   Right to vote at stockholders' meetings or by proxy

   III.   Right to receive a predetermined fixed portion of the corporation's profit in cash when declared

   IV.   Right to buy restricted securities before they are offered to the public

   A.   I, III and IV
   B.   II
   C.   II, III and IV
   D.   II and IV

12. Which of the following best describe warrants?

   I.   Short-term instruments that become worthless after the expiration date

   II.   Most commonly offered in connection with debentures to sweeten the offering

   III.   Issued by a corporation

   IV.   Traded in the securities market

   A.   I and II
   B.   I and III
   C.   I, III and IV
   D.   II, III and IV

13. An owner of preferred stock has which of the following rights?

   I.   Right to determine when dividends will be issued

   II.   Right to vote at stockholders' meetings or by proxy

   III.   Right to a predetermined fixed portion of the corporation's profit in cash when declared

   IV.   Right to buy restricted securities before they are offered to the public

   A.   I, III and IV
   B.   II, III and IV
   C.   II and IV
   D.   III

14. The ex-dividend date is the

   I.   date on and after which the buyer is entitled to the dividend

   II.   date on and after which the seller is entitled to the dividend

   III.   second business day prior to the record date

   IV.   second business day after the record date

   A.   I and III
   B.   I and IV
   C.   II and III
   D.   II and IV

15. A common stockholder's voting rights apply to which of the following?

   I.   Election of the board of directors

   II.   Declaration of dividends

   III.   Authorization or issue of more common shares

   A.   I only
   B.   I and III only
   C.   II and III only
   D.   I, II and III

16. Which of the following option investors are bearish?

   I.   Buyer of a call
   II.   Writer of a call
   III.   Buyer of a put
   IV.   Writer of a put

   A.   I and II
   B.   I and IV
   C.   II and III
   D.   III and IV

17. Belle tells her broker that she thinks the price of ALF is going to go up, but she does not have the money to buy 100 shares right now. How could she use options to profit from a rise in the stock's price?

    I.   Buy calls on ALF.
    II. Write calls on ALF.
    III. Buy puts on ALF.
    IV. Write puts on ALF.

    A. I and II
    B. I and IV
    C. II and III
    D. II and IV

18. Common stockholders' rights include a

    I.   residual claim to assets at dissolution
    II. vote for the amount of stock dividend to be paid
    III. vote in matters of recapitalization
    IV. claim against dividends that are in default

    A. I
    B. I and III
    C. II and III
    D. III and IV

19. Rank the following government securities according to the length of their maturities, from longest to shortest.

    I.   Notes
    II. Bills
    III. Bonds

    A. I, II, III
    B. II, I, III
    C. III, I, II
    D. III, II, I

20. Which of the following statements about debentures are true?

    I.   They are secured by a mortgage or a lien.
    II. They are secured by the good faith of the issuing corporation.
    III. They are considered to be a safer investment than preferred stock.
    IV. They have a senior claim to the corporation's assets when compared to common stock.

    A. I and III only
    B. II, III and IV only
    C. II and IV only
    D. I, II, III and IV

21. Which of the following statements about a bond selling above par value is(are) true?

    I.   The nominal yield is lower than the current yield.
    II. The yield to maturity is lower than the nominal yield.
    III. The yield to maturity is lower than the current yield.
    IV. The nominal yield always stays the same.

    A. I and IV only
    B. II, III and IV only
    C. III only
    D. I, II, III and IV

22. Which of the following statements is(are) true of Treasury bills?

    I.   They are sold at a discount.
    II. They pay a fixed rate of interest semiannually.
    III. They mature in one year or less.
    IV. They mature in ten years or more.

    A. I, II and III
    B. I and III
    C. II and IV
    D. III

23. The interest from which of the following bonds is exempt from federal income tax?

    I.   State of California bonds
    II. City of Anchorage bonds
    III. Treasury bonds
    IV. GNMA bonds

    A. I and II only
    B. I, II and IV only
    C. III and IV only
    D. I, II, III and IV

24. Which of the following are money-market instruments?

    I.   Bankers' acceptances
    II. Treasury bills
    III. Commercial paper
    IV. Treasury bonds maturing in six months

    A. I and II only
    B. I, II and III only
    C. III and IV only
    D. I, II, III and IV

25. Which of the following statements about mortgage bonds are true?

    I.   They are secured by a mortgage or a lien.
    II. They are secured by the good faith of the issuing corporation.
    III. They are considered to be a safer investment than preferred stock.
    IV. They have a senior claim to the corporation's assets when compared to common stock.

    A. I and III only
    B. II, III and IV only
    C. II and IV only
    D. I, II, III and IV

26. Which of the following statements about a bond selling below par value is(are) true?

    I.   The nominal yield is lower than the current yield.
    II. The yield to maturity is lower than the nominal yield.
    III. The yield to maturity is lower than the current yield.
    IV. The nominal yield always stays the same.

    A. I and IV only
    B. II, III and IV only
    C. III only
    D. I, II, III and IV

27. Which of the following statements is(are) true of Treasury bonds?

    I.   They are sold at a discount.
    II. They pay a fixed rate of interest semiannually.
    III. They mature in one year or less.
    IV. They mature in ten years or more.

    A. I, II and III
    B. I and III
    C. II and IV
    D. III

28. Karen Kodiak lives in Detroit, Michigan. She is interested in purchasing bonds that are exempt from state income tax. The interest from which of the following bonds is exempt from Michigan state income tax?

    I.   State of California bonds
    II. Michigan Toll Authority bonds
    III. Treasury bills
    IV. Treasury bonds

    A. I and II only
    B. I and IV only
    C. II, III and IV only
    D. I, II, III and IV

29. Which of the following would NOT be considered money-market instruments?

   I.   Debentures rated Aaa
   II. Treasury notes
   III. Commercial paper
   IV. Treasury bonds maturing in six months

   A. I and II only
   B. I and III only
   C. II, III and IV only
   D. I, II, III and IV

30. Which of the following statements about corporate bonds are true?

   I.   They represent ownership in the corporation.
   II. They generally involve less market risk than common stock.
   III. They pay a variable rate of income.
   IV. They usually mature ten or more years after issue.

   A. I and III only
   B. II and III only
   C. II and IV only
   D. I, II, III and IV

31. Collateral trust bonds may be secured by

   I.   real property of the issuing corporation
   II. equity and debt securities of a subsidiary corporation
   III. equity and debt securities of another corporation
   IV. installment payments based on the corporation's accounts receivable

   A. I
   B. II
   C. II or III
   D. II or IV

32. Belle Charolais owns several Series EE bonds. She wishes to redeem them after three years. She would

   I.   pay federal income tax on the interest she has earned
   II. sell them through her broker
   III. receive the same rate of interest as she would have had she held the bonds to maturity

   A. I only
   B. I and II only
   C. II and III only
   D. I, II and III

33. Which of the following statements about general obligation municipal bonds are true?

   I.   They are second only to U.S. government bonds in safety of principal.
   II. They are backed by the taxing power of the municipality.
   III. They are nonmarketable.
   IV. They pay higher interest rates than corporate debt securities.

   A. I and II
   B. I and IV
   C. II and III
   D. II, III and IV

34. Corporate bonds are considered safer than corporate stock issued by the same company because

   I.   bonds represent equity in the company
   II. the company is more likely to back the original investors
   III. bonds are senior to common stock
   IV. the holder of a corporate bond is a debtor to the company

   A. I and II
   B. II, III and IV
   C. III
   D. III and IV

35. Which of the following securities is(are) issued with a fixed rate of return?

    I. Bonds
    II. Preferred stock
    III. Common stock
    IV. Convertible preferred stock

    A. I, II and IV only
    B. III only
    C. IV only
    D. I, II, III and IV

36. Municipal bonds are issued as either revenue bonds or general obligation bonds. The characteristics of general obligation bonds are

    I. interest from general obligation bonds is exempt from federal income taxes
    II. interest is payable only from the revenue of the facility being financed
    III. these bonds do not have to carry a legal opinion of counsel
    IV. the principal of these bonds is backed by the full faith and credit of the issuing municipality

    A. I and II only
    B. I and IV only
    C. II and IV only
    D. I, II, III and IV

37. Cities and states issue both revenue bonds and general obligation bonds. Which of the following are characteristics of revenue bonds?

    I. Interest from revenue bonds is exempt from federal income taxes.
    II. Interest is payable only from the revenue of the facility being financed.
    III. These bonds do not have to carry a legal opinion of counsel.
    IV. The principal of these bonds is payable only from the revenue of the facility being financed.

    A. I and II only
    B. I, II and IV only
    C. IV only
    D. I, II, III and IV

38. Which of the following bonds would qualify as a municipal bond?

    I. General obligation bond of the City of Denver
    II. Revenue bond issued by the City of Detroit to build the Joe Louis Arena
    III. Sewer bond issued by Cook County, Illinois
    IV. Highway bond issued by the State of New Mexico

    A. I only
    B. I and II only
    C. II and III only
    D. I, II, III and IV

39. Which of the following statements is(are) true of a Treasury STRIP?

    I. The rate of return is locked in.
    II. There is no reinvestment risk.
    III. The interest is taxed as a capital gain.
    IV. The interest is realized at maturity.

    A. I
    B. I, II and III
    C. I, II and IV
    D. IV

40. TCBS currently has earnings of $4 and pays a $.50 quarterly dividend. The market price of TCBS is $40. What is the current yield?

    A. 1.25%
    B. 5%
    C. 10%
    D. 15%

41. If interest rates are increasing and the market prices of bonds are decreasing, what happens to the value of preferred stock during this period?

    A. Its value increases.
    B. Its value decreases.
    C. Its value remains the same.
    D. Interest rates and the price of bonds have no impact on the value of stock.

42. An investor will be in a position to acquire stock under which of the following circumstances?

    I.   She is a buyer of a call.
    II. She is a buyer of a put.
    III. She is a seller of a call.
    IV. She is a seller of a put.

    A. I and III
    B. I and IV
    C. II and III
    D. II and IV

◆ Answers & Rationale

1. **D.** A company may pay a dividend in any of the ways listed. (Page 4)

2. **A.** "Investment bankers" is another term for "broker-dealers." They do everything listed except lend money to corporate clients that require debt financing. (Page 41)

3. **A.** An underwriter manages the offering and helps the corporation to raise capital. (Page 42)

4. **C.** An investment banker is a broker-dealer acting to help an issuer raise money in the capital or money markets. In a firm commitment underwriting, the broker-dealer purchases the securities for resale. An investment banker is not a commercial bank and does not make loans. (Page 41)

5. **B.** A primary offering involves the sale of previously unissued securities. The issuing company receives the proceeds from the sale. Of course, once the securities are sold, there will be more securities outstanding and in the hands of the public. (Page 42)

6. **D.** The broker-dealer can buy and sell securities either as an agent, charging a commission on a transaction and having no risk, or as a dealer, charging a markup or markdown and sharing the risk. (Page 40)

7. **A.** An exchange is an auction market in which securities listed on that exchange are traded. There is no minimum price for securities; rather, the highest price bid and the lowest price offered prevail. Trading activity on the exchanges as well as on the OTC market is regulated by the Securities Exchange Act of 1934. (Page 38)

8. **B.** A customer confirmation must contain information on price, quantity, identity and commission or markup and must be sent by settlement. Broker-to-broker confirmations must be sent within 24 hours (the day of or the day after the trade). (Page 44)

9. **A.** Nasdaq is available on three levels of service, but it is primarily a method for obtaining information on prices (bid and ask) and inventories of OTC-traded securities. (Page 37)

10. **C.** Rights are issued by the corporation that give the subscriber the right to purchase stock within a short period of time at a price lower than the stock's current market price. Rights do not have to be exercised but may be traded in the secondary market. Warrants are commonly used as a sweetener in debenture offerings. (Page 21)

11. **B.** The stockholder has the right to vote and the right to dividends if and when declared (although not to a fixed dividend). A restricted security is one that has prescribed limits on resale generally requiring registration. (Page 5)

12. **D.** Warrants are commonly used as a sweetener in debenture offerings and carry a long life. Rights are issued by the corporation to give the subscriber the right to purchase stock within a short period of time at a price lower than the stock's current market price. Warrants do not have to be exercised but may be traded in the secondary market. (Page 21)

13. **D.** The preferred stockholder generally has no right to vote but carries a prior right to dividends if and when declared. A restricted security is one that has prescribed limits on resale generally requiring registration. (Page 7)

14. **C.** Stocks sold on the ex-dividend date entitle the seller to the dividend. Stocks sell ex-dividend two business days before the record date. (Page 46)

15. **B.** Common stockholders may elect the board of directors (which only indirectly influences the policy on payment of dividends) and may vote on issues concerning the company's capitalization (such as the issuance of more common stock). (Page 5)

16. **C.**   Options investors who are in a position to sell the stock (put buyers and call writers) have a bearish outlook. Remember that diagonal positions (those positions that are total opposites, such as buys versus sells and puts versus calls) are on the same side of the market.   (Page 22)

17. **B.**   The bullish strategies are buying calls and writing puts.   (Page 22)

18. **B.**   As the corporation's owners, common stockholders would have the lowest claim against a company's assets at dissolution or bankruptcy. The owners of cumulative preferred stock have a claim against any dividends that are in default. Holders of common stock are entitled to vote on matters that affect their proportionate ownership. Recapitalization—the alteration of a corporation's capital structure—is an example of a situation that requires a vote of the stockholders.   (Page 5)

19. **C.**   Treasury bills mature in less than a year, notes mature in from one to ten years and bonds mature in more than ten years.   (Page 25)

20. **B.**   Debentures are secured by the good faith and credit of the issuing corporation. They are senior to stock ownership, have a senior claim to assets and are considered a safer investment.   (Page 12)

21. **B.**   Nominal yield is fixed and stays the same on all bonds. A bond selling above par is selling at a premium, so the current yield and yield to maturity will be less than the nominal yield.   (Page 16)

22. **B.**   T bills are sold at a discount and have maturities of up to one year. Although they mature at face value, it is not considered interest.   (Page 25)

23. **A.**   Municipal bonds are exempt from federal income tax. Treasury bonds are exempt from state tax. GNMAs are subject to federal and state income tax.   (Page 31)

24. **D.**   Money markets are made up of short-term high-yield debt issues. All of the items listed here are considered short term—even the Treasury bonds, since they are maturing within six months.   (Page 36)

25. **D.**   Mortgage bonds are secured by the good faith and credit of the issuing corporation evidenced by a pledge of real estate or a similar asset. They are senior to stock ownership, have a senior claim to assets over other debt issues and are considered a safer investment.   (Page 11)

26. **A.**   Nominal yield is fixed and stays the same on all bonds. A bond selling below par is selling at a discount, so the current yield and yield to maturity will be greater than the nominal yield.   (Page 16)

27. **C.**   T bonds are sold at par and pay interest semiannually. They are issued with maturities of ten years or more.   (Page 26)

28. **C.**   Municipal bonds are exempt from federal income tax and from state tax only within the state of issue. U.S. Treasury issues are subject to federal income tax, but would be exempt from state taxes. The California bond would be exempt from state tax in California but not in Michigan.   (Page 31)

29. **A.**   Money markets are made up of short-term high-yield debt issues. Because the Treasury bond is maturing in less than a year, it is also considered a money-market instrument. The debenture and Treasury note are long-term instruments.   (Page 36)

30. **C.**   Bonds represent a creditor relationship; stock represents an ownership interest. Normally bonds are issued with a stated rate of interest and mature in ten or more years.   (Page 57)

31. **C.**   A collateral trust bond is backed by securities of a subsidiary corporation or another company's securities. A mortgage bond is backed by real property.   (Page 11)

32. **A.**   A Series EE bond is a nonnegotiable instrument. The bond is redeemed by the government (usually through a bank). The interest re-

ceived by the bondholder will be less if the bond is redeemed prior to maturity. The difference between purchase price and redemption value represents interest, which is taxable at the federal level.

(Page 27)

33. **A.** General obligation bonds are backed by the general taxing authority of the municipal issuer. As such, they are often considered very safe investments. Municipal issues are marketable and are bought and sold in the secondary marketplace. Because interest received on municipal debt is exempt from federal taxation, yields offered on municipal debt are lower than yields offered on corporate debt.   (Page 32)

34. **C.** A bond represents a legal obligation to repay principal and interest by the company. The holder of a corporate bond is a *creditor* of the company.   (Page 9)

35. **A.** Bonds and preferred stock are typically issued with a stated payment, either in interest or dividends. Common stockholders are entitled to receive a variable distribution of profits if and when a dividend is declared.   (Page 14)

36. **B.** All municipal bonds must carry a legal opinion of counsel affirming that the issue is a municipal issue and interest is exempt from federal taxation. Interest and principal of a revenue bond will be paid only if the facility financed produces the revenue necessary to pay. A GO is a municipal issue backed by the full faith and credit of the municipality.   (Page 32)

37. **B.** A revenue bond is a municipal issue sold to raise funds for the purpose of constructing a revenue-producing facility. All municipal bonds require an opinion of specialized bond counsel stating that the issue does indeed represent a mu-

nicipal obligation and that interest payments are exempt from federal taxation. The interest and principal payments are backed to the extent the facility produces enough revenue to make payments.   (Page 33)

38. **D.** Any bond issued by a state, municipality or governmental unit other than the federal government is categorized as a municipal issue.

(Page 32)

39. **C.** A STRIP has no reinvestment risk because there are no interest payments to have at risk in regards to reinvestment. Because there is no reinvestment risk, the total rate of return is locked in or set at issuance. The interest on the bond is paid at maturity, but it is taxed as interest income over the life of the bond.   (Page 13)

40. **B.** The quarterly dividend is $.50; therefore, the annual dividend is $2.00. $2 divided by $40 (market price) equals 5% annual yield (current yield).   (Page 4)

41. **B.** Preferred stocks are interest rate sensitive as are other fixed-interest rate investment vehicles such as bonds. Because the dividend amount is fixed, if interest rates are increasing, the return provided by the dividend may be less than the return provided by other investments. The value of preferred stock will decrease.   (Page 7)

42. **D.** Warrants are commonly used as a sweetener in debenture offerings and carry a long life. Rights are issued by the corporation to give the subscriber the right to purchase stock within a short period of time at a price lower than the stock's current market price. Warrants do not have to be exercised but may be traded in the secondary market.   (Page 21)

 **44** Investment Companies Exam

1. Which of the following statements about open-end investment companies are true?

   I. They may constantly issue new shares.
   II. They redeem shares at any time.
   III. They may leverage common shares by issuing bonds.

   A. I and II only
   B. I and III only
   C. II and III only
   D. I, II and III

2. Lotta Leveridge owns 150 shares of ArGood Mutual Fund. Which of the following statements are true?

   I. When a dividend is declared by the fund, she will receive a cash dividend for each share owned.
   II. She will have difficulty liquidating her shares.
   III. The amount of her dividend will reflect her proportional interest in the value of the fund portfolio on the record date.
   IV. She will receive dividends from only 150 shares of stock held in the fund portfolio.

   A. I, II and IV
   B. I and III
   C. II and III
   D. II, III and IV

3. Mutual funds are like other types of corporations in that

   I. they may issue equity and debt
   II. their boards of directors make policy decisions
   III. shareholders have ownership rights

   A. I and III only
   B. II only
   C. II and III only
   D. I, II and III

4. ALFA Financial Services charges a fee for its services in managing several mutual funds. Which of the following would be included in the services ALFA supplies?

   I. Ensuring that the fund portfolio meets diversification requirements
   II. Attempting to meet the investment objectives of the fund
   III. Analyzing the market and deciding when securities in the portfolio should be bought or sold
   IV. Changing investment objectives in order to maximize potential gain for the shareholders

   A. I, II and III only
   B. I and III only
   C. II and III only
   D. I, II, III and IV

5. June Polar is explaining mutual funds to a prospective investor. Which of the following statements may she use in her conversation with the client?

    I. "Mutual fund shares are liquid, so an investor can use them as either short-term or long-term investments."

    II. "Mutual funds always redeem shares at NAV, so there is very little chance of a financial loss."

    III. "The redemption value of mutual fund shares fluctuates according to the value of the fund's portfolio."

    IV. "Because mutual funds are required to make payment within seven days of redemption, you will always be able to receive a return of your original investment."

    A. I, II and IV
    B. I and III
    C. III
    D. III and IV

6. A client comes to you for advice regarding the investment company in which he should invest. You should tell him to check the company's

    I. investment policy
    II. track record
    III. portfolio
    IV. sales load

    A. I, II and III only
    B. I and III only
    C. IV only
    D. I, II, III and IV

7. Which of the following would probably be found in the portfolio of a money-market fund?

    I. T bills
    II. T bonds with a short time to maturity
    III. Bank certificates of deposit
    IV. Common stock

    A. I
    B. I and II
    C. I, II and III
    D. II, III and IV

8. Which of the following would be classified as an investment company?

    I. Closed-end company
    II. Open-end company
    III. Qualified plan company
    IV. Fixed annuity company

    A. I and II
    B. I, II and IV
    C. II
    D. III and IV

9. According to the Investment Company Act of 1940

    I. a company must have $1 million in assets before it may begin operations

    II. at least 40% of the board of directors may not be affiliated or hold a position with the fund

    III. the fund must have at least 100 shareholders

    IV. the fund may not borrow more than 33 1/3% of its asset value

    A. I and III only
    B. II, III and IV only
    C. II and IV only
    D. I, II, III and IV

10. Which of the following is(are) characteristic of money-market funds?

    I.   Portfolio of short-term debt instruments
    II.   High beta
    III. Offered without a sales load
    IV.   Fixed NAV

    A. I
    B. I, II and IV
    C. I, III and IV
    D. II, III and IV

11. When the ACE Fund, an open-end investment company, issues and sells new shares, it must comply with the requirements of the

    I.   Securities Act of 1933
    II.   Securities Exchange Act of 1934
    III. Investment Company Act of 1940

    A. I and II only
    B. I and III only
    C. II and III only
    D. I, II and III

12. According to the Investment Company Act of 1940, which of the following are required of investment companies?

    I.   Investment company registration statement filed with the SEC
    II.   Minimum net worth of $100,000 before the offer of shares to the public
    III. Statement of investment policies and of diversification status

    A. I and II only
    B. I and III only
    C. II and III only
    D. I, II and III

13. If Joe Kuhl fails to make payment for the XYZ Mutual Fund shares within the required amount of time, the broker-dealer could

    I.   cancel the order
    II.   fine Joe based on the dollar amount of the sale
    III. sell the securities and charge Joe for any loss

    A. I and II only
    B. I and III only
    C. III only
    D. I, II and III

14. Unrealized gain in a mutual fund portfolio

    I.   affects the value of mutual fund shares
    II.   is the growth in market value of securities held in the portfolio
    III. is realized by shareholders only when they redeem their shares

    A. I and II only
    B. I and III only
    C. II and III only
    D. I, II and III

15. The conduit theory of taxation means that the

    I.   fund is not taxed on earnings it distributes
    II.   retained earnings are taxed as regular corporate income
    III. earnings distributed by a regulated mutual fund are taxed twice

    A. I and II only
    B. I and III only
    C. II and III only
    D. I, II and III

16. ACE Fund invests all of its assets in municipal bonds. This means that

   I. shareholders do not pay federal taxes on dividend distributions
   II. the fund is not subject to federal tax on any interest earnings it retains
   III. shareholders pay all taxes at the preferential capital gains rate

   A. I and II only
   B. I and III only
   C. II and III only
   D. I, II and III

17. Which of the following statements are true of a mutual fund dividend distribution?

   I. The fund pays dividends from net income.
   II. A single taxpayer may exclude $100 worth of dividend income from taxes annually.
   III. An investor is liable for taxes on the distribution, whether it is a cash distribution or reinvested in the fund.
   IV. An investor is liable for taxes only if the distribution is received in cash.

   A. I and II
   B. I, II and III
   C. I and III
   D. II and IV

18. Clara Bullock and Klaus Bruin each has an open account in the ArGood Mutual Fund. Clara has decided to receive all distributions in cash, while Klaus is automatically reinvesting all distributions. How do their decisions affect their investments?

   I. Cash distributions may reduce Clara's proportional interest in the fund.
   II. Clara may use the cash distributions to purchase shares later at NAV.
   III. Klaus's reinvestments purchase additional shares at NAV rather than at the offering price.

   A. I and II only
   B. I and III only
   C. II and III only
   D. I, II and III

19. Which of the following characteristics are true of a contractual planholder?

   I. She receives a plan certificate.
   II. She owns a specific share of the underlying mutual fund shares.
   III. She owns specific shares of securities in the underlying mutual fund's portfolio.
   IV. She must complete the contractual plan.

   A. I and II
   B. I and III
   C. II and IV
   D. III and IV

20. Which of the following statements describe contractual plans?

   I. They cannot be sold in certain states.
   II. They do not obligate the planholder to complete the contracted number of payments.
   III. They have a predetermined fixed schedule of sales charges.

   A. I and II only
   B. I and III only
   C. II and III only
   D. I, II and III

21. Under the Uniform Gifts to Minors Act, you can

    I.   give an unlimited amount of cash
    II. give securities
    III. give up to $10,000 cash
    IV. revoke a gift

    A. I
    B. I and II
    C. I, II and IV
    D. II and III

22. Concerning a fixed-time withdrawal plan offered by a mutual fund

    I.   the amount received each month by the client may vary
    II. a fixed number of shares will be liquidated each month
    III. not all funds offer this type of withdrawal
    IV. this plan is self-exhausting

    A. I
    B. I and II
    C. I, III and IV
    D. II, III and IV

23. Which of the following withdrawal plans offered by the ArGood Mutual Fund will pay the client a fixed monthly payment?

    I.   Fixed-dollar withdrawal
    II. Fixed-percentage withdrawal
    III. Fixed-share withdrawal
    IV. Liquidation over a fixed period of time

    A. I only
    B. II and III only
    C. II, III and IV only
    D. I, II, III and IV

24. In a mutual fund, a shareholder who elects not to receive share certificates can liquidate all or a portion of his holdings and receive payment from the fund if the fund receives which of the following?

    I.   Written request from the shareholder
    II. Signed stock power from the shareholder
    III. Signature guarantee from the shareholder

    A. I
    B. I and II
    C. I and III
    D. II and III

25. Which of the following are characteristic of a mutual fund voluntary accumulation plan?

    I.   Minimum initial purchase
    II. Minimum optional additional purchases
    III. Declining sales charges on new investment as money accumulates
    IV. Obligatory purchase goal

    A. I and II only
    B. I, II and III only
    C. II and IV only
    D. I, II, III and IV

26. Which of the following characteristics describe(s) a contractual planholder?

    I.   He receives unit trust certificates.
    II. He owns an undivided interest in the mutual fund shares underlying the plan.
    III. He owns an undivided interest in the portfolio of the underlying mutual fund.

    A. I and II
    B. I and III
    C. II and III
    D. III

27. A customer opens a new cash account. Which of the following signatures is(are) required before orders can be executed?

    I.   Customer
    II. Registered representative
    III. Registered principal

    A. I only
    B. I and II only
    C. II and III only
    D. I, II and III

28. A change in which of the following should be indicated in a customer's file?

    I.   Name or address
    II. Marital status
    III. Objectives

    A. I only
    B. I and II only
    C. III only
    D. I, II and III

29. The investment adviser in a regulated, diversified open-end investment company will perform which of the following functions?

    I.   Make sure the fund invests in such a manner as to retain its diversified status.
    II. Attempt to fulfill the fund's investment objective through careful investing.
    III. Change investment objectives as he believes is in the best interest of the investors.
    IV. Investigate the tax status of potential investments.

    A. I, II and III
    B. I, II and IV
    C. II and IV
    D. III and IV

30. June Polar wants to buy $1,000 worth of an open-end investment company. She may buy shares through

    I.   the sponsor of the fund
    II. a brokerage firm
    III. the custodian of the fund
    IV. a bank acting as dealer

    A. I and II
    B. I, II and IV
    C. II
    D. III and IV

31. The ACE Fund experienced an unrealized loss last month. This loss will

    I.   result in a lower NAV per share
    II. mean lower dividend payments to shareholders
    III. reduce the proceeds payable to shareholders who liquidate their shares

    A. I and II only
    B. I and III only
    C. II and III only
    D. I, II and III

32. You notice that the total assets of ALFA, a regulated open-end investment company, went down 28% last year. You also notice that the stock in which ALFA deposited its capital did very well. Lastly, you notice that ALFA holds a large number of bonds. Which two of the following most likely occurred?

    I.   ALFA was holding too much cash.
    II. Interest rates went up.
    III. ALFA paid huge commissions to agents for their extra sales effort.
    IV. A large number of ALFA shares was redeemed.

    A. I and II
    B. I and III
    C. II and III
    D. II and IV

33. Which of the following statements about sales charges is(are) true?

    I. Under NASD rules, mutual fund sales charges may not exceed 8.5% of the offering price.

    II. Under NASD rules, mutual fund sales charges may not exceed 8.5% of the share's net asset value.

    III. An investment company must offer rights of accumulation, breakpoints and reinvestment of dividends at NAV in order to charge an 8.5% sales charge.

    IV. Under the Investment Company Act of 1940, the maximum sales charge for purchases of mutual fund shares under a contractual plan is 9%.

    A. I
    B. I and III
    C. I, III and IV
    D. II, III and IV

34. The offering price of the ACE Fund is $9, and its net asset value is $9.40. The offering price of the GEM Fund is $23.80, and its net asset value is $19.45. From these quotes you know that

    I. ACE is an open-end fund
    II. ACE is a closed-end fund
    III. GEM is an open-end fund
    IV. GEM is a closed-end fund

    A. I and III
    B. I and IV
    C. II and III
    D. II and IV

35. The NAV of an open-end investment company

    I. is calculated seven days a week
    II. is calculated as stipulated in the prospectus
    III. takes into account cash held by the fund but not invested
    IV. when divided by the number of shares outstanding equals the net asset value per share

    A. I and IV
    B. II, III and IV
    C. II and IV
    D. III

36. Which of the following characteristics describe the net asset value per share?

    I. Increases if the assets of the fund appreciate in value
    II. Decreases if the fund distributes a dividend to shareholders
    III. Decreases when shares are redeemed
    IV. Increases if shareholders reinvest dividend and capital gains distributions

    A. I and II
    B. I and III
    C. II and III
    D. II and IV

37. Under what circumstances could a mutual fund temporarily suspend the redemption provision?

    I. If the New York Stock Exchange is closed on days other than customary weekends and holidays
    II. If permitted by the SEC
    III. If an emergency condition exists and then only with SEC approval
    IV. At the discretion of the investment company management

    A. I, II and III only
    B. II and III only
    C. II, III and IV only
    D. I, II, III and IV

38. In order for a registered investment company to implement a 12b-1 plan, the plan must be approved by a majority of the

 I. outstanding voting shares of the company
 II. board of directors
 III. uninterested members of the board of directors
 IV. investment advisory board

 A. I
 B. I and II
 C. I, II and III
 D. II, III and IV

39. To qualify for the quantity discount, which of the following could NOT be joined together under the definition of "any person"?

 I. Father and his 35-year-old son investing in separate accounts
 II. Husband and wife investing in a joint account
 III. Husband and wife investing in a separate account
 IV. Trust officer working on behalf of a single trust account

 A. I
 B. II, III and IV
 C. II and IV
 D. III and IV

◆ Answers & Rationale

1. **A.** An open-end company must stand ready to redeem shares within seven days of receiving a customer's request and may continuously offer its shares for sale. Although an open-end company may invest in just about any security, it may issue only one class of voting stock. The company cannot issue any type of debt. (Page 76)

2. **B.** A mutual fund share represents an undivided interest in the fund's portfolio. If a dividend is declared, the shareholder receives a dividend for each mutual fund share held. Dividends are paid in cash unless the shareholder elects to reinvest the cash distribution for the purchase of more fund shares. (Page 111)

3. **C.** Mutual funds may issue only one class of voting stock. Like corporate stockholders, mutual fund shareholders have various rights, one of which is the right to elect the board of directors, which sets policies for the fund. (Page 90)

4. **A.** The objective of the mutual fund may be changed only by a majority vote of the outstanding shares. The fund manager is assigned the day-to-day management responsibilities of the fund. Duties would include attempting to meet the objective as set out by the fund and buying and selling securities to be held in the portfolio. (Page 91)

5. **C.** Mutual funds are very marketable, but because of the sales charge, they are recommended for long-term investments. Shares are redeemed at NAV; however, the NAV will fluctuate, and upon redemption the investor may have more or less money than originally invested. (Page 97)

6. **D.** All of these elements listed should be disclosed when comparing funds. (Page 85)

7. **C.** Money-market instruments are considered short-term, very liquid debt instruments. Because common stock is equity, it would not be in a money-market fund. (Page 83)

8. **A.** Open- and closed-end funds are classified as investment companies. Plan companies offer plans in which an investment company may be selected as an investment vehicle but are not investment companies themselves. Fixed annuities are offered by insurance companies only. (Page 75)

9. **B.** A company must have commitments for at least $100,000 in assets before it begins. All of the other statements are true. (Page 88)

10. **C.** Money-market mutual funds invest in portfolios of short-term debt instruments such as T bills, commercial paper and repos. They are offered without a sales load or charge. The principal objective of such funds is to generate current interest income, and generally the NAV does not appreciate. (Page 83)

11. **D.** A mutual fund issuing shares must comply with the Securities Act of 1933 (registration) and the Investment Company Act of 1940 (one class of security, type of investment company). The Securities Exchange Act of 1934 deals with the people who sell the shares and the markets in which the shares are sold but also details anti-fraud requirements that must be observed by investment companies. (Page 89)

12. **D.** The Investment Company Act of 1940 requires registration of funds and a minimum initial net worth of $100,000, at least 100 shareholders and a specifically defined investment objective. (Page 87)

13. **C.** If Joe fails to pay for the shares within five business days, the broker-dealer must sell the shares to pay for the transaction. Any gain or loss will be settled between the broker-dealer and Joe. The order has taken place and cannot be canceled. (Page 44)

14. **D.** Unrealized gains in portfolio securities are the result of the asset's appreciation in value. This appreciation in value will be reflected in an appreciation of the mutual fund shares themselves. A shareholder wanting to cash in on this appreciation can do so only by selling the shares (realizing the gain). (Page 112)

15. **D.** By qualifying as a regulated investment company (the conduit, or pipeline, tax theory), the fund is liable for taxes only on the income retained. The investor benefits because the income is taxed only twice (at the corporate level and at the individual level) and not three times (also at the fund level).   (Page 112)

16. **A.** A municipal bond fund derives its income from interest paid from the municipal bonds held, which is exempt from federal income tax.
                                     (Page 82)

17. **C.** Funds pay dividends from net income, and the investor is liable for taxes on all distributions. The $100 annual exclusion was eliminated with the new tax code.   (Page 113)

18. **B.** By electing to receive distributions in cash while others are purchasing shares through reinvestment, Clara is lowering her proportional interest in the fund. Most funds allow reinvestment of dividends at net asset value. Cash invested is considered a new purchase, and the shares will be purchased at the public offering price, not NAV.
                                     (Page 115)

19. **A.** An individual investing in a contractual plan receives a certificate evidencing ownership of shares held in trust by the plan company. Remember, plan companies are unit investment trusts that invest in shares of mutual funds. The planholder owns units in the trust, not specific shares of the mutual fund.   (Page 116)

20. **D.** The contractual plan is not legal in several states; the contract is unilateral (only the company is bound); and the prospectus will detail the specific charges to be deducted from each payment over the life of the plan.   (Page 116)

21. **B.** There is no limit to the size of the gift that may be transferred under a Uniform Gifts to Minors Act account. The $10,000 is the gift tax exclusion and relates only to the amount of the gift that may be subject to tax.   (Page 130)

22. **C.** A fixed-time withdrawal plan is considered self-liquidating. Only the time is fixed; the number of shares liquidated, the amount of money received and the percentage of the account liquidated will vary from period to period. Funds may or may not offer withdrawal plans. If they do, the prospectus will describe information concerning the plans.   (Page 121)

23. **A.** In a withdrawal plan, if one variable is fixed, such as fixed dollar, all other aspects of the payment will vary. If a client is receiving a fixed-dollar payment, the plan must be a fixed-dollar plan.   (Page 121)

24. **C.** Orders for redemption without a certificate being issued require a written request and signature guarantee.   (Page 105)

25. **B.** A voluntary accumulation plan is voluntary, not binding. The company may require that the initial investment meet a certain minimum dollar amount. It may also specify that any additions meet set minimums (for example, $50). The sales charge is level, and the plan may qualify for breakpoints based on the accumulated value. (Page 115)

26. **A.** A contractual plan buys mutual fund shares, to hold in trust. The planholder then owns an undivided interest in the mutual fund shares, as evidenced by the unit trust certificate(s).
                                     (Page 116)

27. **C.** When a customer opens a new account, the card is signed by the registered rep introducing the customer to the firm and by the principal, who is accepting the customer for the firm. The customer is not required to sign the new account card. The customer's signature is required only on a margin account.   (Page 124)

28. **D.** All information that affects a registered rep's recommendations or the financial situation of a customer must be noted immediately in the file.
                                     (Page 124)

29. **B.** The investment adviser is responsible for making investments according to the objective stipulated by the fund. The fund's objective may be changed only with a majority vote of the outstanding shares.   (Page 91)

30. **A.** The custodian does not sell the shares but holds them for safekeeping. A bank cannot be a member of the NASD and therefore cannot act as a dealer (although subsidiaries independent of the bank may be set up as broker-dealers). (Page 96)

31. **B.** An unrealized loss is the same as a depreciation in asset value, which results in a lower NAV per share. A shareholder would receive less at redemption than he would have received if redemption took place prior to the depreciation of the asset. (Page 97)

32. **D.** Because ALFA has a portfolio composed of bonds, if interest rates increase, the value of the bonds will decline. If shares are redeemed, the value of the portfolio will decline as the money is paid out. Commissions are paid from sales charges collected; they are not an expense of the fund. (Page 16)

33. **C.** The NASD limits sales charges to 8.5% of the POP as a maximum. If the fund does not allow for breakpoints, reinvestment of dividends at net, or rights of accumulation, the maximum is less than 8.5%. Under the Investment Company Act of 1940, the maximum sales charge on mutual funds is deferred to the NASD rules, while a contractual plan specifically may charge 9% over the life of the plan. (Page 117)

34. **D.** The ACE Fund is selling below its net asset value, so it must be a closed-end fund. GEM is selling above its NAV by more than the 8 1/2%

sales load allowed, so it also must be a closed-end fund. (Page 104)

35. **B.** NAV must be calculated at least every business day but not on weekends or holidays. It takes into account all of the fund's assets and is arrived at by totaling the assets and dividing that amount by the number of shares outstanding. (Page 97)

36. **A.** Share prices increase when assets in the portfolio increase in value. Share prices decrease when the fund distributes a dividend, as the shareholder will receive either cash or additional shares. Redeeming or purchasing shares does not affect share prices, only total assets. Reinvesting dividends or capital gains has no effect on share prices either. (Page 97)

37. **A.** The seven-day redemption guideline is law and may be suspended only with SEC permission or if the NYSE is closed on a day other than customary holidays and weekends. (Page 105)

38. **C.** A 12b-1 plan must be approved by a majority vote of the shareholders, board of directors and uninterested members of the board of directors. The fee must be reapproved annually. (Page 100)

39. **A.** For the purpose of qualifying for breakpoints, the definition of "person" includes family units—but only minor children, not someone 35 years old. (Page 102)

45 Variable Contracts and Retirement Planning Exam

1. To register new securities, an investment company must

   I. supply detailed information about itself to the SEC
   II. supply detailed information about the new securities to the SEC
   III. obtain the SEC's approval of the issue

   A. I and II only
   B. I and III only
   C. II and III only
   D. I, II and III

2. A prospectus for an individual variable annuity contract

   I. must provide full and fair disclosure
   II. is required by the Securities Act of 1933
   III. must be filed with the SEC
   IV. must precede or accompany every sales presentation

   A. I only
   B. I, III and IV only
   C. II and III only
   D. I, II, III and IV

3. Which of the following information must be included in a prospectus describing variable life insurance to clients?

   I. Summary explanation in nontechnical terms of the principal features of the policy
   II. Statement of investment policy of the separate account
   III. Statement of the separate account's net investment return for the past ten years
   IV. Statement of the deductions and charges against the gross premium, including all commissions paid to agents for each policy year the commissions are to be paid

   A. I and II only
   B. I, II and III only
   C. III and IV only
   D. I, II, III and IV

4. If a variable annuity has an assumed investment rate of 5% and the annualized return of the separate account is 4%, the value of the

   I. accumulation unit will rise
   II. annuity unit will rise
   III. accumulation unit will fall
   IV. annuity unit will fall

   A. I and II
   B. I and IV
   C. II and III
   D. III and IV

5. Which of the following statements about a straight-life variable annuity is(are) true?

   I. The number of annuity units a client redeems never changes.
   II. The number of accumulation units a client owns never changes.
   III. If the client dies during the annuity period, the remaining funds will be distributed to the beneficiary.
   IV. The monthly payout is fixed to the Consumer Price Index.

   A. I only
   B. I and II only
   C. II and III only
   D. I, II, III and IV

6. The difference between a fixed annuity and a variable annuity is that the variable annuity

   I. offers a guaranteed return
   II. offers a payment that may vary in amount
   III. will always pay out more money than the fixed annuity
   IV. attempts to offer protection to the annuitant from inflation

   A. I and III
   B. I and IV
   C. II and III
   D. II and IV

7. A variable annuity's separate account is

   I. used for the investment of monies paid by variable annuity contract holders
   II. separate from the general investments of the insurance company
   III. operated in a manner similar to an investment company
   IV. as much a security as it is an insurance product

   A. I only
   B. I and II only
   C. II and III only
   D. I, II, III and IV

8. A mutual fund and a variable annuity's separate account are similar in that

   I. the investment portfolio is professionally managed
   II. the client may vote for the board of directors or board of managers
   III. the client assumes the investment risk
   IV. payout plans guarantee the client income for life

   A. I, II and III only
   B. II and IV only
   C. III and IV only
   D. I, II, III and IV

9. Which of the following factors may determine the amount of payout from a variable annuity?

   I. Mortality experience of the company
   II. Age and sex of the annuitant
   III. Insurability of the annuitant
   IV. Rate of return of the separate account

   A. I, II and IV only
   B. II only
   C. III and IV only
   D. I, II, III and IV

10. If a customer, age 52, cashes in her annuity contract before payout begins, she will

   I. be taxed at the ordinary income tax rate on earnings in excess of cost base
   II. be taxed at ordinary rates on the amount withdrawn that represents cost base, and will be taxed at capital gains rates on the amount withdrawn that exceeds cost base
   III. have to pay a 5% penalty on the amount withdrawn that exceeds cost base
   IV. have to pay a 10% penalty on the amount withdrawn that exceeds cost base

   A. I
   B. I and III
   C. I and IV
   D. II and III

11. An annuity may be purchased under which of the following methods?

    I.   Single payment deferred annuity
    II. Single payment immediate annuity
    III. Periodic payment deferred annuity
    IV. Periodic payment immediate annuity

    A. I and II only
    B. I, II and III only
    C. III and IV only
    D. I, II, III and IV

12. June Polar purchased a variable annuity with an immediate payout plan. In the first month, she received a payment of $328. Which of the following statements about June's investment is(are) true?

    I.   Her next payment is guaranteed to be $328.
    II. She made a lump-sum investment.
    III. She purchased the variable annuity from a registered representative.

    A. II only
    B. II and III only
    C. III only
    D. I, II and III

13. Lotta Leveridge assumes the risk involved with her variable annuity. What does this mean?

    I.   She is not assured of the return of her invested principal.
    II. The underlying portfolio is primarily common stocks, which have no guaranteed return.
    III. As an investor, she can be held liable for the debts incurred by the insurance company.

    A. I and II only
    B. II and III only
    C. III only
    D. I, II and III

14. Joe Kuhl has just purchased an immediate variable annuity. Which of the following describe Joe's investment?

    I.   It was a lump-sum purchase.
    II. Distribution of dividends will occur during the accumulation period.
    III. Accumulation and payment of dividends will occur during the payout period.

    A. I and II only
    B. I and III only
    C. II and III only
    D. I, II and III

15. Which of the following statements about deferred variable annuities are true?

    I.   Purchase payments can be either lump sum or periodic.
    II. Contract holders are guaranteed a rate of return.
    III. Earnings accumulate in the contract holder's account during the prepayment period.

    A. I and II only
    B. I and III only
    C. II and III only
    D. I, II and III

16. A variable annuity contract guarantees a

    I.   rate of return
    II. fixed mortality expense
    III. fixed administrative expense

    A. I and II only
    B. I and III only
    C. II and III only
    D. I, II and III

17. Separate accounts are similar to mutual funds in that both

   I.   may have diversified portfolios of common stock
   II. are managed by full-time professionals
   III. give investors voting rights

   A. I and II only
   B. I and III only
   C. II and III only
   D. I, II and III

18. Klaus Bruin's annuity has a portfolio that contains mostly common stocks. What does this mean for Klaus?

   I.   In a rising market, the value of Klaus's account may rise.
   II. In a rising market, the value of an accumulation unit may rise.
   III. Klaus is protected from loss.

   A. I and II only
   B. I and III only
   C. II and III only
   D. I, II and III

19. At retirement Angus Bullwether decides to annuitize his variable annuity contract. After his final purchase payment, he has 1,857 accumulation units. What factors will be considered when determining the amount of payout he will receive?

   I.   Value of one annuity unit
   II. Conversion value shown in the company's annuity table
   III. Value of Angus's share of the separate account

   A. I and II only
   B. I and III only
   C. II and III only
   D. I, II and III

20. An investor owning which of the following variable annuity contracts would hold accumulation units?

   I.   Periodic payment deferred annuity
   II. Single payment deferred annuity
   III. Immediate life annuity
   IV. Immediate life annuity with ten-year certain

   A. I and II only
   B. I, III and IV only
   C. IV only
   D. I, II, III and IV

21. The annuity unit of a variable annuity changes in value in a manner that corresponds most closely to changes in which of the following?

   I.   Dow Jones Index
   II. Cost of living index
   III. Value of securities held by the insurance company
   IV. Value of the securities kept in a separate account

   A. I and III only
   B. I, III and IV only
   C. IV only
   D. I, II, III and IV

22. Which of the following investors are eligible to establish an IRA?

   I.   Independently wealthy individual whose sole source of income is $125,000 per year in dividend and interest income
   II. Law student who earned $1,200 in a part-time job
   III. Woman who earned $3,500 last year selling cosmetics but whose spouse is covered by a company profit-sharing plan

   A. I and II only
   B. I and III only
   C. II and III only
   D. I, II and III

23. Which of the following fees and expenses may be deducted from the gross premium paid in a variable life insurance contract?

    I.   Mortality risk fee
    II. Expense fees
    III. Amount to provide for insurance
    IV. Sales expenses including commissions paid to agents

    A. I and II only
    B. III only
    C. IV only
    D. I, II, III and IV

24. If the assumed interest rate of the variable life insurance policy is 4% and the separate account earns 6%, the policyholder would expect the

    I.   cash value to increase
    II. cash value to decrease
    III. death benefit to increase
    IV. death benefit to decrease

    A. I and III
    B. I and IV
    C. II and III
    D. II and IV

25. A distinguishing characteristic of scheduled premium VLI is that an increase or a decrease in the value of the separate account used to fund the VLI contract will lead to an increase or a decrease in the

    I.   annual premium payable
    II. death benefit payable exclusive of the minimum guaranteed in the contract
    III. amount of cash value
    IV. number of individuals the insured can name as beneficiaries of the contract

    A. I, II and III only
    B. I and IV only
    C. II and III only
    D. I, II, III and IV

26. Joe Kuhl earned $34,000 this year, and his wife Bea earned $46,000. Which of the following statements is(are) true?

    I.   Joe may contribute $2,250 to his IRA.
    II. Bea may contribute $2,250 to her IRA.
    III. Bea and Joe may each contribute $2,000 to separate IRAs.
    IV. Bea and Joe may contribute a total of $4,000 to an IRA.

    A. I and IV only
    B. II and IV only
    C. III only
    D. I, II, III and IV

27. Which of the following individuals are eligible to participate in a tax-deferred annuity?

    I.   Maintenance engineer at a state university
    II. Teacher in a public school system
    III. Minister

    A. I and II only
    B. I and III only
    C. II and III only
    D. I, II and III

28. Under a defined-contribution plan, the

    I.   participant is guaranteed a contribution that is based on an agreed-upon percentage or rate
    II. participant's retirement benefits are based on the balance in his individual account
    III. employer may discriminate among employees as to participation

    A. I and II only
    B. I and III only
    C. II and III only
    D. I, II and III

◆ Answers & Rationale

1.   **A.**   The SEC does not approve anything. The registration statement and prospectus filed with the SEC must disclose all material facts of the issuer and the security being issued.   (Page 89)

2.   **D.**   A variable annuity is a security and therefore must be registered with the SEC. As part of the registration requirements, a prospectus must be filed and distributed to prospective investors prior to or during any solicitation for sale.
(Page 89)

3.   **D.**   All of the information listed here must be presented in the prospectus distributed to clients.
(Page 89)

4.   **B.**   The accumulation unit will increase in value because the portfolio earned 4%; however, the annuity unit value will decrease because the actual return of the portfolio (4%) was less than the assumed interest rate of 5% necessary to maintain payments.   (Page 154)

5.   **A.**   Annuity units are fixed; their current value when cashed in determines the payout amount. A life-only annuity ceases payments at the death of the client. The company keeps any undistributed payments. Accumulation units will fluctuate in value and number during the accumulation period.   (Page 147)

6.   **D.**   Variable annuities differ from fixed because the payments vary and they are designed to offer the annuitant protection against inflation.
(Page 142)

7.   **D.**   The separate account is used for the moneys invested in variable annuities. It is kept separate from the general account and operated very much like an investment company. It is considered both an insurance product and an investment product.   (Page 142)

8.   **A.**   Both a mutual fund and a variable annuity offer professional management and a board of managers or directors, and the client assumes the investment risk. Only variable annuities have payout plans that guarantee the client income for life.
(Page 142)

9.   **A.**   Mortality experience, age, sex and rate of return all have a bearing on the size of payout. The insurability of the annuitant has no bearing.
(Page 148)

10.   **C.**   Cashing in an annuity will cause the customer taxation at the ordinary income tax rate on all earnings in excess of the cost base. Any withdrawal prior to age 59 1/2 is subject to a 10% penalty unless it is for death or disability, or if the contract has been annuitized for a period of five years or life, whichever is greater.   (Page 149)

11.   **B.**   A periodic payment immediate annuity would be rather difficult to provide. As the annuitant is contributing, he would also be receiving.
(Page 144)

12.   **B.**   A variable annuity does not guarantee the amount of monthly payments. June's next monthly payment may be more, less or the same as her initial payment. Because June's payments began immediately, she must have made a single lump-sum investment to the company. Finally, because a variable annuity is a security, the salesperson must be a registered representative. (Page 144)

13.   **A.**   The annuitant bears the investment risk in a variable annuity. The portfolio is not guaranteed to return a specified rate, and the principal invested will also fluctuate in value according to the securities held in the separate account portfolio.
(Page 142)

14.   **B.**   There is no accumulation period with an immediate annuity. A single lump-sum investment is made, and payments begin immediately. During payout, the principal and earnings are distributed as the payout.   (Page 144)

15.   **B.**   A variable annuity has no guaranteed earnings rate. A deferred annuity can be purchased either with a lump-sum investment or with periodic payments. During the accumulation period, earn-

ings (losses) of the separate account are credited to (subtracted from) the value of the contract holder's account.   (Page 144)

16. **C.** A variable annuity does not guarantee an earnings rate; however, it does guarantee to make payments for life (mortality) and normally guarantees that expenses will not increase above a specified level.   (Page 142)

17. **D.** Separate accounts as well as mutual funds may contain a diversified portfolio of securities and be managed by a professional investment advisor. Voting rights for policy and management elections are available.   (Page 142)

18. **A.** Klaus assumes the investment risk of the contract, including both upward and downward movements. If the market is rising, the value of the separate account is increasing, which is reflected in an increase in accumulation unit value and ultimately in Klaus's account value.   (Page 147)

19. **C.** In order to calculate the value of the first payment, when annuitizing a contract the company will multiply Angus's account value by a factor summarizing age, sex, option and the AIR. This value is then used to purchase annuity units, the current value of which will determine subsequent payments.   (Page 148)

20. **A.** Accumulation units represent units of ownership in a life insurance company's separate account while the contract is in the deferral stage. Annuity units are the units of ownership while the contract is in the payout stage (annuitized). Immediate annuities purchase annuity units directly.
                                        (Page 147)

21. **C.** The value of an annuity unit will reflect changes in the assets held in the life insurance company's separate account.   (Page 147)

22. **C.** An individual may contribute 100% of earned income up to a maximum of $2,000. Interest and dividend income is passive income, not earned income.   (Page 159)

23. **C.** Sales load is deducted from the gross premium; the other fees are deducted from the separate account (benefit base).   (Page 153)

24. **A.** If the separate account earns at a rate that is greater than the rate assumed, the extra earnings may lead to an increase in the death benefit and cash value.   (Page 148)

25. **C.** The separate account performance will affect the cash value or death benefit only. Premiums are fixed and level.   (Page 152)

26. **C.** Both Joe and Bea can contribute the maximum of $2,000 to separate IRAs. The $2,250 limitation is for married couples with one non-working spouse. Still, the $2,250 must be split between two accounts, with no more than $2,000 contributed in one account.   (Page 159)

27. **D.** Employees of 501c3 and 403b organizations, which include charities, religious groups, sports organizations and school systems, qualify for tax-deferred annuities (TDAs).   (Page 171)

28. **A.** Under a defined-contribution plan, contributions may be based on years of service or, more frequently, salary. Benefits are provided based on what the accumulated contributions will provide at retirement. The plan is qualified and may not discriminate.   (Page 167)

 **46** Final Exam One

1. Treasury bills are

   A. issued at par
   B. callable
   C. issued in bearer form
   D. registered

2. If a bond is purchased at a premium, the yield to maturity is

   A. higher than the nominal yield
   B. lower than the nominal yield
   C. the same as the nominal yield
   D. the same as the current yield

3. A 12% corporate bond issued by the XYZ Company is due in ten years. The bond is convertible into XYZ common stock at a conversion price of $20 per share. The XYZ bond is quoted at 120. Parity of the common stock is

   A. $20
   B. $24
   C. $50
   D. $60

4. When a broker-dealer is holding money and/or securities in its own account, it is

   A. underwriting
   B. hypothecating the securities
   C. taking a position
   D. engaging in none of the above

5. If interest rates are increasing and the market prices of bonds are decreasing, what happens to the value of preferred stock during this period?

   A. Its value increases.
   B. Its value decreases.
   C. Its value remains the same.
   D. Interest rates and the price of bonds have no impact on the value of stock.

6. Which of the following constitutes a discretionary account?

   A. Trading account of the registered representative
   B. Trading account of the broker-dealer
   C. Account where the investor gives the broker written authority to buy or sell securities in the customer's account
   D. Mutual fund account allowing periodic withdrawals

7. Common stockholders' rights include a

   I. residual claim to assets at dissolution
   II. vote for the amount of stock dividend to be paid
   III. vote in matters of recapitalization
   IV. claim against dividends that are in default

   A. I
   B. I and III
   C. II and III
   D. III and IV

8. An investor who purchases a Treasury STRIP is assured of

    I. a locked-in rate of return
    II. a lump-sum payment of principal and interest at maturity
    III. lower taxes because the returns would be taxed at the lower capital gains rate
    IV. little or no reinvestment risk

    A. I
    B. I, II and III
    C. I, II and IV
    D. II and IV

9. Where can you purchase shares of a closed-end investment company after its initial offering?

    A. Directly from the investment company
    B. From other shareholders through a broker-dealer
    C. From either A or B
    D. From neither A nor B

10. Deductions and charges against the variable life insurance separate account may include

    I. expense and mortality risk fees
    II. sales load
    III. state premium taxes
    IV. cost of insurance

    A. I and III
    B. I and IV
    C. II and III
    D. II and IV

11. In describing GNMAs to a potential investor, you would tell him that

    A. the certificates have the full faith and credit backing of the U.S. government
    B. each bond is backed by a pool of insured mortgages
    C. interest payments received by the investor are exempt from both local and federal income taxes
    D. a GNMA can be purchased for as little as $10,000

12. An investment company share normally goes ex-dividend

    A. on the record date
    B. the day after the record date
    C. five days after the record date
    D. seven days after the record date

13. An investor interested in monthly interest income should invest in

    A. GNMAs
    B. Treasury bonds
    C. stock of a utility company
    D. corporate bonds

14. Which of the following would be classified as an investment company?

    I. Closed-end company
    II. Open-end company
    III. Qualified plan company
    IV. Nonqualified plan company
    V. Fixed annuity company

    A. I and II
    B. I, II and V
    C. II
    D. III, IV and V

15. A teacher has placed money into a tax-qualified variable annuity over the past twelve years. The teacher has contributed $26,000, and the value of the annuity today is $36,000. If the teacher withdraws $15,000 today, what are the tax consequences if the teacher is in the 30% tax bracket?

    A. $1,500
    B. $3,000
    C. $4,500
    D. There are no taxes due on this withdrawal.

16. The market price of a convertible bond will depend on

    A. the value of the underlying stock into which the bond can be converted
    B. current interest rates
    C. the rating of the bond
    D. all of the above

40. If TIP Company's dividend decreases by 5% and its stock's market value decreases by 7%, the current yield of the stock will

A. increase
B. decrease
C. remain at 5%
D. remain at 7%

41. If a variable annuity has an assumed investment rate of 5% and the annualized return of the separate account is 4%, what are the consequences?

I. The value of the accumulation unit will rise.
II. The value of the annuity unit will rise.
III. The value of the accumulation unit will fall.
IV. The value of the annuity unit will fall.

A. I and II
B. I and IV
C. II and III
D. III and IV

42. ACE, an open-end investment company, has the following financial information:

Dividend income	$2,000
Interest income	900
Short-term gains	1,000
Long-term gains	1,000
Expenses	900

In order to qualify as a regulated investment company, ACE must distribute what amount to its investors?

A. $1,800
B. $2,700
C. $3,510
D. $3,600

43. June Polar is 65. She had payroll deduction contributions into a nonqualified tax-deferred annuity. Her contributions totaled $10,000, and the current value of her account is $16,000. For tax purposes, what is June's cost basis?

A. $0
B. $10,000
C. $16,000
D. $6,000

44. If Mrs. Polar had payroll deductions totaling $10,000 placed into a qualified tax-deferred annuity and her current value in the account were $16,000, for tax purposes her cost basis would be

A. $0
B. $6,000
C. $10,000
D. $16,000

45. An investor is looking into the purchase of Series EE bonds through payroll deduction at his place of employment. If the investor decides to purchase the Series EE bonds, he will receive the interest earned

A. monthly
B. semiannually
C. annually
D. at redemption

46. Premiums for a scheduled payment variable life policy are

I. fixed as to the premium amount
II. variable as to the premium amount, depending on the face amount of the policy
III. fixed as to time of payment
IV. variable as to time of payment

A. I and III
B. I and IV
C. II and III
D. II and IV

17. Where can open-end investment company shares be purchased and sold?

A. In the secondary marketplace
B. From the open-end company
C. In the primary market
D. All of the above

18. An investor has bonds maturing in two weeks. The investor plans to purchase new bonds with a 10% coupon rate. If interest rates decline in the period before the investor can purchase the new bonds, the investor can expect the income to be received from the new bonds to

A. increase
B. decline
C. stay the same
D. balloon

19. Under the provisions of an UGMA account, when the minor reaches the age of majority, the account

A. should be turned over to the donee
B. should be turned over to the donor
C. remains an UGMA account
D. is liquidated

20. A corporation needs shareholder approval for which of the following?

A. Cash dividend
B. 4-for-1 split
C. 10% stock dividend
D. The repurchase of 100,000 of its own shares

21. Federal funds are used primarily by

A. large commercial banks
B. mutual insurance companies
C. independent broker-dealers
D. savings and loans

22. One of the most important functions of a banker's acceptance is its use as a means of

A. facilitating trades in foreign goods
B. facilitating trades of foreign securities in the U.S.
C. assigning previously declared distributions by foreign corporations
D. guaranteeing payment of an international bank's promissory note

23. If a corporation wanted to offer stock at a given price for the next five years, it would issue

A. rights
B. warrants
C. callable preferred stock
D. put options

24. Which of the following withdrawal plans would an investor select if she wanted to receive a fixed payment monthly from the investment company?

A. Fixed-time
B. Fixed-share
C. Fixed-percentage
D. Fixed-dollar

25. Which of the following comes under NASD guidelines concerning sales literature or advertising?

I. Giving a prepared presentation to the local Kiwanis Club
II. Distributing a letter to all clients
III. Distributing copies of an article from a magazine

A. I only
B. II only
C. II and III only
D. I, II and III

26. The Board of Governors of the NASD has the authority to

    I.   suspend a person, prohibiting him from associating with any exchange
    II. censure a partner of a member firm
    III. suspend or expel a member firm from membership in the NASD
    IV. either suspend or bar a person from further association with a member firm

    A. I and III only
    B. II, III and IV only
    C. II and IV only
    D. I, II, III and IV

27. All of the following would be considered typical of a money-market fund EXCEPT that

    A. the underlying portfolio is normally made up of short-term debt instruments
    B. most or all are offered as no-load investments
    C. such funds have a high beta and are safest in periods of low market volatility
    D. its net asset value normally remains unchanged

28. A customer indicates that she wishes to invest $50,000 in mutual funds. The investments are to be split into three different funds, each with its own management company and all of which are growth-oriented health care funds. The registered representative should advise the customer that

    A. this is an excellent idea because it spreads the risk of investing even more
    B. she will pay greater commissions on the investment when the money is split between three funds than if she put the money into only one fund
    C. she will be able to exchange shares from one fund to another as conditions change without incurring a new sales charge
    D. she should buy individual stocks because mutual funds are only for smaller investors

29. The result of a client investing the same amount of money into a mutual fund at regular intervals over a long period of time is a lower

    A. price per share than cost per share
    B. cost per share than price per share
    C. dollar amount invested
    D. return on the cost basis

30. The NASD Rules of Fair Practice govern the actions of its members. All of the following are considered violations of the rules EXCEPT

    A. churning accounts
    B. the blanket recommending of low-price speculative stocks
    C. using discretionary authority
    D. guaranteeing the customer against loss

31. On February 14th an investor purchases 1,000 shares of the ACE Fund, which has an objective of providing the highest possible level of income on a monthly basis. On February 15th, the investor informs his agent that he has changed his mind and wishes to exchange his bond fund shares for shares of a common stock growth fund with an objective of capital appreciation within the same family of funds. The investor's bond fund shares increased in value prior to the exchange. How will this increase in value be taxed?

    A. As income because the bond fund's objective was to provide for current income on a monthly basis
    B. As a short-term gain because the bond fund was held for less than twelve months
    C. As a long-term gain because the exchange of the bond fund shares was made into a common stock fund with an objective of long-term capital appreciation
    D. Because the shares were exchanged within a family of funds, the increase in value of the bond fund shares is not taxed, but it increases the cost base in the common stock fund investment.

32. If a complaint is filed with the NASD charging that a member or associated person violated one or more of the Association's rules, which of the following codes governs the resolution of such matters?

    A. Code of Arbitration
    B. Code of Procedure
    C. Professional Practice Code
    D. Business Conduct Code

33. What secures an industrial development revenue bond?

    A. State tax
    B. Municipal tax
    C. Trustee
    D. Net lease payments from the corporation

34. What organization or governmental unit sets economic policy?

    A. Federal Reserve Board
    B. Government Economic Board
    C. Congress
    D. Secretary of the Treasury

35. A registered representative of an NASD member firm wishes to open an account with another member firm. The executing member shall take all the following actions EXCEPT

    A. notify the employer member in writing prior to the execution of the transaction of the intention to open or maintain the account for the representative
    B. immediately transmit to the employer member duplicate copies of confirmations or other statements with respect to the representative's account
    C. transmit duplicate copies of confirmations or other statements with respect to the representative's account upon request of the employer member
    D. notify the registered representative of the executing member's intent to notify the employer member

36. In its attempt to increase the money supply, the Federal Open Market Committee is purchasing T bills. This action should cause the yield on T bills to

    A. increase
    B. decrease
    C. remain the same
    D. fluctuate

37. Which of the following does NOT expose the investor to reinvestment risk?

    A. Treasury stock
    B. Treasury bonds
    C. Treasury STRIPS
    D. Treasury notes

38. Distributions to an employee from a profit-sharing plan after retirement are made

    A. from interest accumulating on the plan's assets
    B. only from the profits on the plan's assets
    C. from the amount allocated to the individual's account during the employee's participation in the plan
    D. only from the amount allocated to the individual's account plus accumulated earnings during the employee's participation in the plan

39. An individual calculating taxable income received from a municipal bond fund investment for this year would consider that

    A. part of the income distribution received as a dividend is taxable at ordinary income tax rates
    B. all of the income distribution received as a dividend is taxable at ordinary income tax rates
    C. any capital gains distributions received from the fund are taxable at ordinary income tax rates
    D. all distributions received from the fund, both income and gains, are exempt from federal income tax

47. An investor is in the annuity stage of a variable annuity purchased 15 years ago. During the present month, the annuitant receives a check for an amount that is less than the previous month's payment. Which of the following events caused the annuitant to receive the smaller check?

    A. The performance of the account was less than the previous month's performance.
    B. The performance of the account was greater than the previous month's performance.
    C. The performance of the account was less than the assumed interest rate.
    D. The performance of the account was greater than the assumed interest rate.

48. A registered representative may arrange the purchase of an interest in a privately offered limited partnership only if the representative

    I. informs her broker-dealer after the trade
    II. informs her broker-dealer before the trade
    III. provides all documents and information as required by her broker-dealer
    IV. Because the sale is private, the representative does not have to do anything out of the ordinary.

    A. I and II
    B. II
    C. II and III
    D. IV

49. Which of the following statements is true of the expense ratio of an open-end investment company?

    A. It is computed exclusive of the management fee.
    B. It is computed inclusive of the management fee.
    C. It is computed taking into account the management fee only.
    D. It shows the extent of leverage in the fund.

50. A mutual fund paid $.30 in dividends and $.75 in capital gains during the year. The offering price at the end of the year is $6.50. The fund's current yield for the year is

    A. 4.6%
    B. 6.9%
    C. 11.5%
    D. 16.2%

51. Fees such as mortality and risk expenses are deducted from the

    I. premium payment for flexible premium policies
    II. premium payment for fixed premium policies
    III. benefit base for scheduled premium policies
    IV. benefit base for fixed premium policies

    A. I and II
    B. I and IV
    C. II and III
    D. III and IV

52. The separate account funding a variable annuity that purchases shares in a mutual fund offered by the life insurance company is considered

    A. a unit investment trust
    B. a face-amount certificate company
    C. a management investment company
    D. none of the above

53. In a mutual fund, after opening an account an investor can generally make additional periodic investments in minimum amounts of

    A. $50
    B. $100
    C. $500
    D. The amount varies from fund to fund.

54. Which of the following characteristics describe stock rights?

  I. Short-term instruments that become worthless after the expiration date
  II. Most commonly offered in connection with debentures to sweeten the offering
  III. Issued by a corporation
  IV. Traded in the securities market

  A. I and II
  B. I and III
  C. I, III and IV
  D. II, III and IV

55. Ada and Angus Bullwether are tenants in common in a joint account. Which of the following statements is(are) true?

  I. If one of them dies, the survivor will not automatically assume full ownership.
  II. They need not have equal interest in the account.
  III. They may have a disproportionate interest in the property in the account.

  A. I only
  B. I and II only
  C. II and III only
  D. I, II and III

56. A prospectus for an individual variable annuity contract

  I. must provide full and fair disclosure
  II. is required by the Securities Act of 1933
  III. must be filed with the SEC
  IV. must precede or accompany every sales presentation

  A. I only
  B. I, III and IV only
  C. II and III only
  D. I, II, III and IV

57. In a mutual fund, the amount of increases and/or decreases in the NAV over the past years can be reviewed in the

  A. official statement
  B. customer account form
  C. prospectus
  D. tombstone

58. The NASD's Rules of Fair Practice prohibit members from

  I. lending a client's securities without prior authorization from the client
  II. inducing a client to purchase shares of a mutual fund by implying the client will profit from a pending dividend
  III. receiving discounts in securities transactions from another member

  A. I and II only
  B. II and III only
  C. III only
  D. I, II and III

59. A broker-dealer decides to give a $300 bonus to the registered representative from any other member firm who sells the most shares in a joint sales contest. This arrangement is

  I. unacceptable
  II. acceptable if the SEC approves
  III. acceptable if the underwriter is an NASD member
  IV. acceptable as long as it is not considered compensation

  A. I
  B. I and IV
  C. II
  D. II and III

60. Which of the following statements about sales charges is(are) true?

 I. Under NASD rules, mutual fund sales charges may not exceed 8.5% of the offering price.
 II. Under NASD rules, mutual fund sales charges may not exceed 8.5% of the share's net asset value.
 III. An investment company must offer rights of accumulation, breakpoints and reinvestment of dividends at NAV in order to charge an 8.5% sales charge.
 IV. Under the Investment Company Act of 1940, the maximum sales charge for purchases of mutual fund shares is 9%.

 A. I
 B. I and III
 C. I, III and IV
 D. II, III and IV

61. An owner of common stock has the right to

 I. determine when dividends will be issued
 II. vote at stockholders' meetings or by proxy
 III. receive a predetermined fixed portion of the corporation's profit in cash when declared
 IV. buy restricted securities before they are offered to the public

 A. I, III and IV
 B. II
 C. II, III and IV
 D. II and IV

62. Bea Kuhl is participating in a periodic payment plan. Fifty percent of her first year's payments are taken as a sales charge. What is the maximum the sales charge can average over the life of the plan?

 A. 8.5%
 B. 9%
 C. 16%
 D. 20%

63. In a mutual fund, a shareholder who elected not to receive share certificates can liquidate all or a portion of his holdings and receive payment from the fund if the fund receives which of the following?

 I. Written request from the shareholder
 II. Signed stock power from the shareholder
 III. Signature guarantee from the shareholder

 A. I
 B. I and II
 C. I and III
 D. II and III

64. In order to get cash for an emergency that arose, Angus Bullwether redeemed his shares in a mutual fund that offered reinvestment privileges. Within how many days of redemption could he reinvest in the same fund without having to pay additional sales charges?

 A. 7
 B. 30
 C. 45
 D. 60

65. June Polar wants to buy $1,000 worth of an open-end investment company. She may buy them through

 I. the sponsor of the fund
 II. a brokerage firm
 III. the custodian of the fund
 IV. a bank acting as dealer

 A. I and II
 B. I, II and IV
 C. II
 D. III and IV

66. Contract holders must be given the right to vote on matters concerning separate account personnel at the

    A. beginning of separate account operations

    B. first meeting of contract holders within one year of beginning operations

    C. meeting of contract holders after one year of selling the first variable life policy

    D. Contract holders are not allowed to vote on separate account personnel according to federal law.

67. A separate account funding a variable life contract is considered to be a(n)

    A. investment company issuing periodic payment plan certificates

    B. insurance company issuing periodic payment plan certificates

    C. investment company issuing variable annuity contracts

    D. fixed annuity company issuing variable payment contracts

68. Separate accounts funding a variable life contract and certain personnel working for the account are required to be registered under which of the following securities acts?

    I. Securities Act of 1933
    II. Securities Exchange Act of 1934
    III. Investment Company Act of 1940
    IV. Investment Advisers Act of 1940

    A. I, II and III only
    B. II only
    C. III and IV only
    D. I, II, III and IV

69. Adam Grizzly invests $3,000 in open-end investment company shares. After 60 days, he signs a letter of intent for a $10,000 breakpoint and backdates the letter two months. Six months later, he deposits $10,000 into the fund. He will receive a reduced sales charge on

    A. the $3,000 investment only
    B. $7,000 of the investment only
    C. the $10,000 investment only
    D. the entire $13,000 investment

70. An owner of preferred stock has which of the following rights?

    I. Right to determine when dividends will be issued

    II. Right to vote at stockholders' meetings or by proxy

    III. Right to a predetermined fixed portion of the corporation's profit in cash when declared

    IV. Right to buy restricted securities before they are offered to the public

    A. I, III and IV
    B. II, III and IV
    C. II and IV
    D. III

71. Some open-end investment companies offer their investors a conversion privilege, which permits investors to

    A. exchange general securities for shares in the mutual fund's portfolio

    B. delay payment of taxes on investment company shares that have appreciated in value

    C. purchase additional fund shares from dividends paid by the fund

    D. exchange shares of one mutual fund for those of another fund under the same management, at net asset value

72. Which of the following would be eligible for membership in the NASD?

   A. Bank organized under state and federal laws
   B. Closed-end investment company
   C. Broker or dealer whose regular course of business consists of transactions in securities or the investment banking business
   D. All of the above

73. Joe Kuhl uses the FIFO method to determine his capital gains. What does this mean?

   A. The IRS will assume a liquidation of the first shares that were acquired.
   B. Bernard will indicate the specific shares that were redeemed without regard to when they were purchased.
   C. The last shares purchased are the first shares to be redeemed.
   D. None of the above apply in this case.

74. Tex Longhorn is about to buy a variable annuity contract. He wants to select an annuity that will give him the largest possible monthly payment. Which of the following payout options would do so?

   A. Life annuity with period certain
   B. Unit refund life option
   C. Life annuity with ten-year period certain
   D. Life only annuity

75. Porter Stout has $350,000 in securities and $201,000 in cash with his brokerage firm. If the brokerage firm were forced to liquidate, how much of the account would be covered by SIPC?

   A. $250,000 of the securities and all of the cash
   B. All of the securities and $150,000 of the cash
   C. All of the securities and $100,000 of the cash
   D. All of the cash and $299,000 of the securities

76. If a customer submits a sell order to his broker-dealer after the close of the New York Stock Exchange, the customer will receive a price based on the net asset value computed

   A. the previous business day
   B. the same day regardless of when the order is received
   C. the next time the firm computes it
   D. within the next two business days

77. Hugh Heifer originally invested $20,000 into the ACE Fund and has reinvested dividends and gains of $8,000. His shares in ACE are now worth $40,000. He converts his investment in ACE to the ATF Fund, which is under the same management as ACE. Which of the following statements is true?

   A. He retains his cost basis of $28,000 in the ATF Fund.
   B. He must declare $12,000 as a taxable gain upon conversion into the ATF Fund.
   C. He retains a $20,000 cost basis in the ATF Fund because of the conversion privilege.
   D. He is not liable for taxes in the current year because he did not have constructive receipt of the money at conversion.

78. Which of the following is(are) the responsibility of an underwriter?

   I. Managing the distribution of large blocks of stock to the public and to institutions
   II. Selling a predetermined share of an offering to its customers
   III. Raising capital for corporations by assisting in the distribution of a corporation's new offering
   IV. Lending money to corporate clients that require debt financing

   A. I, II and III only
   B. I, II and IV only
   C. II only
   D. I, II, III and IV

79. Chip Bullock is the sole owner of a business. He earns $160,000 a year and makes the maximum contribution to a defined benefit Keogh plan. How much money may be contributed to his IRA?

   A. $0
   B. $2,000
   C. $15,000
   D. $30,000

80. The Securities Exchange Act of 1934 does which of the following?

   I.   Requires registration of securities
   II. Requires registration of broker-dealers with the SEC
   III. Prohibits inequitable and unfair trade practices
   IV. Provides for regulation of the over-the-counter market

   A. I only
   B. II and III only
   C. II, III and IV only
   D. I, II, III and IV

81. A no-load fund sells its shares to the public

   A. through a network of underwriters and dealers
   B. through a dealer and its sales representatives
   C. by underwriter only
   D. by a direct sale from the fund to the investor

82. Gordy Guernsey owns a variable annuity contract, and the AIR stated in the contract is 5%. In January the realized rate of return in the separate account was 7%, and Gordy received a check based on this return for $200. In February the rate of return was 10%, and Gordy received a check for $210. To maintain the same payment Gordy received in February, what rate of return would the separate account have to earn in March?

   A. 3%
   B. 5%
   C. 7%
   D. 10%

83. Which of the following statements about sales literature for mutual funds is(are) true?

   I.   The material used to solicit the sale of mutual fund shares may require approval by a principal of the firm.
   II. All mutual fund sales literature must be approved by the NASD within three days of its first use.
   III. If the sponsor of the mutual fund has had the literature reviewed by the NASD in advance, no further approvals are required by the firm.

   A. I and III only
   B. II only
   C. III only
   D. I, II and III

84. When would an investor be liable for tax on reinvested distributions from an open-end investment company?

   A. When the shares purchased from the distribution are sold
   B. When the shares purchased with the distribution have been held for twelve months
   C. At the time the distribution is made
   D. None of the above

85. According to the NASD Rules of Fair Practice, a member firm may give certain selling concessions to

   A. the general public
   B. other NASD member firms
   C. nonmember broker-dealers
   D. all of the above

86. An investor who owns shares of a mutual fund actually owns

   A. an undivided interest in the fund's debt capitalization
   B. specific shares of stock in the fund's portfolio
   C. an undivided interest in the fund's portfolio
   D. certain unspecified securities among those owned by the fund

87. A municipal bond is quoted at 6 1/4%. Currently its yield to maturity is 6 3/4%. From this information it can be determined that the municipal bond is trading

A. flat
B. at par
C. at a discount
D. at a premium

88. The Securities Act of 1933 requires that which of the following be offered only by prospectus?

I. Treasury bonds
II. Mutual fund shares
III. Variable annuities
IV. Unit investment trusts

A. I and II
B. II and III
C. II, III and IV
D. III and IV

89. A customer decides to buy shares of an open-end investment company. When is the price of the shares determined?

A. At the next calculation of net asset value the day the fund custodian receives proper notification from the client
B. At the next calculation of net asset value the day the broker-dealer wires the custodian on behalf of the client
C. Both A and B
D. Neither A nor B

90. The ACE Fund has prepared a piece of sales literature to be distributed to individuals who respond to ACE's tombstone ad. If the fund sends the literature to a prospect, the literature must

A. contain directions for obtaining a prospectus
B. include the good points contained in the prospectus
C. contain the SEC disclaimer
D. be accompanied by a prospectus

91. Which of the following are characteristic of a mutual fund voluntary accumulation plan?

I. Minimum initial purchase
II. Minimum optional additional purchases
III. Declining level sales charges as money accumulates
IV. Obligatory purchase goal

A. I and II only
B. I, II and III only
C. IV only
D. I, II, III and IV

92. Your customer tells you he wants a source of retirement income that is stable but that also could offer some protection against purchasing power risk in times of inflation. You should recommend

A. a variable annuity
B. a fixed annuity
C. a combination annuity
D. common stocks and municipal bonds

93. The NASD was established to

I. set and standardize charges and commissions
II. encourage just and equitable principles of trade
III. adopt and enforce Rules of Fair Practice among brokers and dealers

A. I only
B. II and III only
C. III only
D. I, II and III

94. Which of the following characteristics describe(s) a contractual planholder?

I. He receives unit trust certificates.
II. He owns an undivided interest in the mutual fund shares underlying the plan.
III. He owns an undivided interest in the portfolio of the underlying mutual fund.

A. I and II
B. I and III
C. II and III
D. III

95. Which type of nonmarketable security pays semiannual interest?

   A. Series EE bonds
   B. Treasury bonds
   C. Series HH bonds
   D. Agency issues

96. Which of the following statements about a straight-life variable annuity is(are) true?

   I.   The number of annuity units a client redeems never changes.
   II. The number of accumulation units a client owns never changes.
   III. If the client dies during the annuity period, the remaining funds will be distributed to the beneficiary.
   IV. The monthly payout is fixed to the Consumer Price Index.

   A. I
   B. I and II
   C. I, II and III
   D. II, III and IV

97. The Investment Company Act of 1940 requires that mutual funds pay dividends from their

   A. capital gains
   B. net income
   C. gross income
   D. portfolio earnings

98. Tex Longhorn is 61 years old. He would like to take a lump-sum distribution from his Keogh plan. What would be the tax treatment of this distribution?

   A. It is eligible for five-year income averaging.
   B. It will be taxed at long-term capital gains rates.
   C. There will be a 10% penalty.
   D. There will be a 50% penalty.

99. An NASD broker-dealer trading in shares of an open-end investment company is prohibited from buying shares of the fund

   A. to cover existing orders
   B. for the firm's own investment purposes
   C. at a discount
   D. for the purpose of resale at a later date

100. Which of the following has the authority to approve an investment adviser's contract with the investment company?

   A. NASD District Business Conduct Committee
   B. Board of directors of the fund
   C. Board of Governors of the NASD
   D. SEC

◆ Answers & Rationale

1. **D.** A registered security is one whose owner is designated on records maintained for this purpose. Even though T bills are book-entry securities and no certificates are issued, ownership records are maintained and therefore they are considered registered. (Page 25)

2. **B.** A bond purchased at a premium is purchased for an amount greater than the face amount of the bond at maturity. The premium paid reduces the yield of the bond if held until maturity. (Page 16)

3. **B.** The bond is quoted as 120; therefore, it is selling for $1,200. Parity of the stock in which the holder of the bond can convert is equal to $24 as follows. The bondholder would be able to convert the bond into 50 shares of stock (face amount $1,000 ÷ $20 per share = 50 shares), because the bond has a current price of $1,200; dividing this amount by 50 equals parity price of the underlying stock. (Page 19)

4. **C.** When a dealer is holding securities for its own account, it is considered to be taking a position. (Page 39)

5. **B.** Preferred stocks are interest rate sensitive as are other fixed-interest rate investment vehicles such as bonds. Because the dividend amount is fixed, if interest rates are increasing, the return provided by the dividend may be less than the return provided by other investments. The value of preferred stock will decrease. (Page 7)

6. **C.** A discretionary account is an account where a representative has been given authority to select the amount and type of investment for a client. The authorization must be written. (Page 128)

7. **B.** As the corporation's owners, common stockholders would have the lowest claim against a company's assets at dissolution or bankruptcy. The owners of cumulative preferred stock have a claim against any dividends that are in default. Holders of common stock are entitled to vote on matters that affect their proportionate ownership. Recapitalization—the alteration of a corporation's capital structure—is an example of a situation that requires a vote of the stockholders. (Page 5)

8. **C.** Even though an investment in a Treasury STRIP does not yield a regular cash flow, paying all of its interest at maturity, the difference between the purchase price and the mature value is still taxed as ordinary income and must be accrued on a yearly basis. (Page 13)

9. **B.** Closed-end investment company shares are traded in the secondary marketplace (OTC or exchange). Therefore shares are purchased from other shareholders through broker-dealers. Closed-end funds (unlike open-end funds) cannot issue shares directly to shareholders. (Page 76)

10. **B.** Cost of insurance and mortality and expense risk fees are deducted from the separate account. Sales loads and premium taxes are deducted from the premium. (Page 153)

11. **A.** The certificates issued by the GNMA represent interests in government-insured mortgages pooled by mortgage brokers who guarantee the monthly cash flow, but it is the U.S. government that actually backs GNMA pass-through certificates. GNMA pass-throughs are issued in minimum denominations of $25,000, and all interest earned is subject to federal income tax. (Page 29)

12. **B.** An investor purchasing shares on the record date becomes a shareholder of record and is entitled to the dividend declared. Orders received after the pricing of shares or the record date would be processed the next day and would purchase shares ex-dividend. (Page 110)

13. **A.** The mortgages underlying GNMA modified pass-through certificates pay interest on a monthly basis. GNMA then passes this monthly income through to investors in GNMA pass-through certificates. (Page 29)

14.   **A.**   Open- and closed-end funds are classified as investment companies. Plan companies offer plans in which an investment company may be selected as an investment vehicle, but are not investment companies themselves. Fixed annuities are offered by insurance companies only.
(Page 75)

15.   **C.**   Contributions to a tax-qualified annuity are taxable when withdrawn at ordinary income tax rates. Because in this case the teacher is withdrawing $15,000, that amount is subject to tax. Thirty percent of $15,000 equals a tax liability of $4,500.
(Page 149)

16.   **D.**   All of the factors listed affect the price of a convertible bond. The rating of a bond reflects the issuing company's health and therefore indirectly affects the value of the investment.
(Page 18)

17.   **B.**   Open-end company shares are bought and sold from the investment company.   (Page 76)

18.   **C.**   Fluctuations in interest rates may affect the price of a bond but will not affect the income payable from the bond. The percentage interest payable for use of money is stated on the face of a bond and is part of the bond indenture, a legal obligation on the part of the issuing company.
(Page 9)

19.   **A.**   At the age of maturity, proceeds must be handed over to the child (donee) under the terms of the Uniform Gifts to Minors Act.   (Page 130)

20.   **B.**   Shareholders have a right to vote on such items as mergers, reorganizations, recapitalizations and stock splits.   (Page 5)

21.   **A.**   The federal funds rate is the rate of interest at which member banks of the Federal Reserve System can borrow excess funds from other members, usually on an overnight basis.   (Page 50)

22.   **A.**   A banker's acceptance is a time draft typically used to facilitate overseas trading ventures. It is guaranteed by a bank on behalf of a corporation in payment for goods or services.
(Page 35)

23.   **B.**   A warrant is a purchase option for stock for a long period of time. The warrant allows the holder to purchase common stock for a set price. Rights and options have a short life.   (Page 21)

24.   **D.**   A fixed-dollar plan is the only type of plan that fixes a definite dollar payment.
(Page 121)

25.   **D.**   Sales literature is any public solicitation concerning securities.   (Page 215)

26.   **B.**   The Board of Governors of the NASD may censure, suspend or expel a member or a person associated with a member. It has no jurisdiction over the exchanges and cannot prohibit any person from associating with them.   (Page 212)

27.   **C.**   Money-market funds have no price volatility; the rate of interest on money-market funds fluctuates in conjunction with that of the instruments underlying the original money-market certificates.   (Page 84)

28.   **B.**   Because the funds are under separate management, the load charged on each separate investment will most likely be at the maximum. If the customer invested the entire sum within one fund or a family of funds, a reduced sales charge may have been available.   (Page 102)

29.   **B.**   By investing a predetermined amount of money periodically for a long period of time, the investor is investing using the concept of *dollar cost averaging*. The result is to reduce the cost per share compared to the average market price.
(Page 120)

30.   **C.**   Use of discretionary authority is not a violation of the Rules of Fair Practice, but abuse of that authority by excessive trading and the misuse of a customer's funds or securities is. Answers A, B and D are clear violations. Recommendations should be based on the customer's financial status and objectives. Low-priced stocks may result in a higher percentage of commission. Brokers that

make a practice of selling low-priced stocks are often called *penny brokers*.   (Page 206)

31. **B.**   Because the bond fund shares were held for less than twelve months, the gain is short term. An exchange privilege does not exempt the transfer of funds from taxation. The exchange is a taxable event.   (Page 105)

32. **B.**   Complaints charging that a member firm or an associated person violated one or more of the NASD's rules are handled under the Code of Procedure. Complaints, which charge that a specific rule was violated, should not be confused with disputes, which tend to deal more with business ethics, failures to perform and misunderstandings. Disputes are submitted for resolution under the NASD's Code of Arbitration.   (Page 211)

33. **D.**   IDRs are issued by municipalities to construct a facility that will be used by, or is being constructed for the benefit of a corporation. When this is done, the corporation is required to sign a long-term lease. Although classified as a municipal security, IDRs are backed by the revenues of the corporation participating in the project.   (Page 33)

34. **C.**   Congress sets fiscal policy, while the FRB sets monetary policy.   (Page 50)

35. **B.**   When an employee opens an account with another member, the employee will be notified by the executing member that the employing member will be notified that the account is to be opened, and copies of confirmations and other reports will be available upon request.   (Page 126)

36. **B.**   The purpose of the FOMC purchase is to increase the attractiveness of the market price of T bills. Because the price will be driven up by an increased market demand and a decreased supply, yields should decrease.   (Page 52)

37. **C.**   STRIPS are special bonds issued by the Treasury department and split into individual principal and interest payments, which are then resold in the form of zero-coupon bonds. Because zeros pay no interest, the investor realizes gains in the form of increased basis as the bond matures and there are no income payments to reinvest.   (Page 13)

38. **D.**   Distributions from a profit-sharing plan are made from the individual's account, reflecting the accrued amount of contributions and earnings on the contributions. Contributions to the plan are normally based on a predetermined percentage of profits.   (Page 169)

39. **C.**   Interest in the form of dividends paid from a municipal bond fund would be exempt from federal income tax. Gains from the sale of portfolio securities would be subject to ordinary income tax.   (Page 107)

40. **A.**   Because the dividend rate decreased at a rate less than the market value of the stock, the current yield will be greater.   (Page 4)

41. **B.**   The accumulation unit will increase in value because the portfolio earned 4%; however, the annuity unit value will decrease because actual return of the portfolio (4%) was less than the assumed interest rate of 5% necessary to maintain payments.   (Page 148)

42. **A.**   To qualify as a regulated investment company, at least 90% of net investment income (without regard to gains) must be distributed. Net investment income would equal dividend income ($2,000 in this case) plus interest income ($900) minus expenses ($900), to equal $2,000. Ninety percent of $2,000 is $1,800.   (Page 112)

43. **B.**   Contributions to a nonqualified annuity are made aftertax. The growth of the annuity is deferred, representing ordinary income when withdrawn. Cost basis is $10,000.   (Page 149)

44. **A.**   If contributions are made into a tax-qualified annuity, the contributions are made before tax. The growth is deferred. Mrs. Polar has no cost basis in this question. The entire $16,000 will be taxed as ordinary income.   (Page 149)

45. **D.**   Interest on Series EE bonds is received at redemption of the bonds.   (Page 27)

46. **A.** Scheduled payment VLI contracts have fixed premiums and payment periods. (Page 152)

47. **C.** In the annuity stage of a variable annuity, the amount received will depend on the performance of the account compared to the assumed interest rate. If actual performance is less than the AIR, the value of the payout will decline. (Page 148)

48. **C.** In a private securities transaction the representative must obtain permission for the sale from his broker-dealer prior to the transaction. The transaction must be through the books of the broker-dealer, and any information requested by the broker-dealer must be supplied. The broker-dealer is still responsible for actions of the representative in this private transaction. (Page 204)

49. **B.** The expense ratio includes the expenses of operating the fund compared to fund assets. Expenses included in the ratio are management fees, administrative fees, brokerage fees and taxes. (Page 85)

50. **A.** Current yield of a mutual fund is current income ($.30 dividend in this case) divided by the net asset value ($6.50). Gains are not included in calculation of current yield; they are accounted for separately. (Page 110)

51. **D.** Expenses are deducted from the benefit base (cash value) for both scheduled and flexible premium VLI contracts. (Page 153)

52. **A.** A separate account purchasing shares of mutual funds to fund variable contracts does not actively manage the securities held; instead, the account holds the shares in trust for the contract holders. This account is classified as a unit investment trust under the act of 1940. (Page 142)

53. **D.** Minimum amounts are different from fund to fund, and a registered rep must refer to the prospectus for each fund. (Page 79)

54. **C.** Rights are issued by the corporation, giving the subscriber the right to purchase stock within a short period of time at a reduced price from the stock's current market price. The right does not have to be exercised, but may be traded in the secondary market. Warrants are commonly used as a sweetener in debenture offerings. (Page 21)

55. **D.** Under tenants in common, owners may have a fractional interest in the undivided ownership of an asset. The interest passes to the decedent's estate at death unlike JTWROS, wherein the survivor succeeds to the interest. (Page 127)

56. **D.** A variable annuity is a security and therefore must be registered with the SEC. As part of the registration requirements, a prospectus must be filed and distributed to prospective investors prior to or during any solicitation for sale. (Page 170)

57. **C.** Changes in NAV will be found in the prospectus for at least ten years if the fund has existed that long. (Page 218)

58. **A.** The Rules of Fair Practice prohibit unauthorized borrowing (theft) and selling dividends. Discounts are allowed to other NASD members if a dealer agreement has been signed. (Page 207)

59. **A.** Gifts in excess of $100 per person per year are not allowed. (Page 206)

60. **C.** The NASD limits sales charges to 8.5% of the POP as a maximum. If the fund does not allow for breakpoints, reinvestment of dividends at net or rights of accumulation, the maximum is less than 8.5%. Under the Investment Company Act of 1940, the maximum sales charge on mutual funds is deferred to the NASD rules, while a contractual plan specifically may charge 9% over the life of the plan. (Page 98)

61. **B.** The stockholder has the right to vote and the right to dividends if and when declared (although not a fixed dividend). A restricted security is one that has prescribed limits on resale generally requiring registration. (Page 5)

62. **B.** The maximum sales charge on a contractual plan whether front-end load or spread load is 9% over the life of the plan. (Page 117)

63. **C.** Orders for redemption without a certificate being issued requires a written request and a signature guarantee. A signed stock power would be required if the shareholder had possession of the mutual fund certificates.   (Page 79)

64. **B.** Funds offering the reinstatement privilege allow the investor to redeem and reinvest shares within 30 days without an additional sales charge. The privilege can be used only once, and only the amount withdrawn can be reinstated.
(Page 79)

65. **A.** The custodian does not sell the shares, but holds them for safekeeping. A bank cannot be a member of the NASD and therefore cannot act as a dealer (although subsidiaries independent of the bank may be set up as broker-dealers). (Page 76)

66. **B.** Contract holders must be given the right to vote on company personnel (directors, adviser, custodian, etc.) at the first meeting held within one year of the start of operations.   (Page 141)

67. **A.** The Investment Company Act of 1940 defines an insurance company offering VLI contracts as an investment company offering periodic payment plan certificates. The separate account may be organized as either an open-end investment company or as a unit investment trust. (Page 142)

68. **D.** Companies offering VLI contracts must register under the Investment Company Act of 1940; the VLI contract must be registered under the Securities Act of 1933; representatives selling the contract must register under the Securities Exchange Act of 1934; and the adviser managing the separate account must register under the Investment Advisers Act of 1940.   (Page 142)

69. **D.** The entire investment qualifies for the reduced load. A letter of intent covers purchases within a 13-month period and may be backdated 90 days. Adam Grizzly actually had eleven months in which to make the additional investment.
(Page 103)

70. **D.** The preferred stockholder generally has no right to vote but carries a prior right to dividends

if and when declared. A restricted security is one that has prescribed limits on resale generally requiring registration.   (Page 7)

71. **D.** The exchange, or conversion, privilege allows an investor to exchange shares of one fund for another fund under the same management without paying an additional sales charge (although the exchange is still a taxable event).   (Page 105)

72. **C.** Broker-dealers in the securities business may become members; banks cannot. A closed-end fund is an investment company and not a broker-dealer.   (Page 194)

73. **A.** FIFO means "first in, first out." Answer C describes LIFO (last in, first out); answer B describes share identification.   (Page 114)

74. **D.** Generally a life only contract will pay the most per month because payments cease at the death of the annuitant.   (Page 146)

75. **C.** SIPC covers cash and securities up to $500,000, but only $100,000 in cash.   (Page 192)

76. **C.** Orders to redeem shares will be executed at the next computed price.   (Page 106)

77. **B.** The exchange privilege offers exchange without an additional sales charge, but the exchange is still taxable. Hugh is taxed on the gain of $12,000 ($40,000 – $28,000).   (Page 114)

78. **A.** An underwriter manages the offering and helps the corporation to raise capital.
(Page 42)

79. **B.** The question asks what Chip's IRA contribution may be; the maximum is the lesser of 100% earned income or $2,000.   (Page 158)

80. **C.** The Securities Act of 1933 (paper act) requires registration of securities. The act of 1934 (people act) requires registration of people and exchanges transacting securities business in order to prevent manipulative and deceptive practices.

The NASD is the SRO of the OTC market, but the SEC has final authority.   (Page 186)

81. **D.** Because there is no load, there is no underwriter. The fund makes sales directly to the public.   (Page 96)

82. **B.** If the actual rate of return equals the assumed interest rate, the check will stay the same. Recall that the payout is based on an accumulated value to be distributed over the life of the annuitant (like compounding). Therefore, for Gordy to receive the $210 in March, the account must earn 5%.   (Page 148)

83. **A.** Sales literature must be approved by a firm's principal prior to use. If the literature has been reviewed by the NASD, it need not be submitted by every broker-dealer intending to use it.   (Page 220)

84. **C.** Reinvested income and gains distributions are taxable in the year they are received.   (Page 113)

85. **B.** Members may give other members concessions, but must deal with the public and non-members at the public offering price.   (Page 96)

86. **C.** Each shareholder owns an undivided (mutual) interest in the portfolio of the mutual fund.   (Page 79)

87. **C.** The YTM is greater than the nominal yield, meaning the price must be less than par. The bond is selling at a discount.   (Page 15)

88. **C.** Treasury securities are exempt from registration requirements as are municipal issues and do not require a prospectus.   (Page 182)

89. **C.** The price for mutual fund shares is the next price calculated by the fund after receipt of the request. Answer B describes a repurchase transaction.   (Page 106)

90. **D.** Any solicitation requires a prospectus to be delivered prior to or during the solicitation. (Sales literature is solicitation.)   (Page 216)

91. **B.** A voluntary accumulation plan is voluntary, not binding. The company may require that the initial investment meets a certain minimum dollar amount. It may also specify that any additions meet set minimums (for example, $50). The plan may qualify for breakpoints based on the accumulated value.   (Page 115)

92. **C.** Because the investor wants the objectives provided by both a fixed and variable annuity, a combination annuity would be suitable.   (Page 144)

93. **B.** The commissions charged are not set, but must be fair and reasonable for the service provided as enumerated in the NASD Rules of Fair Practice.   (Page 194)

94. **A.** A contractual plan buys mutual fund shares to hold in trust. The planholder then owns an undivided interest in the mutual fund shares evidenced by the unit trust certificate(s). (Page 116)

95. **C.** Series EE bonds are sold at a discount and mature to face value; T bonds and agency issues are marketable debt. HH bonds are nonmarketable and pay interest semiannually.   (Page 27)

96. **A.** Annuity units are fixed; their current value, when cashed in, determines the payout amount. A life only annuity ceases payments at the death of the annuitant. The company keeps any undistributed payments. Accumulation units will fluctuate in value and number during the accumulation period.   (Page 147)

97. **B.** Dividends are paid from net income (interest plus dividends plus short-term gains when identified minus expenses).   (Page 110)

98. **A.** The distribution would be taxed as ordinary income but would also qualify for five-year income averaging (TRA 1986). A 10% penalty would apply if Tex were under age 59 1/2; the 50% penalty would apply if he did not take the distribu-

tion according to his life expectancy by April 1st of the year following the year he turned 70 1/2.

(Page 166)

99. **D.** A broker-dealer may purchase shares only to fulfill existing orders or for its own investment account, not for inventory. (Page 93)

100. **B.** The investment adviser's contract is approved by the board of directors of the fund and often a majority vote of the outstanding fund shares. An investment adviser must be *registered* with the SEC, not approved. (Page 91)

47 Final Exam Two

1. Equity ownership of a corporation is split into two types. These types are commonly referred to as

   A. stocks and bonds
   B. common stocks and preferred stocks
   C. preferred stocks and bonds
   D. common stocks and convertible bonds

2. An individual purchasing a flexible premium variable life contract should know that

   I. premiums are discretionary as to timing and amount
   II. the death benefit may equal the contract's face amount
   III. the death benefit may equal the contract's face amount plus cash value
   IV. cash value and duration of the policy are directly affected by the performance of the separate account

   A. I, II and III only
   B. I, III and IV only
   C. IV only
   D. I, II, III and IV

3. What is(are) the responsibilities of a respondent when the party learns that it is involved in an arbitration dispute?

   I. The respondent must file the appropriate forms with the Director of Arbitration within 20 calendar days of the receipt of service.
   II. In its answer, the respondent must put forth all defenses to the statement of claim.
   III. The respondent may set forth a counterclaim, if any, against the initiating party or a third party.

   A. I only
   B. I and II only
   C. III only
   D. I, II and III

4. Which of the following securities pays interest monthly?

   A. T bill
   B. Commercial paper
   C. Municipal general obligation bond
   D. Government National Mortgage Association pass-through certificate

5. The market value of a stock is determined by

   A. the board of directors
   B. what individuals are willing to pay for it
   C. a vote of the stockholders
   D. the company's financial condition

6. Which of the following Treasury securities allows an investor to lock in a yield for an extended period of time by minimizing reinvestment risk?

   A. Treasury bill
   B. Treasury STRIP
   C. Treasury bond
   D. Treasury note

7. Which of the following debt instruments pays no interest?

   A. STRIP
   B. T note
   C. T bond
   D. T stock

8. A mutual fund previously invested in bonds with a medium-length maturity. As the bonds matured, the fund reinvested the proceeds and purchased long-term bonds with maturities of up to 20 years. What would have happened to the fund if the reinvestment had occurred during a period when interest rates were rising?

   I. Decrease in yield
   II. Decrease in income
   III. Increase in yield
   IV. Increase in income

   A. I and II
   B. I and IV
   C. II and III
   D. III and IV

9. A company that has paid its common stockholders a dividend would be required to also have made distributions to which of the other securities issued by the company?

   I. Bonds
   II. Convertible bonds
   III. Preferred stock
   IV. Convertible preferred stock

   A. I and II only
   B. I and III only
   C. II and III only
   D. I, II, III and IV

10. Which of the following corporate bonds is usually backed by other investment securities?

    A. Mortgage bond
    B. Equipment trust certificate
    C. Collateral trust bond
    D. Debenture

11. Which of the following would be the best time for an investor to purchase long-term fixed-interest rate bonds?

    A. When short-term interest rates are high and are beginning to decline
    B. When short-term interest rates are low and are beginning to rise
    C. When long-term interest rates are low and are beginning to rise
    D. When long-term interest rates are high and are beginning to decline

12. If not appealed to the Board of Governors, findings by a District Business Conduct Committee become effective

    A. immediately
    B. only after review by the SEC
    C. no sooner than 10 days from the date of the decision
    D. no sooner than 45 days from the date of the decision

13. Interest rates have been rising for the past few days. What has happened to the price of bonds traded in the bond market during this time?

    A. Increase
    B. Decrease
    C. Stay the same
    D. Bond prices are not affected by interest rates.

14. Which of the following investments would provide high appreciation potential together with high risk?

    A. Balanced fund
    B. Bond fund
    C. Income fund
    D. Sector fund

15. Which of the following statements is(are) true of Treasury bills?

    I. They are sold at a discount.
    II. They pay a fixed rate of interest semiannually.
    III. They mature in one year or less.
    IV. They mature in ten years or more.

    A. I, II and III
    B. I and III
    C. II and IV
    D. III

16. The formula used to determine the tax-equivalent yield between a taxable and a nontaxable bond and to compare corporate return with municipal return is

    A. nominal yield divided by 100% minus the investor's tax bracket
    B. nominal yield plus 100% minus the investor's tax bracket
    C. nominal yield multiplied by 100% minus the investor's tax bracket
    D. nominal yield minus 100% minus the investor's tax bracket

17. The interest from which of the following bonds is exempt from federal income tax?

    I. State of California bonds
    II. City of Anchorage bonds
    III. Treasury bonds
    IV. GNMA bonds

    A. I and II only
    B. I, II and IV only
    C. III and IV only
    D. I, II, III and IV

18. Your customers would like to have $40,000 set aside when their child starts college, but do not want to invest in anything that could endanger their principal. In this situation, you should recommend

    A. zero-coupon bonds or Treasury STRIPS
    B. corporate bonds with a high rate of interest payment
    C. municipal bonds for their long-term tax benefits
    D. Treasury bills

19. Which of the following are money-market instruments?

    I. Bankers' acceptances
    II. Treasury bills
    III. Commercial paper
    IV. Treasury bonds maturing in six months

    A. I and II only
    B. I, II and III only
    C. III and IV only
    D. I, II, III and IV

20. When trading common stock, either at an exchange or over the counter, the typical size of the trading unit is how many shares?

    A. 10
    B. 50
    C. 100
    D. There is no standard unit.

21. The annuity unit of a variable annuity changes in value in a manner that corresponds most closely to changes in which of the following?

    I. Dow Jones Index
    II. Cost of living index
    III. Value of securities held by the insurance company
    IV. Value of the securities kept in a separate account

    A. I and III only
    B. I, III and IV only
    C. IV only
    D. I, II, III and IV

22. Which of the following is(are) the responsibility of an investment banker?

    I.   Distributing large blocks of stock to the public and to institutions
    II. Buying previously unissued securities from an issuer and selling them to the public
    III. Raising long-term capital for corporations by underwriting new issues of securities
    IV. Lending money to corporate clients that require debt financing

    A.   I, II and III only
    B.   I, II and IV only
    C.   III only
    D.   I, II, III and IV

23. The federal funds rate is charged to banks for

    A.   short-term bank loans from the government
    B.   loans offered by major New York City banks
    C.   loans from other banks and can change daily
    D.   loans from broker-dealers

24. The over-the-counter market could be characterized as which of the following?

    A.   Auction market
    B.   Double-auction market
    C.   Negotiated market
    D.   None of the above

25. The ex-dividend date is the

    I.   date on and after which the buyer is entitled to the dividend
    II. date on and after which the seller is entitled to the dividend
    III. second business day prior to the record date
    IV. second business day after the record date

    A.   I and III
    B.   I and IV
    C.   II and III
    D.   II and IV

26. Geographic diversification of municipal securities investments protects against all of the following EXCEPT

    A.   adverse legislation in a certain area
    B.   economic decline in a certain area
    C.   a change in interest rates
    D.   default by a particular issuer

27. August Polar has $800 to invest in the Amusement Technology Fund. If the shares are currently priced at $21.22 each, August will be able to purchase

    A.   no shares because the minimum trading unit is 100 shares
    B.   37 shares and $14.85 in change
    C.   37.7 shares
    D.   38 shares

28. When examining the portfolio of a diversified common stock fund, you would most likely find

    A.   all growth stocks within one particular industry
    B.   stocks of many companies within many industries
    C.   mostly convertible bonds and other debt instruments
    D.   There is no telling what you would find.

29. A customer who watches the T bill auctions noticed that the average return to investors in the latest T bill auction fell to 4.71%, down from 4.82% at the previous week's sale. When he asks you for your interpretation, you tell him that

    A.   the decline in yields indicates that the supply of short-term funds has decreased relative to demand
    B.   investors who purchased bills at this auction paid more for them than purchasers at the previous week's sale
    C.   investors who purchased T bills twelve weeks ago paid less than purchasers since that time
    D.   the federal funds rate and other short-term interest rate indicators are probably rising

30. Which of the following statements are true concerning flexible premium contracts?

   I.   The contract holder determines premium amounts.
   II. The contract holder determines the death benefit.
   III. Cash value is affected by separate account performance.
   IV. The contract may lapse due to insufficient cash value.

   A. I and II only
   B. I, II and III only
   C. III and IV only
   D. I, II, III and IV

31. Federal Open Market Committee activities are closely watched by Wall Street because of the effect of its decisions on all of the following EXCEPT

   A. money supply
   B. interest rates
   C. exchange rates
   D. money velocity

32. Which of the following statements describes a balanced fund?

   A. It has some portion of its portfolio invested in both debt and equity instruments at all times.
   B. It has equal amounts of common stock and corporate bonds at all times.
   C. It normally has equal amounts of common and preferred stock at all times.
   D. None of the above statements is true.

33. All of the following are advantages of mutual fund investment EXCEPT

   A. the investor retains personal control of her investment in the fund portfolio
   B. exchange privileges within a family of funds managed by the same management company
   C. the ability to invest almost any amount at any time
   D. the ability to qualify for reduced sales loads based on accumulation of investment within the fund

34. According to the Investment Company Act of 1940

   I.   a company must have $1,000,000 in assets before it may begin operations
   II. at least 40% of the board of directors may not be affiliated or hold a position with the fund
   III. the fund must have at least 100 shareholders
   IV. the fund may not borrow more than 33 1/3% of its asset value

   A. I and III only
   B. II, III and IV only
   C. II and IV only
   D. I, II, III and IV

35. An investor in a 28% tax bracket has a $5,000 loss after netting all capital gains and losses realized. How much may the investor deduct from income that year?

   A. $0
   B. $2,500
   C. $3,000
   D. $5,000

36. The NAV of an open-end investment company

   I.   is calculated seven days a week
   II. is calculated as stipulated in the prospectus
   III. takes into account cash held by the fund but not invested
   IV. when divided by the number of shares outstanding equals the net asset value per share

   A. I and IV
   B. II, III and IV
   C. III
   D. IV

37. The net asset value per share of a mutual fund will fluctuate in value relative to the

   A. value of the fund's portfolio
   B. law of supply and demand
   C. number of shareholders
   D. S&P 500 market index

38. The net asset value per share will

   I.   increase if the assets of the fund appreciate in value
   II. decrease if the fund distributes a dividend to shareholders
   III. decrease when shares are redeemed
   IV. increase if shareholders reinvest dividend and capital gains distributions

   A.   I and II
   B.   I and III
   C.   II and III
   D.   II and IV

39. Typically, no-load mutual funds are sold to the public in which of the following ways?

   A.   The fund sells directly to the investor.
   B.   The fund sells to a plan company, which in turn sells to the investor.
   C.   The fund sells to a dealer, who in turn sells to the investor.
   D.   The fund sells to investors through federal banks.

40. A secondary distribution is

   A.   a distribution that is accomplished without an investment banker
   B.   used to achieve a better price than the current market
   C.   a method of redistributing a large block of stock without significantly affecting the market price
   D.   a new issue of stock or bonds that is being offered by a "second tier" company

41. The net asset value of a mutual fund is $9.30. If its sales charge is 7%, its offering price is

   A. $9.95
   B. $9.97
   C. $10
   D. $10.70

42. If a mutual fund charges an 8 1/2% sales charge, all of the following must be offered by the fund EXCEPT

   A.   exchange privileges
   B.   breakpoints
   C.   rights of accumulation
   D.   dividend reinvestment at NAV

43. If an investment company offers rights of accumulation and an investor wishes to get a reduced sales charge, the client must deposit sufficient funds within

   A.   45 days
   B.   13 months
   C.   There is no time limit.
   D.   Each fund may have its own requirements.

44. Amusement Technology Fund permits rights of accumulation. Max Leveridge has invested $9,000 and has signed a letter of intent for a $15,000 investment. His reinvested dividends during the 13 months total $720. How much money must Max contribute to fulfill the letter of intent?

   A. $5,280
   B. $6,000
   C. $9,000
   D. $15,000

45. You have decided to buy 100 shares of the ACE Fund, which prices its shares at 5:00 pm every business day. You turn in your order at 3:00 pm when the shares are priced at $10 NAV, $10.86 POP. The sales load is 7.9%. What will your 100 shares cost?

   A. $1,000
   B. $1,079
   C. $1,086
   D.   100 times the offering price, which will be calculated at 5:00 pm

46. When comparing definitions in the stock market and mutual funds, the bid price is similar to the NAV, and the ask price is similar to

   A. the net asset value
   B. the sales load
   C. the public offering price
   D. none of the above

47. Hugh Heifer is redeeming 1,000 shares of the ACE Fund. Hugh has submitted his request for redemption, which ACE receives at noon. ACE prices its shares at the close of the NYSE each day, at which time the shares are priced at $12.50 NAV, $13.50 ask. ACE also charges a 1% redemption fee. Hugh will receive what amount for his shares?

   A. $12,375
   B. $12,500
   C. $13,365
   D. $13,500

48. The ex-dividend date for shares of a mutual fund is

   A. two business days prior to the record date
   B. seven days prior to the record date
   C. the same day as the record date
   D. the day following the record date

49. Klaus Bruin buys shares of the ZBest Invest Mutual Fund shortly before the ex-dividend date. Before he buys the shares, Klaus should understand that

   A. the price of the shares will decline on the ex-dividend date by the amount of the distribution
   B. if he reinvests the dividend, he will not be liable for taxes on the dividend received
   C. there is a great advantage to his purchasing the shares immediately so that he can receive the dividend
   D. all of the above may occur

50. Which of the following makes up the net investment income of an open-end investment company?

   A. Net gains on sales of securities
   B. Dividends, interest and unrealized gains
   C. Income from dividends and interest paid by securities held by the fund minus the operating expenses
   D. Ninety percent of the net asset value of the fund

51. Which of the following are true of mutual fund dividend distributions?

   I. The fund pays dividends from net income.
   II. A single taxpayer may exclude $100 worth of dividend income from taxes annually.
   III. An investor is liable for taxes on distributions whether the dividend is a cash distribution or reinvested in the fund.
   IV. An investor is liable for taxes only if the distribution is received in cash.

   A. I and II
   B. I, II and III
   C. I and III
   D. II and IV

52. Greta Guernsey redeemed 200 of her 500 mutual fund shares. She has not designated which shares were redeemed. Which of the following methods does the IRS use to determine which shares have been redeemed?

   A. Identified shares
   B. Wash sale rules
   C. LIFO
   D. FIFO

53. ACE, an open-end investment company, operates under the conduit or pipeline tax theory. Last year it distributed 91% of all net investment income as a dividend to shareholders. Therefore ACE paid

A. taxes on 9% of its net investment income last year
B. taxes on 9% of its net investment income and capital gains last year
C. taxes on 91% of its net investment income last year
D. no taxes last year because it qualified as a regulated investment company under IRC Subchapter M

54. Your client has a $21,000 net capital loss this year. He plans to apply the maximum deduction towards his ordinary income for the year. After the year, he may

A. carry $3,000 of the loss forward
B. carry the loss forward for six years and deduct $3,000 per year
C. carry the loss forward for seven years and deduct $3,000 per year
D. not carry the loss forward

55. On January 10, 1987, Adam Grizzly purchased 1,000 shares of the ArGood open-end investment company. On January 22, 1987, ArGood sells 25,000 shares of TCB at a profit. ArGood originally purchased the TCB on June 24, 1984. On February 15, 1987, ArGood distributes the gain from the sale of TCB to shareholders. How will Adam be taxed on this distribution?

A. The income will be taxed as a long-term gain taxable as ordinary income.
B. The income will be taxed as a long-term gain qualifying for the 60% exclusion.
C. If Adam is using automatic reinvestment, he will not be taxed at all.
D. Adam will not be taxed because he did not sell the TCB; ArGood is liable for all taxes.

56. Which of the following is the usual source of a mutual fund's capital gains distribution?

A. Net long-term gains resulting from the sale of the company's mutual fund shares
B. Net short-term gains resulting from the sale of the company's mutual fund shares
C. Net long-term gains resulting from the sale of securities in the fund's investment portfolio
D. Net short-term gains resulting from the sale of securities in the fund's investment portfolio

57. Your open-end investment company client has decided not to take automatic reinvestment of dividend and capital gains distributions. This will

A. not change the tax status of these distributions
B. lower the client's proportionate ownership in the fund each time a distribution is made
C. be the way individuals requiring income payments will often invest
D. result in all of the above

58. Gwinneth Stout has a large investment in the ATF open-end investment company. She has selected a fixed-time withdrawal plan. The computation for the withdrawal plan will be based on the

A. NAV each period
B. NAV at the first payment
C. POP each period
D. POP at the first payment

59. A customer is receiving funds from an open-end investment company under the provisions of a withdrawal plan. This means

    A. the client must continue to make investments into the fund
    B. the client will generally be discouraged from making further investments into the fund
    C. the client will always exhaust the plan within a predetermined period of time
    D. that if the client withdraws only dividend and gains distributions, the principal amount of the investment will always remain intact

60. A customer chooses a voluntary accumulation plan and signs up for automatic checking account deductions of $100 a month. She tells the registered representative that she intends to continue the plan for ten years. Which of the following statements is true?

    A. Her decision to invest is binding, and she must continue to invest for ten years.
    B. She can terminate the plan at her option.
    C. She will be charged a late fee on investments not made in a timely fashion.
    D. She can terminate the plan if she agrees to pay the balance in lump sum.

61. Voting rights extended to contract holders of variable life insurance contracts funded by a separate account shall be one vote on company matters for each

    A. contract owned
    B. dollar of cash value credited to the contract
    C. $100 of cash value funded by the insurance company's general account
    D. $100 of cash value funded by the insurance company's separate account

62. The investment objective of a separate account funding variable life insurance may be changed

    A. with a majority vote of shares
    B. by order of the state insurance commissioner
    C. if either A or B occurs
    D. under no circumstances

63. A separate account registering as an investment company offering variable life contracts under the Investment Company Act of 1940 is required to have a minimum net capital of

    A. $100,000 before operations may begin
    B. $1,000,000 before operations may begin
    C. The separate account may operate if the insurer has capital of $1,000,000.
    D. both A and C

64. Under the Uniform Gifts to Minors Act, the owner of the securities held in the account is the

    A. custodian
    B. minor
    C. parent of the minor
    D. donor of the securities

65. Joe and his wife Bea own shares in the ACE Fund as joint tenants with rights of survivorship. If Joe dies, what happens to the shares in the account?

    A. One half of the shares would belong to Bea, and the remaining half would be distributed to Joe's estate.
    B. Bea would own all the shares.
    C. Ownership of the shares would have to be determined by probate court.
    D. None of the above would occur.

66. Armand A. Legge has been investing $100 a month in the Amusement Technology Fund over the past five months. His purchases are as follows:

Month	Price/Share	Quantity
1	10	10
2	20	5
3	25	4
4	5	20
5	10	10

What is the difference between Armand's average cost and the average price he paid for the shares?

A. $3.80
B. $7.14
C. $10.20
D. $14

67. The price of closed-end investment company shares is determined by

A. supply and demand
B. the New York Stock Exchange
C. the board of directors
D. the net asset value plus the sales charge

68. The offering price of the Amusement Technology Fund is $9, and its net asset value is $9.40. The offering price of the ACE Fund is $23.80, and its net asset value is $19.45. From these quotes you know that

I. ATF is an open-end fund
II. ATF is a closed-end fund
III. ACE is an open-end fund
IV. ACE is a closed-end fund

A. I and III
B. I and IV
C. II and III
D. II and IV

69. Customers could pay a commission, rather than a sales charge, for shares of a(n)

A. no-load fund
B. mutual fund
C. open-end investment company
D. closed-end investment company

70. According to the NASD, the maximum sales charge on a variable annuity contract is

A. 8.5% of the total amount invested
B. 8.5% of the net amount invested
C. 9% of the total amount invested
D. unlimited

71. The value of a variable annuity separate account fluctuates in relationship to the

A. general account maintained by the insurance company
B. value of the separate account portfolio
C. Consumer Price Index
D. S&P 500 market index

72. At age 65, Randy Bear purchased an immediate variable annuity contract. Randy made a lump-sum $100,000 initial payment and selected a life income with ten-year period certain payment option. Randy lived until age 88. The insurance company made payments to Randy

A. until his initial payment of $100,000 was exhausted
B. for ten years
C. for 23 years
D. at a fixed rate for ten years and at a variable rate up until his death

73. The difference between a fixed annuity and a variable annuity is that the variable annuity

I. offers a guaranteed return
II. offers a payment that may vary in amount
III. will always pay out more money than the fixed annuity
IV. attempts to offer protection to the annuitant from inflation

A. I and III
B. I and IV
C. II and III
D. II and IV

74. The variable annuity's separate account is

    I.   used for the investment of monies paid by variable annuity contract holders
    II. separate from the general investments of the insurance company
    III. operated in a manner similar to an investment company
    IV. as much a security as it is an insurance product

    A. I only
    B. I and II only
    C. II and III only
    D. I, II, III and IV

75. Similarities between a mutual fund and a variable annuity's separate account include which of the following?

    I.   The investment portfolio is professionally managed.
    II. The client may vote for the board of directors or board of managers.
    III. The client assumes the investment risk.
    IV. The payout plans guarantee the client income for life.

    A. I, II and III only
    B. II and IV only
    C. III and IV only
    D. I, II, III and IV

76. Stock rights (also called *subscription rights*) are

    I.   short-term instruments that become worthless after the expiration date
    II. most commonly offered in connection with debentures to sweeten the offering
    III. issued by a corporation
    IV. traded in the securities market

    A. I and II
    B. I and III
    C. I, III and IV
    D. II, III and IV

77. Your client is 68 years old, retired and in good health. She is concerned about budgeting funds. She needs funds for day-to-day living expenses starting now. As her representative, you might suggest that she purchase

    A. all the whole life insurance that she can afford
    B. a periodic-payment deferred variable annuity
    C. a single-payment deferred variable annuity
    D. an immediate annuity

78. An insurance company offering a variable annuity makes payments to annuitants on the 15th of each month. The contract has an assumed interest rate of 3%. In July of this year the contract earned 4%. In August the account earned 6%. If the contract earns 3% in September, the payments to annuitants will be

    A. greater than the payments in August
    B. less than the payments in August
    C. the same the payments in August
    D. less than the payments in July

79. Which of the following factors may determine the amount of payout from a variable annuity?

    I.   Mortality experience of the company
    II. Age and sex of the annuitant
    III. Insurability of the annuitant
    IV. Rate of return of the separate account

    A. I, II and IV only
    B. II only
    C. III and IV only
    D. I, II, III and IV

80. According to the NASD Rules of Fair Practice, a member firm may give certain selling concessions to

    A. the general public
    B. other NASD member firms
    C. nonmember broker-dealers
    D. all of the above

81. If a customer, age 52, chooses to cash in his or her annuity contract before payout begins, the client will

 I. be taxed at the ordinary income tax rate on earnings in excess of cost base
 II. have to pay a 10% penalty on the amount withdrawn that exceeds cost base
 III. have to pay a 5% penalty on the amount withdrawn that exceeds cost base
 IV. be taxed at ordinary rates on the amount withdrawn, which represents cost base, and will be taxed at capital gains rates on the amount withdrawn that exceeds cost base

 A. I
 B. I and II
 C. I and III
 D. III and IV

82. If a customer, age 35, invests $100 a month in a variable annuity for seven years and suddenly dies

 A. the customer's beneficiaries will not receive any money until the year in which the customer would have turned 59 1/2
 B. the insurance company gets to keep all the contributions made to date because the contract was not annuitized
 C. the customer's beneficiaries will receive only the amount contributed
 D. if the contract were insured, the customer's beneficiaries would receive the greater of the contributions or current value of the account

83. When a customer withdraws money from an IRA after age 59 1/2, the

 A. amount withdrawn is subject to a 10% penalty
 B. amount withdrawn is subject to taxes at the capital gains rate
 C. entire amount in the IRA is subject to taxation at the ordinary rate, regardless of the amount withdrawn
 D. amount withdrawn is subject to taxation at ordinary income tax rates

84. Which of the following statements is(are) true about a qualified, noncontributory defined benefit plan?

 I. Contributions are taxable.
 II. Distributions are taxable.
 III. Contributions may vary.

 A. I and II
 B. II
 C. II and III
 D. III

85. If an employer installs a Keogh plan, that plan must include all full-time employees with how many years of service?

 A. One
 B. Three
 C. Five
 D. None of the above

86. Keogh plans are retirement programs designed for use by nonincorporated businesses. These plans allow the self-employed individual to contribute on a tax-deductible basis

 A. the lesser of 25% of earned income or $30,000
 B. the lesser of 25% of all income or $30,000
 C. the greater of 25% of earned income or $30,000
 D. the greater of 25% of all income or $30,000

87. June Polar is a retired teacher participating in a qualified tax-sheltered annuity. Contributions made on her behalf total $15,000. This year she received a lump-sum payment of $21,000. How would this payment be taxed?

 A. As a capital gains distribution
 B. As ordinary income
 C. $6,000 as capital gains and the remainder as ordinary income
 D. As ordinary income, except for the $15,000, which represents return of her contribution

88. ALFA Securities, an NASD member, wants to buy shares in the ATF Mutual Fund from the fund's sponsor at a discount. This arrangement is possible if the sponsor of the ATF Mutual Fund

    A. is not an NASD member
    B. is also an NASD member and a sales agreement between the two firms is in effect
    C. has a sales agreement with ALFA Securities
    D. meets any of the above restrictions

89. Under what conditions does the Investment Company Act of 1940 require a written statement disclosing the source of dividend payments?

    A. Whenever a dividend is paid
    B. Whenever net income is part of the dividend
    C. Whenever all or part of the dividend payment comes from a source other than current income or accumulated undistributed net income
    D. The Investment Company Act of 1940 does not require disclosure, only the Internal Revenue Code requires disclosure of the amount of the dividend.

90. When using the annual report as sales literature, the

    I. principal of the firm must approve its use as such
    II. prospectus must accompany the report
    III. figures contained in the report must be as of a specific date
    IV. report must contain the complete portfolio list

    A. I, II and III only
    B. I and IV only
    C. II, III and IV only
    D. I, II, III and IV

91. In the sale of open-end investment company shares, the prospectus

    A. is not necessary
    B. must be delivered to the client either before or during the sales solicitation
    C. must be delivered before the sales solicitation
    D. must be delivered at or before the delivery of the fund share certificate

92. Which of the following persons would most likely become a member of the NASD?

    I. Person convicted of a crime involving fraudulent conversion in the securities business within the past ten years
    II. Person who transacts business for his own account and for others in the over-the-counter market
    III. Person acting as a specialist on the New York Stock Exchange only

    A. I and III only
    B. II only
    C. II and III only
    D. I, II and III

93. When deciding on the suitability of a particular investment for a client, that client's need for liquidity is

    A. not necessary to be determined
    B. only necessary to be determined if the individual is planning on retirement
    C. an important element to be considered when determining the suitability of an investment
    D. only important if the client has no other liquid investments

94. Which of the following individuals may not purchase shares of a hot issue of stock?

    A. General partner of a member firm
    B. Spouse of the person who is the managing underwriter of the issue
    C. Senior officer of a bank
    D. All of the above

95. A sale of securities in a dollar amount just below the point at which an investor could take advantage of a lower sales charge by making a larger purchase

    I.   is called a breakpoint sale
    II. would not be a conflict of interest
    III. is contrary to just and equitable principles of trade
    IV. requires the approval of the District Business Conduct Committee

    A. I
    B. I and III
    C. I and IV
    D. II

96. NASD rules permit members to

    A. execute an order to sell shares of a customer's securities, knowing that delivery of these shares will be two weeks later
    B. continue to compensate a registered representative for sales that were made while the representative was working for the firm according to a previous contract
    C. arrange for a customer to receive $5,000 worth of credit in order to purchase mutual fund shares
    D. give a selling concession to a nonmember firm because of the large number of shares the nonmember is purchasing

97. While recommending the purchase of a security, a registered representative presented material indicating a possible upward move in the price of the recommended security. This recommendation to buy was probably

    I.   fraudulent
    II. in violation of the Rules of Fair Practice
    III. not suitable for all investors
    IV. acceptable if the statements about prices and earnings were clearly labeled as forecasts

    A. I
    B. I and II
    C. III
    D. III and IV

98. An employee who is involved in the management of an NASD member's business, particularly in the supervision of business solicitation or in training, would have to be registered as a

    A. broker
    B. dealer
    C. partner
    D. principal

99. Which Federal Reserve Board regulation prohibits brokers and dealers from extending credit for the purchase of open-end investment company shares?

    A. Regulation A
    B. Regulation G
    C. Regulation U
    D. Regulation T

100. The NASD's Code of Procedure contains guidelines for

    A. handling violations of the NASD's Rules of Fair Practice
    B. reviewing and approving accounts, trades, correspondence and sales literature
    C. resolving disputes between two NASD members
    D. resolving disputes between NASD members and non-NASD firms

◆ Answers & Rationale

1. B. Equity ownership comes with two types of securities. These are common and preferred stocks. (Page 3)

2. D. Flexible premium policies allow for the insured to determine the amount and timing of premium payments. Depending on the policy, the death benefit may equal the face value of the contract, a percentage of cash value or a combination of the two. If performance of the separate account is such that cash value drops below an amount necessary to maintain the policy in force, the policy will lapse. (Page 156)

3. D. Anyone can bring charges of rule violations against a member firm or an associated person, including customers, which is the reason each branch office must maintain library copies of the NASD's Bylaws, Rules of Fair Practice and Code of Procedure. (Page 211)

4. D. Government National Mortgage Association (GNMA) pass-through certificates pay investors interest and a return of principal on a monthly basis. Treasury bills and most commercial paper are sold on a discounted basis and mature for a par amount. The dollar difference between the discounted amount and par is the earned interest. Municipal bonds pay interest on a semiannual basis. (Page 29)

5. B. Market value of stock is determined by supply and demand. (Page 6)

6. B. This is actually a three-part question pertaining to locking in yield, a long period of time and reinvesting with minimum risk. The long time aspect is easily handled in that bonds are longer term securities than notes or bills. STRIPS (Separate Trading of Registered Interest and Principal of Securities) are T bonds with the coupons removed. The choice between bonds and STRIPS is simplified when reinvestment risk is considered. STRIPS don't pay interest; instead, they are sold at a deep discount and mature at face par value. Conse-

quently, there are no interest payments to be reinvested and no reinvestment risk. This is also how the investor locks in a yield. (Page 26)

7. A. STRIPS (Separate Trading of Registered Interest and Principal of Securities) are T bonds with the coupons removed. STRIPS don't pay interest; instead, they are sold at a deep discount and mature at face par value. (Page 12)

8. D. The longer the maturity of a bond, the greater the risk to the investor. As a result, long-term bonds pay higher interest rates than medium- or short-term bonds. If the fund replaces medium-term bonds with long-term bonds, you would expect the long-term bonds to pay higher interest rates and thus more income. Additionally, as interest rates increase, so do yields. For example, the fund has a medium-term bond paying 8%. The income from the bond is $80 annually. The bond matures and the fund receives $1,000 as a return of principal. The fund is purchasing a long-term bond paying 9%, or $90, annually (income to the fund will increase by $10). Additionally, if interest rates are rising, price is declining. Thus, the 9% long-term bond will not cost $1,000, but say $950. Therefore, the current yield of the 9% bond will be 9.47% ($90 ÷ $950)—yield is up. (Page 17)

9. D. Because common stock is paid last (most junior), other securities issued by the firm will receive distributions (interest payments on debt securities and dividends on senior equity securities). (Page 5)

10. C. Collateral trust bonds are backed by other securities, while mortgage bonds are backed by real estate. Equipment trust certificates are backed by equipment. Debentures are secured by the company's promise to pay. (Page 11)

11. D. The best time to buy long-term bonds is when long-term interest rates have peaked. In addition to the high return, as interest rates fall the value of existing bonds will rise. (Page 16)

12. D. If not appealed, District Business Conduct Committee decisions become final 45 days after the decision date. (Page 212)

13. **B.**   When interest rates rise, bond prices fall. (Page 16)

14. **D.**   A sector or specialized fund offers a higher appreciation potential (coupled with higher risk) than an income-oriented fund.   (Page 82)

15. **B.**   T bills are sold at a discount and are for a duration of up to one year. Although they mature at face, it is not considered interest.   (Page 25)

16. **A.**   Tax-equivalent yield on bonds issued between municipalities and corporations is determined by dividing the municipal bond's nominal yield by the difference in the investor's tax bracket. In reality, since municipal securities are quoted in yield to maturity, the truest measure of equivalency uses the bond's yield to maturity.   (Page 31)

17. **A.**   Municipal bonds are exempt from federal income tax. Direct federal debt, such as Treasury bonds, are subject to federal income tax but would be exempt from state tax. GNMA bonds are subject to both federal and local taxes.   (Page 31)

18. **A.**   Zero-coupon bonds represent the lowest risk coupled with the highest return of all the investments listed. They offer no current income.   (Page 26)

19. **D.**   Money-market securities are made up of short-term high-yield debt issues. All of the items listed here are considered short term—even the bonds, because they will mature in less than one year.   (Page 36)

20. **C.**   Common stock trades in round lots of 100 shares each.   (Page 3)

21. **C.**   The value of an annuity unit will reflect changes in the assets held in the life insurance company's separate account.   (Page 147)

22. **A.**   "Investment banker" is another term for "broker-dealer." Investment bankers do everything listed except lend money to corporate clients that require debt financing.   (Page 41)

23. **C.**   The federal funds rate is the rate of interest at which member banks of the Federal Reserve System can borrow excess funds from other members, usually on an overnight basis. The rate is subject to change and often does on a daily basis.   (Page 51)

24. **C.**   The New York Stock Exchange is an auction market, and the OTC market is a negotiated market.   (Page 39)

25. **C.**   Stocks sold on the ex-dividend date entitle the seller to the dividend. Stocks sell ex-dividend two business days before the record date.   (Page 46)

26. **C.**   If the interest rates change, geographic diversification will not help you. A change in interest rates will affect all of the yields.   (Page 33)

27. **C.**   August will be able to purchase 37.7 shares. Mutual fund shares may be sold in full or fractional amounts and do not trade in round lots of 100 shares.   (Page 79)

28. **B.**   A diversified common stock fund will contain stocks from many companies and many industries.   (Page 81)

29. **B.**   As rates for T bills drop, T bill prices climb; T bill rates and prices have an inverse relationship. T bills are priced at their yield, so an investor who bids 4.71% is actually paying more for a T bill than one who bids 4.82%.   (Page 25)

30. **D.**   All of the statements listed are true.   (Page 156)

31. **C.**   The FOMC is one of the most influential committees in the Federal Reserve System, and its decisions affect money supplies, interest rates and even the speed at which dollars turn over (money velocity). The foreign exchange rate is set in the interbank market.   (Page 52)

32. **A.**   Balanced funds carry both equity and debt issues. An equal amount of these issues is not necessary to maintain.   (Page 83)

33. **A.** The control of the investment is given over to the investment manager. All of the other items mentioned are considered advantages.
(Page 73)

34. **B.** A company must have commitments for at least $100,000 in assets before it begins. All of the other items are true. (Page 87)

35. **C.** The maximum deduction of capital losses in any one year is $3,000. Any remaining losses can be carried forward into the next year.
(Page 109)

36. **B.** NAV must be calculated at least every business day but not on weekends or holidays. It takes into account all of the fund's assets and is arrived at by totaling the assets and dividing that amount by the number of shares outstanding.
(Page 97)

37. **A.** Share prices fluctuate in relation to the assets held in the fund's portfolio. (Page 97)

38. **A.** Share prices will increase when assets in the portfolio increase in value. Share prices decrease when the fund distributes a dividend because the shareholder will receive either cash or additional shares. Redeeming or purchasing shares does not affect share prices, only total assets. Reinvesting dividends or capital gains has no effect on share prices either. (Page 97)

39. **A.** No-load funds sell directly to the investor through their own sales force. (Page 96)

40. **C.** A secondary distribution is the sale of stock that has been previously issued and owned. A key purpose of a secondary distribution is to redistribute a large block of stock without significantly affecting the market price. Like a primary distribution, an underwriting manager makes distribution arrangements and a syndicate may be formed. In a secondary distribution, the securities are usually offered at a fixed price that is closely related to the current market price so as not to upset the market significantly. (Page 43)

41. **C.** To determine the selling price of the shares when given the NAV, you must divide the NAV by 100% minus the sales load:

$$\frac{NAV}{100\% - SL\%} = \text{Selling price}$$

In this case,

$$\frac{\$9.35}{100\% - 7\%} = \$10$$
(Page 101)

42. **A.** Funds charging the full 8 1/2% sales load must offer breakpoints, rights of accumulation and dividend reinvestment at NAV. Exchange privileges are the exception. (Page 102)

43. **C.** Rights of accumulation are good for not less than ten years, while the letter of intent has a 13-month limit. (Page 102)

44. **B.** Max must put in the full $15,000, an additional $6,000. Reinvested dividends and changes in the NAV do not affect the amount required. (Page 103)

45. **D.** Mutual funds use forward pricing. You will pay the offering price calculated at 5:00 pm.
(Page 106)

46. **C.** Bid and NAV are similar in that they are both the price at which the customer sells shares. The ask price is similar to the public offering price (POP) because this is the price the customer pays for the purchase of shares. (Page 97)

47. **A.** Hugh will receive $12.50 per share less a redemption fee of 1%; $12.50 times 100 shares is $12,500. A 1% redemption fee is $125, so Hugh receives $12,375. (Page 106)

48. **D.** Mutual fund record dates are set by the fund's board of directors. Since funds use forward pricing and transactions occur the day an order is received, an investor would be a shareholder of record if the transaction is completed by the time the fund prices its shares. Corporate stocks in the secondary market have the ex-dividend date of two business days before the record date. (Page 110)

49. **A.**   Share prices decline on the ex-dividend date. Dividend distributions cause a tax liability, and so the purchase of shares right before an ex-dividend date is not a good idea because of this.
(Page 46)

50. **C.**   Dividends and interest paid on the securities held in the portfolio make up investment income. From this the fund's expenses are paid before it becomes net investment income.
(Page 110)

51. **C.**   Funds pay dividends from net income, and the investor is liable for taxes on all distributions.
(Page 110)

52. **D.**   When a customer does not choose a method, the IRS uses FIFO.
(Page 114)

53. **A.**   ACE pays taxes on any portion of income it does not distribute as long as it distributes at least 90%. ACE paid taxes on 9%.
(Page 112)

54. **B.**   Capital losses can be used to offset capital gains. A client can use $3,000 of capital losses per year to offset ordinary income. After using $3,000 this year, your client will have $18,000 to carry forward.
(Page 109)

55. **A.**   Adam owned shares of the mutual fund when it distributed the gain, and he is liable for the taxes. This is considered a long-term gain, which is currently taxed as ordinary income.
(Page 113)

56. **C.**   Capital gains come from the sale of securities held in the company's portfolio. Most of these gains will be the sale of securities held for long periods of time.
(Page 113)

57. **D.**   Reinvestment does not change the tax status, while taking distributions will lower proportionate ownership. An investment of this type will allow an investor to take distributions without touching the principal.
(Page 112)

58. **A.**   At first, withdrawal of funds will be based on the NAV. Subsequently, it will be determined each time a payment is made.
(Page 121)

59. **B.**   Taking money out of a fund at the same time a person is putting money into the fund is generally discouraged.
(Page 121)

60. **B.**   Voluntary accumulation plans allow for just that. The client can terminate at any time if she so chooses, and there is no penalty for doing so.
(Page 116)

61. **D.**   Contract holders receive one vote per $100 of cash value funded by the separate account. Additionally, if the insurance company votes the shares, the company must vote according to proxies received from the contract holders.
(Page 156)

62. **C.**   The insurance commissioner has the authority to change an investment objective if the objective is in violation of state law; otherwise, the objective may be changed only by majority vote of the separate account's outstanding shares.
(Page 156)

63. **D.**   According to the act of 1940, a separate account may begin operations as long as the insurance company offering the contract has a net worth of $1,000,000 or the account has a net worth of $100,000.
(Page 142)

64. **B.**   The minor is the owner of the securities in an UGMA account while they are held in the name of the custodian.
(Page 130)

65. **B.**   In a JTWROS account, securities pass to the surviving owner.
(Page 127)

66. **A.**   Armand paid a total of $500 for 49 shares of stock, or $10.20 per share. The average price of the shares during this time was the total of the share prices ($70) divided by the number of investment periods (5), or $14. The difference between the two is $3.80.
(Page 120)

67. **A.**   Closed-end investment company shares trade in the secondary market; hence, price is determined by supply and demand.
(Page 76)

68. **D.**   ATF is selling below its net asset value, so it must be a closed-end fund. ACE is selling

above its NAV by more than the 8 1/2% sales load allowed, so it also must be closed end. (Page 85)

69. **D.** Sales charges could be paid on all types of open-end funds, while commissions are paid on securities traded in the secondary market, such as a closed-end company. (Page 76)

70. **A.** NASD rules allow a maximum sales charge on a variable annuity contract of 8 1/2%. (Page 144)

71. **B.** The value of the separate account fluctuates in relation to the securities held in the account. (Page 142)

72. **C.** An annuity with life and ten-year certain will pay for the greater of ten years or the life of the annuitant. Randy lived for 23 more years, which is more than the ten certain. (Page 146)

73. **D.** Variable annuities are different from fixed annuities because the payments vary and they are designed to offer the annuitant protection against inflation. (Page 142)

74. **D.** The separate account is used for the monies invested in variable annuities. It is kept separate from the general account and operated very much like an investment company. It is considered both an insurance product and an investment product. (Page 142)

75. **A.** Both a mutual fund and a variable annuity's separate account offer professional management and a board of managers or directors, and the client assumes the investment risk. Only variable annuities have payout plans that guarantee the client income for life. (Page 142)

76. **C.** Rights are issued by the corporation that give the subscriber the right to purchase stock within a short period of time at a price lower than the stock's current market price. Rights do not have to be exercised but may be traded in the secondary market. Warrants are commonly used as a sweetener in debenture offerings. (Page 21)

77. **D.** Your client needs immediate income. Of the options listed, only the immediate annuity offers this. (Page 144)

78. **C.** The contract earned 3% in September. The assumed interest rate for the contract is 3%. Payment size will not change from the payment made the previous month. (Page 148)

79. **A.** Mortality experience, age, sex and rate of return all have a bearing on the size of payout. The insurability of the annuitant has no bearing. (Page 147)

80. **B.** Members may give other members concessions, but must deal with the public and nonmembers at the public offering price. (Page 96)

81. **B.** Cashing in an annuity prior to age 59 1/2 is a taxable event. The amount withdrawn in excess of cost base is taxed as ordinary income. Additionally, the amount subject to tax is also subject to a penalty of 10%, unless the distribution is annuitized for a period of at least five years, or the distribution is the result of death or disability. (Page 149)

82. **D.** The customer's beneficiaries would receive the current market value, but if the contract were insured, they would receive the greater of the amount invested or the current market value. (Page 146)

83. **D.** Money withdrawn from an IRA after age 59 1/2 is subject to ordinary taxation on the amount withdrawn, but there is no 10% penalty. (Page 161)

84. **C.** Contributions to a qualified, noncontributory plan are made by the employer, not the employee. Contributions are not taxed until they are received as distributions by the participant. Because the benefits provided by this type of qualified plan may vary (depending upon the participant's age, sex, income, etc.), the contributions made on his behalf will vary. All distributions from the plan are taxed upon receipt by the participant. (Page 168)

85. **A.** Keogh plans must allow for the inclusion of all full-time employees, age 21, with one year of service.   (Page 165)

86. **A.** Keogh plans allow contributions for the lesser of 25% of earned income or $30,000.
(Page 164)

87. **B.** Contributions into a TSA, as in all qualified plans, are made before taxes. Payments from these plans require the payment of taxes at the ordinary income tax rate.   (Page 149)

88. **B.** This arrangement is possible if both firms are NASD members and there is a sales agreement in effect.   (Page 96)

89. **C.** The Investment Company Act of 1940 requires disclosure when all or part of the dividend payment comes from a source other than current income or accumulated undistributed net income.
(Page 110)

90. **D.** The principal of the firm must approve the use of the annual report as sales literature, and the figures contained must be current and complete. A prospectus is always required.   (Page 218)

91. **B.** The sale of mutual fund shares requires that the client receives the prospectus before or during the sales solicitation.   (Page 183)

92. **B.** A person conducting business in the over-the-counter market must be a member of the NASD. Transacting business on the Exchange requires membership with the NYSE.   (Page 194)

93. **C.** Liquidity is very important when determining suitability for a client.   (Page 64)

94. **D.** None of the people listed may purchase hot issues.   (Page 209)

95. **B.** This is called a "breakpoint sale" and is contrary to just and equitable principles of trade.
(Page 105)

96. **B.** Registered reps may continue to be compensated for sales that were made while working for the firm and were in accordance with the contract.   (Page 206)

97. **D.** No investment is suitable for all investors. Statements about future prices and earnings may be used if they are clearly labeled as forecasts.
(Page 217)

98. **D.** Supervision of business solicitation or training requires being registered as a principal.
(Page 198)

99. **D.** Regulation T regulates the extension of credit by brokers and dealers for investment company shares.   (Page 88)

100. **A.** The Code of Procedure contains the guidelines for handling violations of the NASD Rules of Fair Practice.   (Page 212)

48 Final Exam Three

1. T bills are issued with all of the following maturities EXCEPT

   A. one month
   B. three months
   C. six months
   D. twelve months

2. Which of the following statements about a bond selling above par value is(are) true?

   I. The nominal yield is lower than the current yield.
   II. The yield to maturity is lower than the nominal yield.
   III. The yield to maturity is lower than the current yield.
   IV. The nominal yield always stays the same.

   A. I and IV only
   B. II, III and IV only
   C. III only
   D. I, II, III and IV

3. All of the following are true of a Treasury receipt EXCEPT

   A. it may be issued by a securities broker-dealer
   B. it is backed by the full faith and credit of the federal government
   C. the interest coupons are sold separately
   D. it may be purchased at a discount

4. Which of the following does not issue commercial paper?

   A. Commercial bank
   B. Finance company
   C. Service company
   D. Broker-dealer

5. A newly issued bond has call protection for the first five years after it is issued. This feature would be most valuable if, during this five-year period, interest rates are generally

   A. fluctuating
   B. stable
   C. falling
   D. rising

6. The newspaper indicates that T bill yields have gone down. This means that T bill prices

   A. are up
   B. are down
   C. are mixed
   D. cannot be determined

7. A 5% bond is purchased with an 8% yield to maturity. After the capital gains tax is paid, the effective yield is

   A. less than 5%
   B. 5%
   C. between 5% and 8%
   D. 8%

275

8. If a registered representative violates NASD rules, the

   A. NASD may only impose a fine
   B. rep may be expelled only by the NASD
   C. NASD may recommend that disciplinary action be taken, but only the SEC can take such action
   D. NASD may fine, censure, suspend or expel the rep

9. Which of the following statements about general obligation municipal bonds are true?

   I. They are second only to U.S. government bonds in safety of principal.
   II. They are backed by the taxing power of the municipality.
   III. They are nonmarketable.
   IV. They pay higher interest rates than corporate debt securities.

   A. I and II
   B. I, II and IV
   C. II, III and IV
   D. III

10. A 10% corporate bond issued by ABC Company is due in ten years. The bond is convertible into ABC common stock at a conversion price of $25 per share. The ABC bond is quoted at 90. Parity of the common stock is

    A. $22.50
    B. $25
    C. $36
    D. $100

11. All of the following are true of taxable zero-coupon bonds EXCEPT

    A. the discount is accreted
    B. tax is paid annually
    C. interest is paid semiannually
    D. bonds are purchased at a discount

12. Which of the following statements is true about a bond quoted as QRS Zr 12?

    A. The bond pays $12 interest annually.
    B. The bond pays $120 interest annually.
    C. The bond pays no interest until maturity.
    D. None of the above statements is true.

13. The maximum fine in a summary complaint proceeding is

    A. $1,000
    B. $2,500
    C. $5,000
    D. $10,000

14. The Code of Arbitration is used when there are disputes between a broker-dealer and

    A. the Securities and Exchange Commission
    B. another broker-dealer
    C. the general public
    D. the National Association of Securities Dealers

15. An economic downturn that lasts for six months is called

    A. a recession
    B. a depression
    C. progressive
    D. regressive

16. Which of the following statements best describes the federal funds rate?

    A. It is the average rate for short-term bank loans last week.
    B. It is the rate charged by major New York City banks.
    C. It is a rate that changes daily and that banks charge each other.
    D. It is the rate major New York City banks charge broker-dealers.

17. An owner of common stock has which of the following rights?

   I.   Right to determine when dividends will be issued
   II. Right to vote at stockholders' meetings or by proxy
   III. Right to receive a predetermined fixed portion of the corporation's profit in cash when declared
   IV. Right to buy restricted securities before they are offered to the public

   A. I, III and IV
   B. II
   C. II, III and IV
   D. II and IV

18. A company in which you own stock is about to have a stock rights offering. You do not plan on subscribing to the offer. Your proportionate interest in the company will be

   A. increased
   B. reduced
   C. the same
   D. More information is needed to answer this question.

19. Under a defined-contribution plan, the

   I.   participant is guaranteed a contribution that is based on an agreed-upon percentage or rate
   II. participant's retirement benefits are based on the balance in his individual account
   III. employer may discriminate among employees as to participation

   A. I and II only
   B. I and III only
   C. II and III only
   D. I, II and III

20. An investor's portfolio includes ten bonds and 200 shares of common stock. If both positions increase by 1/2 of a point, what is the gain?

   A. $50
   B. $105
   C. $110
   D. $150

21. The investment policy of a mutual fund can be changed by a majority vote of the

   A. board of directors
   B. fund's managers
   C. SEC investment committee
   D. outstanding shares

22. What of the following attributes of 401K thrift plans is NOT allowed in most other retirement plans?

   A. Tax-deferred earnings
   B. Deductible contributions to the plan
   C. Matching employer contributions
   D. No penalties for premature distributions

23. Which of the following statements is true of the calculation of the expense ratio of an open-end investment company?

   A. The expense ratio is computed exclusive of the management fee.
   B. The expense ratio is computed inclusive of the management fee.
   C. The expense ratio is computed taking into account the management fee only.
   D. The expense ratio shows the extent of leverage in the fund.

24. Bud Charolais opened an account about twelve years ago with the ACE Mutual Fund. Today his NAV is $20,000. The ACE Fund offers rights of accumulation. Its breakpoints are as follows:

$1 to $24,999	8%
$25,000 to $49,999	6%
$50,000 to $99,999	4%

Bud wishes to deposit $6,000 in the account today. Which of the following would represent his sales charge?

A. $1,000 at 8%, and $5,000 at 6%
B. $4,999 at 8%, and $1,001 at 6%
C. The full $6,000 at 6%
D. The full $6,000 at 8%

25. June Polar has invested in a mutual fund and has signed a statement of intention to invest $25,000. Her original investment was for $13,000, and her current account value is $17,000. For her to complete the letter, she would need to deposit

A. $8,000
B. $12,000
C. $13,000
D. $27,000

26. Adam Grizzly invests $3,000 in open-end investment company shares. After 60 days, he signs a letter of intent for a $10,000 breakpoint and backdates the letter two months. Six months later, he deposits $10,000 into the fund. He will receive a reduced sales charge on

A. the $3,000 investment only
B. $7,000 of the investment only
C. the $10,000 investment only
D. the entire $13,000 investment

27. Some open-end investment companies offer their investors a conversion privilege, which permits investors to

A. exchange general securities for shares in the mutual fund's portfolio
B. delay payment of taxes on investment company shares that have appreciated in value
C. purchase additional fund shares from dividends paid by the fund
D. exchange shares of one mutual fund for those of another fund under the same management, at net asset value

28. ArGood Mutual Fund permits rights of accumulation. Klaus Bruin has invested $9,000 and has signed a letter of intent for a $15,000 investment. His reinvested dividends during the 13 months total $720. How much money must he contribute to fulfill the letter of intent?

A. $5,280
B. $6,000
C. $9,000
D. $15,000

29. If an investment company offers rights of accumulation and an investor wishes to get a reduced sales charge, the client must deposit the sufficient funds within

A. 45 days
B. 13 months
C. There is no time limit.
D. Each fund has its own requirements.

30. The death benefit of a life insurance contract funded by a separate account and offered with fixed premiums is determined at least

A. daily
B. weekly
C. monthly
D. annually

31. A husband and wife are both employed, and each qualifies to open an IRA. To make their maximum allowable contributions, they should open

    A. a joint IRA and deposit $2,000
    B. a joint IRA and deposit $4,000
    C. two separate IRAs and deposit $2,000 each
    D. two separate IRAs and deposit $2,250

32. Which of the following would be eligible under the Keogh plan?

    I. Self-employed doctor
    II. Engineer receiving extra compensation as an outside consultant
    III. Advertising executive who made $5,000 during the year freelancing
    IV. Executive employed by a corporation who received $5,000 in stock options

    A. I, II and III only
    B. I, III and IV only
    C. II and IV only
    D. I, II, III and IV

33. Which of the following statements are true regarding the withdrawal of funds from a qualified retirement plan?

    I. The employee will be taxed at the ordinary income tax rate on his cost base.
    II. Funds may be withdrawn after retirement (as defined) with no tax on the withdrawn amount.
    III. Funds may be withdrawn early by the beneficiary if the covered person dies.
    IV. All qualified plans must be in written form.

    A. I and II only
    B. II, III and IV only
    C. III and IV only
    D. I, II, III and IV

34. Adam Grizzly invests in a tax-qualified variable annuity. What is the tax treatment of the distributions he receives?

    A. Partially tax-free; partially ordinary income
    B. Partially tax-free; partially capital gains
    C. All ordinary income
    D. All capital gains

35. All of the following statements concerning IRA contributions are true EXCEPT

    A. between January 1st and April 15th, contributions may be made for the current year, the past year or both
    B. contributions for the past year may be made after April 15th, provided an extension has been filed on a timely basis
    C. if you pay your tax on January 15th, you can still deduct your IRA contribution even if not made until April 15th
    D. contributions can be paid into this year's IRA from January 1st of this year until April 15th of next year

36. If you invest in a mutual fund and you choose to have automatic reinvestment, you would expect that

    I. dividend distributions will be reinvested at net asset value
    II. dividend distributions will be reinvested at public offering price
    III. capital gains distributions will be reinvested at net asset value
    IV. capital gains distributions will be reinvested at public offering price

    A. I and III
    B. I and IV
    C. II and III
    D. II and IV

37. Under what conditions does the Investment Company Act of 1940 require a written statement disclosing the source of dividend payments?

   A. Whenever a dividend is paid
   B. Whenever net income is part of the dividend
   C. Whenever all or part of the dividend payment comes from a source other than current income or accumulated undistributed net income
   D. The Investment Company Act does not require disclosure; only the Internal Revenue Code requires disclosure of the amount of the dividend.

38. In a nonqualified variable annuity, which of the following best describes the risks borne by the annuitant?

   A. The annuitant must pay taxes on the earnings in the current period.
   B. Mortality risks
   C. Interest rate risks
   D. Operating expense risks

39. In calculating the investment performance of a separate account, you would take into account

   A. realized capital gains
   B. unrealized capital gains
   C. dividend income
   D. all of the above

40. The capital gains tax rate that an individual pays on appreciation in the reserves held for his variable annuity in a separate account while the contract is in the accumulation period is

   A. 0%
   B. 10%
   C. 25%
   D. 50%

41. A customer, age 42, has been depositing money in a variable annuity for five years. He plans to stop investing, but has no intention of withdrawing any funds for at least 20 years. He most likely is holding

   A. accumulation units
   B. annuity units
   C. accumulation shares
   D. mutual fund units

42. During the accumulation period of a periodic payment deferred variable annuity, the number of accumulation units

   A. varies and the value per unit is fixed
   B. is fixed and the value per unit is fixed
   C. is fixed and the value per unit varies
   D. varies and the value per unit varies

43. A doctor has compensation of $160,000. What is the maximum he may contribute to his Keogh plan?

   A. $5,000
   B. $22,000
   C. $28,000
   D. $30,000

44. In the sale of open-end investment company shares, the prospectus

   A. is not necessary
   B. must be delivered to the client either before or during the sales solicitation
   C. must be delivered before the sales solicitation
   D. must be delivered at or before the delivery of the fund share certificate

45. Which Federal Reserve Board regulation prohibits brokers and dealers from extending credit for the purchase of open-end investment company shares?

   A. Regulation A
   B. Regulation G
   C. Regulation U
   D. Regulation T

46. Which of the following would constitute a discretionary account?

    A. Trading account of the registered representative
    B. Trading account of the broker-dealer
    C. Account where the investor gives the broker-dealer the authority to buy or sell securities in the customer's account
    D. Mutual fund account allowing periodic withdrawals

47. When a client opens an account, which of the following pieces of information will need to be noted on the application?

    I. Client's name and Social Security number
    II. Whether the client is employed by an NASD member firm
    III. Signature of the registered rep
    IV. Signature of the office manager, partner or other designated principal
    V. Statement that the client understands the risks involved

    A. I only
    B. I, II, III and IV only
    C. II and IV only
    D. I, II, III, IV and V

48. In general, a registered representative could have power of attorney for accounts of each of the following EXCEPT a(n)

    A. corporation
    B. individual
    C. partnership
    D. custodian

49. Which of the following statements is true of a limited power of attorney that a customer gives his rep?

    A. The rep needs written permission from the customer for each trade.
    B. The customer must renew the power of attorney every year.
    C. The customer can still enter independent orders.
    D. The branch manager must initial each order before it is entered.

50. Your customer works as a nurse in a public school. He wants to know more about participating in his school's TSA plan. You should tell him

    I. his contributions are tax exempt
    II. he is not eligible to participate
    III. distributions before age 59 1/2 are normally subject to penalty tax
    IV. mutual funds and CDs are available investment vehicles

    A. I, II and II
    B. I and III
    C. I, III and IV
    D. II

51. A registered representative of an NYSE member firm who wishes to work outside the firm after hours would require permission from the

    A. member firm
    B. NASD
    C. NYSE
    D. SEC

52. General communications by a broker-dealer firm, such as advertising or research reports, must be approved by which of the following?

    A. Member
    B. Principal of a member
    C. Supervisory analyst
    D. Certified financial analyst

53. Sales literature for a mutual fund must

    A. promise delivery of a prospectus when the shares are delivered to the purchaser
    B. contain a warning that the SEC supervision of the company does not guarantee against a decrease in the market value of the shares
    C. be preceded or accompanied by a prospectus
    D. contain the statement "A prospectus relating to these securities is available upon request"

54. Sales literature and advertising material that have been prepared by the firm's principal underwriter and are to be used by a member firm in connection with the offering of investment company shares must be reviewed by the

   I.   firm's advertising manager
   II. NASD
   III. SEC

   A. I
   B. I and II
   C. II
   D. II and III

55. A customer wants to purchase mutual fund shares just before the ex-dividend date. You should tell him that this is

   A. not advisable under any circumstances
   B. not advisable because of the tax consequences.
   C. advisable because the client will receive a dividend.
   D. advisable because it will allow the client to pay more per share, thus increasing his chance of getting to the breakpoint

56. Randy Bear buys shares of the GEM Fund shortly before the ex-dividend date. Before he buys the shares, Randy Bear should understand that

   A. the price of the shares will decline on the ex-dividend date by the amount of the distribution
   B. if he reinvests the dividend he will not be liable for taxes on the dividend received
   C. there is a great advantage to him purchasing the shares immediately so that he can receive the dividend
   D. all of the above apply

57. A customer indicates he wishes to invest $50,000 in mutual funds. The investments are to be split in three different funds, each with its own management company and not related in any way. The registered representative should advise the client that

   A. this is an excellent idea because it spreads the risk of investing even more
   B. the customer will pay greater commissions on the investment when the money is split between three funds than if the investor put the money into only one fund
   C. the customer will be able to exchange shares from one fund to another as conditions change without incurring a new sales charge
   D. the investor should buy individual stocks because mutual funds are only for smaller investors

58. Sales literature and advertising used in connection with the solicitation or sale of variable life products is defined as

   I.   circulars and leaflets describing the variable life product
   II. prepared presentations used at a seminar open to the public
   III. newspaper advertising of the benefits of variable life insurance
   IV. a letter that is sent to 50 of the agent's present clients describing variable life insurance

   A. I and II only
   B. I and III only
   C. III only
   D. I, II, III and IV

59. Which of the following situations might fall into the category of a hot issue?

   A. New issue is offered at $30 and immediately appreciates to $35.
   B. New issue is offered at $30 and immediately decreases to $25.
   C. Market maker buys at $17 and immediately sells with a spread of $2.
   D. Broker-dealer sells inventory at $60 three weeks after buying at $30.

60. Except under limited circumstances, NASD rules on freeriding and withholding prohibit the purchase of a hot issue by which of the following people?

   I. Finder
   II. Bank officer who has a significant relationship with the issuer
   III. Officer of a broker-dealer firm that is a member of the NASD
   IV. Registered representative

   A. I and II only
   B. I, III and IV only
   C. III and IV only
   D. I, II, III and IV

61. Which of the following is(are) actively traded?

   I. Warrants
   II. Nondetachable rights
   III. Common stock
   IV. Options on stock

   A. I, III and IV only
   B. II only
   C. II and IV only
   D. I, II, III and IV

62. Which of the following statements is(are) true regarding rights and warrants?

   I. Warrants are issued with an exercise price higher than the underlying stock.
   II. Rights are issued with an exercise price lower than the underlying stock.
   III. Warrants are long lived, may even be perpetual and may be issued to anyone.
   IV. Rights are short lived and issued only to present shareholders.

   A. I only
   B. I and II only
   C. II and III only
   D. I, II, III and IV

63. A corporation's capitalization includes $1,000,000 of 7% preferred stock and $1,000,000 of 7% convertible debentures. If all the convertible debentures were converted into common stock, what would happen to the company's earnings?

   A. They would increase.
   B. They would decrease.
   C. There would be no change.
   D. It cannot be determined.

64. Chip Bullock owns 100 shares of TCB Company. A dividend is declared on August 30th. The dividend will be paid to stockholders of record on Thursday, September 15th. When will the stock sell ex-dividend?

   A. September 11th
   B. September 12th
   C. September 13th
   D. September 15th

65. The ex-dividend date is the

    I.   date on and after which the buyer is entitled to the dividend
    II. date on and after which the seller is entitled to the dividend
    III. second business day prior to the record date
    IV. second business day after the record date

    A. I and III
    B. I and IV
    C. II and III
    D. II and IV

66. Your firm is the underwriter of a new mutual fund organized under a 12b-1 plan. Which of the following statements may you make in any mailings or phone calls to your clients?

    A. "The fund has the added advantage of being a no-load investment."
    B. "You will not have to pay any sales charges with this fund because we're buying it as a long-term investment."
    C. "Investments in no-load funds of this type do have some risks, and you will want to review the prospectus carefully."
    D. None of the above

67. The exchange privilege offered by some mutual funds that are in a family of funds managed by the same company refers to the right of the shareholder to

    A. convert mutual fund shares to securities listed on the New York Stock Exchange
    B. reinvest dividends and capital gains without a sales charge
    C. convert shares to a different investment company within the family of funds on a dollar-for-dollar basis
    D. switch shares to an investment company within the family of funds and defer the taxes on any capital gains due to the exchange

68. An annuity is purchased with a life contingency offering a fully paid contribution to the annuity in the event of the owner's death. This life contingency applies during

    A. the accumulation period
    B. the annuity period
    C. both A and B
    D. neither A nor B

69. Failure by a shareholder to provide or verify her Social Security number to the investment company will result in which of the following taxes?

    A. Surtax
    B. Alternative minimum tax
    C. Noncertification tax
    D. Withholding tax

70. In order for a registered investment company to terminate its 12b-1 plan, the termination must be approved by a majority of the

    I.   outstanding voting shares of the company
    II. board of directors
    III. uninterested members of the board of directors
    IV. investment advisory board

    A. I and II
    B. I, II and III
    C. I and III
    D. II, III and IV

71. How often are 12b-1 fees paid?

    A. Monthly
    B. Quarterly
    C. Semiannually
    D. Annually

72. Which of the following are characteristics of money-market instruments?

   A. They are backed by promises to repay a sum of money within a stated period of time.
   B. They are used to borrow money for short periods of time.
   C. They are issued by corporations and governmental bodies.
   D. All of the above

73. The transfer agent of a mutual fund

   I. redeems shares
   II. sells shares
   III. holds custody of fund securities
   IV. handles name changes of mutual fund ownership

   A. I and III
   B. I and IV
   C. II and III
   D. II and IV

74. 12b-1 fees may be used to pay

   A. distributor expenses not identified in the plan document
   B. sales and promotional expenses
   C. transfer fees
   D. investment advisory fees

75. The maximum fee that can be charged under a 12b-1 plan is

   A. an amount equal to the share's net asset value
   B. the difference between the share's POP and NAV
   C. an amount that is reasonable in light of the distribution services offered and described in the plan
   D. 9% over the life of the plan

76. A college graduate has $1,000 in savings and owes $15,000 on college tuition loans to be paid over the next ten years. What type of mutual fund investment would you recommend to him?

   A. Open an account in an income fund with $1,000 and invest periodically using dollar cost averaging.
   B. Invest $1,000 in a capital appreciation fund.
   C. Invest $1,000 in any fund; because he is young, he can absorb any losses.
   D. Defer investment of the $1,000 until he has enough money accumulated to allow investment without adversely affecting his ability to meet emergency expenses.

77. To what does the term "selling dividends" refer?

   A. Encouraging mutual fund customers to sell their holdings just before the fund declares a dividend payment
   B. Enticing customers to buy mutual fund shares just before an ex-dividend date
   C. Withdrawing dividends rather than reinvesting these amounts in additional shares
   D. Encouraging investors to postpone purchases of mutual fund shares until after the ex-date for a dividend distribution

78. An individual has periodically invested $24,000 in a unit investment trust over ten years. What is the maximum sales charge?

   A. $2,040
   B. $2,160
   C. $4,800
   D. $12,000

79. A 45-year-old woman wants the greatest possible monthly income. Preservation and stability of capital are important, although secondary, objectives. Which of the following investments would you recommend?

   A. Money-market mutual fund
   B. High-grade bond fund
   C. Growth mutual fund
   D. Combination fund

80. A registered rep may NOT do which of the following without prior approval from her firm?

   I. Work part-time as piano player
   II. Work part-time as a bartender
   III. Invest passively in a night club
   IV. Receive a salary as a manager and general partner of an apartment building offering investment interests to passive partners

   A. I, II and IV only
   B. II and IV only
   C. III only
   D. I, II, III and IV

81. Gwinneth Stout invested $10,000 in the ACE Fund in February. Gwinneth sold the shares the following January for $9,000. The result is a

   A. capital loss in the year of sale
   B. capital gain in the year of sale
   C. capital loss in the year of purchase
   D. capital gain in the year of purchase

82. ATF Mutual Fund has incurred the following on a per share basis: dividend income of $1.10, interest income of $.90, long-term gains of $1.00, management fees of $.50. What is the maximum dividend the fund can distribute per share?

   A. $1.50
   B. $2.00
   C. $2.50
   D. $3.00

83. Under the Code of Arbitration, the statute of limitations for filing a complaint against a member or associated person is

   A. six months
   B. one year
   C. two years
   D. six years

84. The NASD Rules of Fair Practice govern the actions of its members. All of the following are considered violations of the rules EXCEPT

   A. churning accounts
   B. the blanket recommending of low-price speculative stocks
   C. using discretionary authority
   D. guaranteeing the customer against loss

85. The District Business Conduct Committee may

   A. expel a registered representative from the securities business
   B. fine a registered representative an amount not exceeding $15,000
   C. not bar a registered representative from associating with other members or associated persons
   D. not suspend a member

86. When you inherit a mutual fund upon the death of the owner, what is your cost basis in the shares?

   A. The market value of the shares upon the decedent's death
   B. The same cost basis as the decedent's
   C. The cost basis of the decedent plus the final distribution made by the fund
   D. The market value of the shares twelve months from the date of death

87. Which of the following would be underwriting an issue of securities?

    A. Chip Bullock sells his stock in TCB through his broker.

    B. Angus Bullwether, a director of Microscam, Inc., purchases Microscam stock.

    C. Greide S. Goode & Co., a broker-dealer, sells a block of outstanding stock in Datawaq to Acme Zootech.

    D. ALFA Securities, a broker-dealer, sells a new issue of TIP Bonds to the public.

88. What is the maximum sales charge on a 12b-1 in the first year?

    A. 50%

    B. 20%

    C. 9%

    D. 8.5%

89. What is the maturity of a T bill?

    A. 20 years

    B. 10 years

    C. 5 years

    D. 1 year or less

90. Which of the following is a nontransferable government instrument?

    A. T bond

    B. T bill

    C. T note

    D. EE savings bond

91. What sales charge is refunded in a variable life contract after six months?

    A. No refund is allowed.

    B. All sales charges collected are refunded.

    C. Sales charges exceeding an amount over 30% are refunded.

    D. Sales charges less management fees are refunded.

92. A 12b-1 asset based fee must be disclosed

    A. in the prospectus

    B. on the share certificate

    C. on the application for investment

    D. on all of the above

93. A fixed-premium variable life insurance contract offers

    I. a guaranteed maximum death benefit

    II. a guaranteed minimum death benefit

    III. a guaranteed cash value

    IV. a cash value that fluctuates according to the performance of the contract

    A. I and III

    B. I and IV

    C. II and III

    D. II and IV

94. Which of the following affect the parity of a convertible bond with the underlying stock?

    A. Interest rates

    B. Company earnings performance

    C. Stock market movement and trends

    D. All of the above

95. The prime rate is

    A. the interest rate offered to the bank's best corporate customers

    B. the interest rate at which banks borrow from the Federal Reserve Board

    C. the interest rate at which individuals borrow from banks for mortgages on residential purchases

    D. the points or premium paid to obtain a mortgage on a residential purchase

96. Tex Longhorn, age 65, will receive a lump-sum distribution from his pension plan. He had invested the money in a growth fund in the pension plan. Tex is reconsidering his investment options; he doesn't want to commit the funds for at least eight or nine months. What would you recommend?

    A. Reinvest the money in a growth fund to match his previous objectives until he decides what he wants to do.
    B. Reinvest the money in a one-year CD to preserve capital.
    C. Reinvest the money in a money-market mutual fund.
    D. Hold onto the check from the pension plan until he decides what he wants.

97. If a registered representative uses a prospectus as a sales aid, what must accompany the prospectus in her presentation?

    A. All sales literature describing the investment
    B. All advertising describing the investment
    C. The company's balance sheet
    D. No other information is required unless requested.

98. What of the following attributes of 401K thrift plans is NOT allowed in most other retirement plans?

    A. Tax-deferred earnings
    B. Deductible contributions to the plan
    C. Matching employer contributions
    D. No penalties for premature distributions

99. Which of the following is a statutory disqualification preventing an individual from participating in the securities business as a registered person of the SEC or other self-regulatory organization?

    I. The individual has been convicted within 10 years of a securities-related crime.
    II. The individual has willfully violated the provisions of a federal securities act.
    III. The individual has been expelled or suspended from an SRO.
    IV. The individual is subject to an order of the Commission denying, suspending or revoking registration.

    A. I only
    B. I and II only
    C. II and III only
    D. I, II, III and IV

100. During a recessionary period, will a growth fund or a balanced fund perform better?

    A. The growth fund will do better because its objective is to grow regardless of the economic environment.
    B. The balanced fund will do better because of the downside protection that the bonds and other debt securities held by the fund will provide.
    C. The growth fund will do better because stocks of growth companies typically fare well during recessionary periods.
    D. The balanced fund will do better because any convertible securities held by the fund will increase.

◆ Answers & Rationale

1. **A.** T bills are issued with three-, six- and twelve-month maturities. (Page 25)

2. **B.** Nominal yield is fixed and stays the same on all bonds. A bond selling above par is selling at a premium, so the current yield and yield to maturity will be less than the nominal yield. (Page 16)

3. **B.** Although the Treasury securities underlying Treasury receipts are backed by the full faith and credit of the federal government, the stripped securities are not. (Page 26)

4. **A.** Commercial paper is not issued by commercial banks. The commercial paper market was developed to circumvent banks so that corporations could lend to and borrow from each other more economically. Commercial paper is unsecured corporate IOUs. (Page 35)

5. **C.** In this case "call protection" means that the bonds cannot be called by the issuer for at least five years. If interest rates are falling, the issuer would have reason to want to call the bonds in and, perhaps, issue new bonds at a lower interest rate. Therefore, the call feature protects the investor for a specific period of time. (Page 59)

6. **A.** If the yields have gone down, that means that the discount has been reduced; therefore, the dollar cost of bills has gone up. (Page 25)

7. **C.** This bond, because the yield is above the coupon, is trading at a discount. Therefore, if it is held to maturity, the customer will realize a return on the bond of 8% and have a capital gains tax. Because the tax paid will reduce the return on the customer's investment, the effective yield will be less than 8%. (Page 15)

8. **D.** Under the Code of Procedure, a member or its employees may be censured, suspended, expelled or fined for a violation of NASD rules. (Page 212)

9. **A.** General obligation bonds are backed by the general taxing authority of the municipal issuer. As such, they are often considered very safe investments. Municipal issues are marketable and are bought and sold in the secondary marketplace. Because interest received on municipal debt is exempt from federal taxation, yields offered on municipal debt are lower than yields offered on corporate debt. (Page 32)

10. **A.** The bond is quoted as 90; therefore, it is selling for $900. Parity of the stock in which the holder of the bond can convert is equal to $22.50 as follows: The bondholder would be able to convert the bond into 40 shares of stock ($1,000 face amount ÷ $25 per share = 40 shares) because the bond has a current price of $900; dividing this amount by 40 equals the parity price of the underlying stock. (Page 20)

11. **C.** A portion of the original issue discount on taxable zero-coupon bonds must be declared as income and taxed annually until the bond matures. This is known as accreting the discount. (Page 13)

12. **C.** The QRS is a zero-coupon bond maturing in 2012. Zero-coupon bonds are bought at a discount and mature at face value. If held to maturity, the difference between the purchase price and the maturity price is considered interest. (Page 230)

13. **B.** The maximum fine in a summary complaint is $2,500, according to the NASD Code of Procedure. (Page 213)

14. **B.** The Code of Arbitration covers inter-dealer disputes. (Page 213)

15. **A.** When the economy is bad for six months (or two consecutive quarters), we are in a recession; if it continues, we go into a depression. (Page 48)

16. **C.** The federal funds rate is what banks charge each other for overnight loans. It can fluctuate hourly. (Page 51)

17. **B.**   The stockholder has the right to vote and the right to dividends if and when declared (although not to a fixed dividend). A restricted security is one that has prescribed limits on resale generally requiring registration.   (Page 5)

18. **B.**   A preemptive right enables the stockholder to maintain a proportionate share of ownership in the corporation. Because the shares have already been authorized, should the stockholder decline to participate in the rights offering, the stockholder's interest is reduced.   (Page 20)

19. **A.**   Under a defined-contribution plan, contributions may be based on years of service or, more frequently, salary. Benefits are provided based on what the accumulated contributions will provide at retirement. The plan is qualified and may not discriminate.   (Page 167)

20. **D.**   The gain would be $50 for the bonds (1/2 point for one bond is $5 times 10 bonds) and $100 for the common stock (1/2 point is $.50 times 200 shares).   (Page 9)

21. **D.**   Any changes in a mutual fund's investment policies must be made by a majority vote of the fund's outstanding shares.   (Page 80)

22. **C.**   Thrift or 401K plans allow the employer to match employee contributions up to a stipulated percentage.   (Page 169)

23. **B.**   The expense ratio includes the costs of operating the fund compared to fund assets. Expenses included in the ratio are management fees, administrative fees, brokerage fees and taxes.   (Page 85)

24. **C.**   Under rights of accumulation, if an additional investment plus the client's current account value (or money invested) puts the client's account value over a breakpoint, the entire additional investment qualifies for the reduced sales charge. In this case, Bud's additional investment of $6,000 plus his account value of $20,000 puts his account value over the $25,000 breakpoint. The entire $6,000 investment qualifies for the 6% sales charge.   (Page 104)

25. **B.**   Under a letter of intent, the full contribution stated in the letter must be contributed in order for the letter to be completed. Appreciation is not considered.   (Page 103)

26. **D.**   The entire investment qualifies for the reduced load. A letter of intent covers purchases within a 13-month period and may be backdated 90 days. Adam actually had eleven months in which to make the additional investment.   (Page 103)

27. **D.**   The exchange or conversion privilege allows an investor to exchange shares of one fund for another fund under the same management without paying an additional sales charge (although the exchange is still a taxable event).   (Page 105)

28. **B.**   Klaus must put in the full $15,000 or the additional $6,000. Reinvested dividends and changes in the NAV do not affect the amount required.   (Page 104)

29. **C.**   Rights of accumulation are good forever, while the letter of intent has a 13-month limit.   (Page 104)

30. **D.**   The variable death benefit of a scheduled premium variable life contract is determined annually.   (Page 153)

31. **C.**   Each individual with earned income may open an IRA and deposit 100% of this earned income up to $2,000 per year.   (Page 159)

32. **A.**   A Keogh plan (HR-10) may be opened only by an individual with self-employment income.   (Page 164)

33. **C.**   Cost base in a retirement plan is money contributed aftertax; upon receipt there is no tax liability. Money withdrawn from a qualified plan will be taxed as ordinary income upon receipt.   (Page 166)

34. **C.**   In a tax-qualified annuity, the annuitant has no basis unless voluntary aftertax contributions were made. Such aftertax contributions are the exception and are not mentioned in this question.

Because the annuitant has no basis, all payments are considered ordinary income. In a nonqualified annuity, contributions are made with aftertax dollars, which establish the annuitant's basis. Annuity payments from nonqualified annuities are treated as ordinary income to the extent that they exceed the basis.   (Page 173)

35. **B.** Contributions can be made to an IRA only until the first tax filing deadline (April 15th) even though you may have filed an extension. Anyone with earned income can make a contribution to an IRA.   (Page 158)

36. **A.** Most mutual funds offer automatic reinvestment of income and gains distributions at net asset value. If income distribution reinvestment is subject to a sales charge, then the maximum allowable sales charge for any purchases is reduced.   (Page 111)

37. **C.** The Investment Company Act of 1940 requires disclosure when all or part of the dividend payment comes from a source other than current income or accumulated undistributed net income.   (Page 112)

38. **C.** In a variable annuity, performance of the account is not guaranteed; the investor accepts the risk the account will not perform at the assumed interest rate.   (Page 142)

39. **D.** Performance of a separate account will depend on increases and decreases of the securities held in the portfolio. Whether gains are realized or unrealized, the account will reflect the gain or loss.   (Page 147)

40. **A.** Gains in a separate account are tax deferred. The annuitant will pay ordinary income tax on the distribution upon receipt.   (Page 149)

41. **A.** The customer is in the deferral stage of the annuity and would be holding accumulation units. The value of the customer's account would be converted into annuity units when and if the customer decides to annuitize the contract.
                                            (Page 147)

42. **D.** The value of an accumulation unit varies according to the value of the insurance company's separate account. During the accumulation stage of a variable annuity, the number of units will also vary as the income distributions and additional contributions will be purchasing more units. At the conversion of accumulation units into annuity units, only then is the number of units fixed, but the value still fluctuates according to the value of the separate account.   (Page 147)

43. **D.** Keogh contributions are limited to 25% of aftertax income (the equivalent of 20% of pretax income) to a maximum of $30,000. In this case the doctor's $160,000 income times 20% equals $32,000, $2,000 more than the maximum contribution.   (Page 164)

44. **B.** The sale of mutual fund shares requires that the client get the prospectus before or during the sales solicitation.   (Page 93)

45. **D.** Regulation T regulates the extension of credit by brokers and dealers for investment company shares.   (Page 88)

46. **C.** A discretionary account is an account where a representative has been given authority to select the amount and type of investment for a client. The authorization must be in writing.
                                            (Page 128)

47. **D.** When opening an account, the minimum information needed is the name of the customer, whether the customer is employed with another NASD firm and the customer's tax identification number. Additionally, the registered representative must have discussed the risks of the investment with the customer and must sign the appropriate forms. All accounts will be reviewed by a supervisor (principal of the firm).   (Page 124)

48. **D.** A custodian for an UGMA account cannot grant trading authority to a third party.
                                            (Page 131)

49. **C.** The registered rep must have prior written authority from the customer and have received approval from a supervisory person before accept-

ing discretionary authority. While a designated principal must frequently review the account, the branch manager need not initial each order before it is entered.   (Page 129)

50. **C.** Because he is employed by a public school system, your customer is eligible to participate in the tax-sheltered annuity plan. Employee contributions to a TSA plan are excluded from gross income in the year in which they are made. Like other retirement plans, a penalty tax is assessed on distributions received before age 59 1/2. A TSA plan may invest in various instruments, including mutual funds, stocks, bonds and CDs, in addition to annuity contracts.   (Page 173)

51. **A.** A rep would always need to get permission from the firm before working for another firm.   (Page 204)

52. **B.** All advertising and other communications made by a broker-dealer must be approved by a qualified principal of the firm.   (Page 220)

53. **C.** All sales literature or advertising used in connection with the solicitation of mutual fund shares must be accompanied or preceded by the prospectus.   (Page 215)

54. **C.** All sales literature used in connection with a new offering must be filed for review with the NASD. A principal of the firm must approve its use and is responsible for corrections required by the NASD.   (Page 220)

55. **B.** The value of shares will drop by the amount of the dividend on the ex-dividend date. This loss will not be made up by the dividend as the dividend is subject to ordinary income tax.   (Page 111)

56. **A.** Share prices decline on the ex-dividend date. Dividend distributions cause a tax liability, and the purchase of shares right before an ex-dividend date is not a good idea because of the tax liability.   (Page 46)

57. **B.** Because the funds are under separate management, the load charged on each separate

investment will likely be at the maximum. If the client invested the entire sum within one fund or a family of funds, a reduced sales charge may have been available.   (Page 105)

58. **D.** All of the materials listed are considered as either sales literature or advertising when used in connection with the solicitation of variable life insurance.   (Page 215)

59. **A.** When a stock goes up in price dramatically upon issue, it is said to be hot. Although there is no mathematical formula, a rise in price of 1/8th point or more upon issue is generally considered an example of a hot issue.   (Page 209)

60. **D.** Officers and directors of broker-dealers can never buy a hot issue and neither can the firm for its own inventory. A registered rep never can buy a hot issue. Those persons listed in choices I and II, as well as relatives, cannot buy a hot issue unless the amount they are purchasing is insignificant and they have an underwriter to assist in the solicitation of public interest during the 20-day cooling-off period.   (Page 209)

61. **A.** Warrants, common stock and options all have an active secondary market.   (Page 21)

62. **D.** Warrants are usually issued as a sweetener to a deal. For example, if a company wants to issue bonds at an interest rate lower than general market rates, it could throw in some warrants to make the bonds more attractive. Warrants are usually issued with a very long life and give the holder the right to purchase stock above the current market price. When a corporation has common stock outstanding and wants to issue more common stock, it must offer the shares to the current shareholders first (preemptive rights).   (Page 21)

63. **A.** Bond interest is an expense of the firm, and when it is paid, it reduces the earnings of the firm. If the bonds were to convert, there would be no more interest payments; therefore, the company would have higher earnings. There will be more shares of common stock outstanding, and this will normally translate to lower earnings per share for the common. Interest costs would be reduced, earn-

ings would increase and the number of shares would increase.   (Page 18)

64. **C.** The ex-dividend date is always two business days before the record date. In this case the record date is Thursday, September 15th, so the ex-date will be Tuesday, September 13th.
(Page 46)

65. **C.** Stocks sold on the ex-dividend date entitle the seller to the dividend. Stocks sell ex-dividend two business days before the record date.
(Page 46)

66. **D.** Any statement or reference to a mutual fund offered under a 12b-1 fund that implies that the fund is a no-load fund is considered misleading and a violation of the Rules of Fair Practice.
(Page 100)

67. **C.** The exchange privilege allows a shareholder to exchange shares from one fund to another within a family of funds under the same management without paying an additional sales charge (dollar for dollar). The shareholder is liable for any tax on gains as a result of the exchange.
(Page 105)

68. **A.** An annuity with a life contingency (death benefit) promising a full contribution amount applies to the annuity during the accumulation stage. A guaranteed payout to a beneficiary in the event of an annuitant's death applies to the annuity period.   (Page 146)

69. **D.** Failure to provide a Social Security or federal tax identification number results in an automatic withholding tax of 20% on the account.
(Page 114)

70. **C.** In order to terminate a 12b-1 charge, the termination must be approved by a majority vote of the shareholders or a majority of the uninterested members of the board of directors. Approval by the full board of directors is not required. (Page 100)

71. **B.** A 12b-1 fee is a percent of the annual average net assets of the fund. The fee is typically paid in quarterly installments.   (Page 99)

72. **D.** Money-market instruments are unsecured short-term debt instruments used by corporations and federal, state and city governments to borrow money.   (Page 34)

73. **B.** The transfer agent redeems shares of a mutual fund at the price next calculated after receiving a request for redemption. The transfer agent also handles transfer of account ownership for such transactions as an inheritance or gift. The fund custodian holds custody of fund securities. A fund underwriter or the fund itself sells shares; the transfer agent then records ownership.   (Page 92)

74. **B.** Amounts paid under a 12b-1 plan may be used only to pay for specific sales or promotional services or activities described in the plan. Such services or activities must be or will be provided in connection with the distribution of the shares.   (Page 99)

75. **C.** The maximum charged under a 12b-1 plan must bear a relationship to the distribution services offered and must be reasonable. The fee charged may pay only for those distribution, selling and promotional expenses specifically described in the plan. Shares offered under a 12b-1 fund are sold at net asset value; there is no POP. The 9% maximum refers to shares sold under contractual plan agreements.   (Page 99)

76. **D.** Without knowing more about the graduate's financial situation, you should tell him that he is better off deferring the investment of $1,000 at this time. Should he invest the full $1,000 in any of the mutual funds described in the question, and should an emergency occur, he would most likely have to liquidate his investment. However, if one of the choices were a money market fund, the $1,000 could be considered an emergency fund and this type of investment would be appropriate.
(Page 61)

77. **B.** "Selling dividends" is an unethical sales practice in which a seller intentionally or unintentionally misleads customers into believing they will be getting the equivalent of a rebate on their investments because the fund will soon be paying a distribution. The customers suffer out-of-pocket

losses because the cash immediately coming back is dividend income, subject to tax.   (Page 207)

78. **B.** First, the method of investment describes a contractual plan (i.e., a periodic investment into a unit investment trust over a period of time). The maximum sales charge over the life of a contractual plan is 9%. In this case, 9% of $24,000 equals $2,160.   (Page 118)

79. **B.** A high-grade bond fund would provide income that is greater than that provided by a money-market fund while still offering stability and preservation of capital. Many bond funds provide for monthly payment of interest income, whereas stock funds typically offer distributions only on a quarterly or less frequent basis. The objective of a growth fund typically is not to offer income distributions; rather, the objective is appreciation. A combination fund invests in growth and income stocks and attempts to provide both growth and current income; however, the NAV can fluctuate widely.   (Page 83)

80. **A.** A registered representative may make passive investments for her own account at will. A registered representative may not, without prior notification to and approval from her member, receive compensation for employment outside her regular duties with the member. Additionally, a registered representative is not allowed to participate in private securities transactions without first notifying the member in writing.   (Page 204)

81. **A.** A gain or loss is claimed in the year of sale, not in the year of purchase.   (Page 108)

82. **A.** A mutual fund may distribute net investment income as a dividend. Net investment income is defined as interest and dividends (and short-term gains if identified) less fees. Long-term gains must be distributed separately and no more often than annually. Therefore, dividend income of $1.10 plus interest income of $0.90 minus expenses of $0.50 equals a maximum $1.50 per share dividend distribution.   (Page 110)

83. **D.** The time limit for filing a grievance under the Code of Arbitration is six years. How-

ever, the limitation of six years cannot extend state law, which is typically limited to two years.
(Page 213)

84. **C.** Use of discretionary authority is not a violation of the Rules of Fair Practice, but abuse of that authority by excessive trading and the misuse of a customer's funds or securities is. Answers A, B and D are clear violations. Recommendations should be based on the customer's financial status and objectives. Low-priced stocks may result in a higher percentage of commission. Brokers that make a practice of selling low-priced stocks are often called *penny brokers.*   (Page 205)

85. **A.** Following hearings by the District Business Conduct Committee and/or the Board of Governors, penalties for violation of the NASD Rules of Fair Practice may be assessed as follows: fines (unlimited) on a member or person associated with a member, censure of any member or person associated with a member, suspension of membership of any member, or the registration of any person associated with a member, expulsion of any member or revocation of the registration of any person associated with a member, suspension of or barring of the member or person associated from association with all firms, or any other penalty deemed appropriate.   (Page 212)

86. **A.** The basis of property inherited is either stepped up (or down) to its fair market value (FMV) at the date of the decedent's death. No adjustment of basis is necessary for a period prior to the death of the decedent.   (Page 114)

87. **D.** Underwriting is the effort of a broker-dealer to market and raise capital for a company issuing new securities. The money raised goes to the issuer, as opposed to the seller of a previously outstanding security (secondary transaction) as is the case in answers A, B and C.   (Page 42)

88. **D.** The maximum sales charge on open-end investment companies under NASD rules is 8.5% of the public offering price. For 12b-1 funds, the annual fee cannot exceed on a per-share basis what could have been charged on a load fund with a 12b-1 asset-based fee. This maximum applies un-

less the fund can prove the 12b-1 charge is reasonable for the promotional, distribution and sales services provided.   (Page 99)

89. **D.**   A Treasury bill matures in one year or less.   (Page 25)

90. **D.**   An EE bond is nontransferable. It may only be redeemed by the owner of record.
(Page 27)

91. **C.**   The refund provisions for variable life contracts extend for two years from issuance of the policy. If, within the two-year period, the contract holder terminates participation in the contract, the insurer must refund from the premium the cash value on the contract (the value calculated after receipt of the redemption notice) *plus* all sales charges deducted in excess of 30% in the first year of the contract and 10% in the second year. After the two-year period has lapsed, only the cash value need be refunded; the insurer retains all sales charges collected to date.   (Page 156)

92. **A.**   The 12b-1 fee must be fully disclosed in the prospectus that is used as the offering document for the mutual fund.   (Page 98)

93. **D.**   A fixed-premium variable life contract offers a minimum death benefit (typically $25,000) and a cash value that fluctuates with the performance of the separate account funding the variable life contract. The performance of the separate account will determine the amount of life benefit above the minimum guaranteed by the contract.
(Page 152)

94. **D.**   Parity is the equivalent value between a convertible bond and the underlying common stock into which the bond may be converted. Imbalances can occur when sudden moves in interest rates affect the value of the bond, when company earnings affect the stock's price and when bond or stock market movements affect the value of an individual security traded in the respective market.
(Page 19)

95. **A.**   The prime rate is the interest charged the bank's best corporate customers. Answer B is the discount rate (set by the Fed).   (Page 51)

96. **C.**   Tex wants to park the money from his pension plan distribution for a short period of time so he requires a short-term investment vehicle. The money market fund is best suited to meet his needs. The CD has a maturity that exceeds Tex's time horizon. The growth fund would be likely to entail a load. To do nothing prevents Tex from earning any money during his decision period.   (Page 83)

97. **D.**   Although the prospectus is required prior to or during any solicitation for sale, no other literature or documentation is required.   (Page 93)

98. **C.**   Thrift or 401K plans allow the employer to match employee contributions up to a stipulated percentage.   (Page 169)

99. **D.**   Conviction of a securities crime, suspension or expulsion from a self-regulatory organization, infraction of a securities law or suspension by ruling of the SEC represent a statutory disqualification. The term "statutory" means *written in law.* If an individual is found to fall under any of the above categories he or she can be summarily barred from participation in the securities industry.
(Page 200)

100. **B.**   A balanced fund's objective is to offer stability of return. Typically, a balanced fund is invested in both common stock and debt securities. During market advances, the common stock portion of the portfolio will show superior returns. During down markets, the debt portion of the portfolio will offer returns that are greater than those of common stock. The value of convertible securities is linked in part to the value of the common stock into which the security can be converted. As a result, the convertible security offers some downside protection but not as much as would a straight-debt instrument.   (Page 83)

Notes

Notes